The World Encyclopedia of Comics

Edited by Maurice Horn

VOLUME 3

THE CONTRIBUTORS

Manuel Auad (M.A.), *The Philippines*
Bill Blackbeard (B.B.), *U.S.*
Gianni Bono (G.B.), *Italy*
Joe Brancatelli (J.B.), *U.S.*
MaryBeth Calhoun (M.B.C.), *U.S.*
Javier Coma (J.C.), *Spain*
Bill Crouch (B.C.), *U.S.*
Giulio Cesare Cuccolini (G.C.C.), *Italy*
Mark Evanier (M.E.), *U.S.*
Wolfgang Fuchs (W.F.), *Germany*
Luis Gasca (L.G.), *Spain*
Robert Gerson (R.G.), *U.S.*
Denis Gifford (D.G.), *Great Britain*
Paul Gravett (P.G.), *Great Britain*
Peter Harris (P.H.), *Canada*
Hongying Liu-Lengyel (H.Y.L.L.), *China*
Maurice Horn (M.H.), *France/U.S.*
Pierre L. Horn (P.L.H.), *U.S.*
Slobodan Ivkov (S.I.), *Yugoslavia (Serbia)*
Bill Janocha (B.J.), *U.S.*
Orvy Jundis (O.J.), *The Philippines*
Hisao Kato (H.K.), *Japan*
John A. Lent (J.A.L.), *Asia*
Richard Marschall (R.M.), *U.S.*
Alvaro de Moya (A.M.), *Brazil*
Kalmán Rubovszky (K.R.), *Hungary/Poland*
Ervin Rustemagić (E.R.), *Yugoslavia*
John Ryan (J.R.), *Australia*
Matthew A. Thorn (M.A.T.), *Japan*
Dennis Wepman (D.W.), *U.S.*

The World Encyclopedia of Comics

Edited by Maurice Horn

VOLUME 3

Chelsea House Publishers
Philadelphia

Acknowledgments

The editors of *The World Encyclopedia of Comics* wish to extend their sincere thanks to the following persons: Bill Anderson, Jerry Bails, Larry Brill, Mary Beth Calhoun, Frank Clark, Bill Crouch, Leonard Darvin, Tony Dispoto, Jacques Glénat-Guttin, Ron Goulart, George Henderson, Pierre Horn, Pierre Huet, S. M. "Jerry" Iger, Jessie Kahles Straut, Rolf Kauka, Heikki Kaukoranta, Roland Kohlsaat, Maria-M. Lamm, Mort Leav, Vane Lindesay, Ernie McGee, Jacques Marcovitch, Victor Margolin, Doug Murray, Pascal Nadon, Harry Neigher, Walter Neugebauer, Syd Nicholls, Tom Peoples, Rainer Schwarz, Silvano Scotto, Luciano Secchi, David Smith, Manfred Soder, Jim Steranko, Ernesto Traverso, Miguel Urrutía, Jim Vadeboncoeur, Jr., Wendell Washer, Peter Wiechmann, Mrs. John Wheeler and Joe Willicombe.

We would also like to thank the following collectors who donated reproductions of art from their collections: Wendy Gaines Bucci, Mike Burkey, Tony Christopher, Russ Cochran, Robert Gerson, Roger Hill, Bill Leach, Eric Sack, and Jim Steranko.

Special thanks also to Michel Mandry, Bernard Trout, José Maria Conget of Instituto Cervantes in New York, Four-Color Images Gallery, Frederik Schodt, David Astor, Alain Beyrand, Manuel Halffter, Dominique Petitfaux, Annie Baron-Carvais, Janice Silverman.

Our appreciation also to the following organizations: Associated Newspapers Ltd., Bastei Verlag, Bulls Pressedienst, Comics Magazine Association of America, Editions Dupuis, ERB Inc., Field Newspaper Syndicate, Globi Verlag, The Herald and Weekly Times Ltd., Kauka Comic Akademie, King Features Syndicate, Marvel Comics Group, San Francisco Academy of Comic Art, Strip Art Features, Walt Disney Archives and Walt Disney Productions.

Finally, we wish to thank Don Manza for his photographic work.

Chelsea House Publishers
1974 Sproul Road, Suite 400
P.O. Box 914
Broomall PA 19008-0914

Typeset by Alexander Graphics, Indianapolis IN

Library of Congress Cataloging-in-Publication Data

The world encyclopedia of comics / edited by Maurice Horn.
    p. cm.
    Includes bibliographical references and index.
    ISBN 0-7910-4854-3 (set). — ISBN 0-7910-4857-8 (v. 1). — ISBN 0-7910-4858-6 (v. 2). — ISBN 0-7910-4859-4 (v. 3). — ISBN 0-7910-4860-8 (v. 4). — ISBN 0-7910-4861-6 (v. 5). — ISBN 0-7910-4862-4 (v. 6). — ISBN 0-7910-4863-2 (v. 7)
    1. Comic books, strips, etc.—Dictionaries. I. Horn, Maurice.
PN6710.W6 1998
741.5'03—dc21   97-50448
                                                              CIP

GAI LURON (France) On September 30, 1962, French cartoonist Marcel Gotlib created a new feature in the pages of the *Vaillant* comic magazine, *Nanar et Jujube*, about the young boy Nanar and his pet fox Jujube, who were later joined by a little girl, Piette. Only with the arrival some months later of the unseemly mutt Gai Luron did the feature assume its definitive character: one by one the other protagonists left the strip, which was successively retitled: *Nanar, Jujube et Piette, Jujube et Gai Luron,* and finally (in 1966) *Gai Luron.*

Gai Luron (his name meaning "jolly fellow" is a misnomer) is a canine philosopher whose hangdog face reflects all the vicissitudes of a world-weary life. Disabused and sarcastic, he comments on (in a uniform, slightly disparaging tone) and reacts to (with a visible reluctance of effort) the various indignities that an uncaring world keeps throwing at him. There are few supporting characters: Belle Lurette, Gai Luron's girlfriend and a mimicking mouse, who are the only ones capable of cheerfully accepting Gai Luron's definitely morose attitude.

In 1970 Gotlib relinquished the strip to his former assistant Dufranne. While the drawing style remained essentially the same, Dufranne was not able to maintain the original tone and wit of *Gai Luron,* which was

"Gai Luron," Marcel Gotlib. © Vaillant.

subsequently downgraded from two weekly pages of gags to only one in 1973. Gai Luron faded out of the comic pages in 1976, only to be revived by his creator 10 years later in the humor monthly *Fluide Glacial.* More disabused and as cynical as ever, the hangdog canine has now become embroiled in a number of political and sexual escapades.

A number of *Gai Luron* episodes drawn by Gotlib were reprinted in book form by Editions Vaillant.

M.H.

GAINES, WILLIAM M. (1922-1992) American comic book editor and publisher born on March 1, 1922, in New York. The son of M. C. Gaines, celebrated as the father of comic books, "Bill" Gaines inherited his father's flagging company, E.C. Publications, in 1947.

He made several attempts at love, Western, and funny animal books with little success. In 1950, however, Gaines decided to try horror comics. The genre took hold, and he and editor Al Feldstein ushered in the vaunted E.C. "New Trend" line of horror, science-fiction, war, crime, and humor stories. Written mostly by editors Feldstein, Johnny Craig, and Harvey Kurtzman, the stories were unique in comics, several cuts above anything else then produced. In addition, Gaines lined up a bevy of the finest artists available; among them were Frank Frazetta, Al Williamson, George Evans, Reed Crandall, Bernie Krigstein, Jack Davis, Will Elder, Wally Wood, John Severin, and Graham Ingels. In 1952, Kurtzman invented *Mad,* perhaps the zaniest and most offbeat comic ever to appear. It quickly became an unbelievable success story. Gaines' 11 titles—*Haunt of Fear, Crypt of Terror, Vault of Horror, Crime SuspenStories, Shock SuspenStories, Weird Science, Weird Fantasy, Two-Fisted, Frontline Combat, Mad,* and *Panic*—were all artistic and financial successes. Imitations flourished profusely, and Gaines became a wealthy man.

But the bubble burst in 1953. Excesses of gore and violence in imitators' titles—and later Gaines' books—led to heavy public scrutiny. Magazines and newspapers lobbied against comics, and Fredric Wertham's 1953 book, *Seduction of the Innocent,* claimed crime comics were a cause of juvenile delinquency. The adverse publicity mounted quickly and was highlighted by Gaines' appearance on national television before The Kefauver Senate Subcommittee hearings on crime. Distributors began shying away from comics in general and Gaines' books in particular. By 1954, his empire had collapsed, and after two ill-fated attempts at survival, Gaines gave up the ghost in 1956.

All that remained was Kurtzman's *Mad.* Gaines transformed it into a 25-cent, 48-page black-and-white magazine. It was even more successful than the comic book version, survived Kurtzman's departure, absorbed Feldstein as editor, and now sells over two million copies per issue. Gaines made *Mad* his sole publication, and it has made him fabulously wealthy. He later sold

"The Cosmic Ray Bomb Explosion" (Featuring publisher Bill Gaines and editor Al Feldstein). Illustrated by Al Feldstein.
© William M. Gaines, Agent, Inc.

the magazine to the Kinney conglomerate, but he has stayed on as the autonomous publisher.

Lyle Stuart, Inc. published his biography, *The Mad World of William M. Gaines*, in 1972. Gaines died in his sleep at his Manhattan home on June 3, 1992.

J.B.

GAKI DEKA (Japan) Created by Tatsuhiko Yamagami, *Gaki Deka* ("The Boy Policeman") made its first appearance in the weekly *Shōnen Chambion* in September 1974. Soon *Gaki Deka* became immensely popular, and it is now the topmost boy's strip.

Komawari-kun (nicknamed "Gaki Deka") is a pupil at Sakamuke elementary school. He always wears a police officer's cap, a long and extra-wide polka dot necktie, has extraordinarily swollen cheeks, a wild look in his eyes, a snub nose, an extremely wide mouth and a very dirty mind. He is also impudent, undependable,

"Gaki Deka," Tatsuhiko Yamagami. © Shōnen Chambion.

filthy, stupid, and vulgar. As one can see, Gaki Deka is hardly a credit to the human race.

Regarding himself as a policeman, Gaki Deka indulges in the weirdest acts. He once fought against a dog and put handcuffs on him; later he arrested himself and handcuffed himself. To stay away from school he purposely created a traffic accident; at another time (while late for school) he entered his classroom after breaking the windows. Other shenanigans included tearing a girl's panties with his bare hands (he pretended to be a crab), practicing for the broad jump with a photograph of a nude girl in front of him, and fighting with aquarium sea lions for fish.

The other characters in this unusual strip include Komawari's classmate and rival Sai jō-kun, Sai jō's girl-friend Momo-chan and her younger sister Junchan, Kamawari's parents, and the teacher, Miss Abe.

Gaki Deka became the most talked-about strip of the moment, and its hero's ritualistic poses (such as the "death penalty pose" in which Komawari simulates shooting an enemy) were widely imitated among Japanese youth. *Gaki Deka*, a revolutionary strip in its own way, completely renewed the tradition of Japanese humor strips by introducing absurd and nihilistic elements into its story line. In 1981 Yamagami abruptly decided to terminate the strip; he abandoned comics altogether, in favor of writing short stories and novels.

H.K.

GAMBOLS, THE (G.B.) George and Gaye Gambol made their debut in the *Daily Express* on March 16, 1950. Gaye, clearing up the paper muddle at the end of the football season, encounters George bearing armfuls of more paper muddle for the start of the racing season. She promptly goes home to mother!

Fortunately, she does not stay; fortunately for readers of the *Express* and for creators Barry Appleby and his ex-schoolgirl sweetheart Dobs, long Mrs. Appleby. She writes the scripts, he draws. As implied by their first gag and by the pun of their name, the Gambols

"The Gambols," Barry Appleby. © Daily Express.

began as gamblers, which suited their venue, the sports page. They evolved from a daily "single" gag panel and became a daily strip on June 4, 1951; before then they had made thrice-weekly appearances on "big paper days." By 1956 they expanded to the *Sunday Express* as well, and boosted to three banks of strips to suit overseas syndication. The Gambols toned down to a cozy domestic scene, occasionally enjoying an outing to the races, an echo of their past obsession. To expand their appeal, a ready-made family was introduced through two children, Flivver (nephew) and Miggy (niece). This was deemed preferable to Gaye becoming pregnant at her age. Flivver and Miggy come and go during school holidays, making things conveniently cozy for Christmas.

Barry Appleby, born in Birmingham, learned to draw through Percy V. Bradshaw's Press Art School course, to which he subscribed by post in 1930. By 1937 he had a cartoon in *Punch*, by 1938 a daily panel in the London evening *Star*, and by 1940 had entered comics by taking over *Skit, Skat and the Captain,* and *Pinky Green* from the conscripted Basil Reynolds in *Mickey Mouse Weekly.*

The first paperback collection of *The Gambols* was published in 1952 (the 1953 edition reproduces examples of Appleby's "roughs"), and since then many volumes have appeared. Appleby's style, always very ordinary, has improved over the years since he eliminated all background detail from his panels.

Tragically Appleby lost his wife and collaborator Dobs, but his cartoon characters continued to supply a daily laugh to his readers. After Barry's own unexpected death, the strip was carried on for some time using the stock in hand; and in fact it continues to be published under the title *Barry Appleby's Gambols,* with drawings by Roger Mahoney.

D.G.

GARFIELD (U.S.) Currently the most widely syndicated comic strip in history, Jim Davis's *Garfield* was first launched into 41 newspapers by United Feature Syndicate on June 19, 1978. Reportedly born in the kitchen of Mama Leone's Italian Restaurant, the corpulent, self-indulgent feline is joined by Odie, a witless, slobbering pooch, and cartoonist Jon Arbuckle, their unassertive, nerdy owner.

During the strip's first years, a nondescript housemate, Lyman, shared the spotlight but was soon omitted. Infrequent appearances by Garfield's love interest Arlene, his teddy bear Pookie, and rival Nermal, "the world's cutest kitten," help diversify the otherwise limited ensemble. Creator Davis was previously an assistant on *Tumbleweeds*, and modeled much of Garfield's pacing and sharp delineation on T.K. Ryan's work.

Consciously avoiding any social or political commentary, the feature centers primarily on the cynical cat's pursuit of creature comforts; food, sleep, television, and full control of his domestic domain. Davis's command of direct, universal esprit and low comedy create an aura of slapstick and general silliness, giving the work a broad appeal. All action is presented front and center with few words of dialogue, making it effortless to read and easily translatable into the many languages used in its worldwide circulation. The consistency of clean artwork and honed script is due much to the talented assistants Gary Barker, Valette Green, Brett Koth, and Jeff Wesley, in addition to the dozens of others who oversee the generation of a countless number of licensed products.

Since 1980, the entire strip has been chronicled in book form, with seven titles listed simultaneously on the *New York Times* best-seller list in 1982. That same year the first of thirteen prime-time television specials was aired, and in 1988 the animated show *Garfield and Friends* made its debut on Saturday mornings.

The fat cat has been a float in the Macy's Thanksgiving Day parade and has a permanent exhibit in the Muncie Children's Museum in Indiana. The National Cartoonists Society awarded it the Best Humor Strip for 1981 and 1985, and four years later honored it with the coveted Rueben Award.

Now syndicated by Universal Press, the strip that started as a simple premise has blossomed into an epic phenomenon of pop culture, and it is sure to continue its popularity in the years to come.

B.J.

GARFIELD AND FRIENDS (U.S.) Jim Davis's *Garfield* had been a hit for almost 10 years in newspapers when CBS decided to add an animated version of the strip to its Saturday-morning lineup of cartoons. The show, called *Garfield and Friends,* premiered on October 15, 1988, with the author supervising the production.

All the familiar characters from the comic strip are there going through their usual paces. Garfield plays all kinds of underhanded tricks on his favorite foil, Odie the dog, and runs circles around his putative master, the cartoonist Jon Arbuckle. The plots revolve around the smug feline's love of food and sleep. Although limited, the animation is nicely done, and the series exudes a charm and freshness too often absent from most "kidvid" fare.

The "Friends" promised by the title are Orson the piglet, the four-legged hero of Davis's short-lived *U.S. Acres* comic strip, and his cohorts. These include Roy the rooster, who uses a bugle to wake up the neigh-

Jim Davis, "Garfield." © United Feature Syndicate.

borhood; Booker the chick, who believes Orson is his mother; and Orville, Sylvia, Woodrow, and Fred, the early worms Booker is constantly (and vainly) trying to catch. These animals cavort in separate segments of the series, and the off-the-wall humor of these small vignettes often makes them funnier than the main feature.

In advance of the regularly scheduled program, there had been a number of *Garfield* animated specials, many of which won Emmy Awards, including the first one, *Here Comes Garfield* (1982). Produced by Lee Mendelson and directed by Bill Melendez, the team responsible for the *Peanuts* cartoons, it went on to spawn many sequels. In contrast to the serenity of most of the *Peanuts* shorts, the *Garfield* episodes were filled with action and movement. In one of them the gutsy cat fought against ghosts and goblins; in another adventure he had a run-in with unfriendly natives on a tropical isle. In these specials Garfield often played a variety of tough characters, including Cave Cat, Space Cat, and the no-nonsense private eye, Sam Spayed. In all of the cartoons, the cat's thoughts are voiced by Lorenzo Music, while Tom Hoge and Greg Berger play the other regulars.

M.H.

GARTH (G.B.) "Whence did Garth come! The answer may be forever unknown. For Garth is not as other men. He is a powerful, mysterious, fascinating figure; moving at will through the maze of Time, lending his mighty strength to the cause of Right." Thus reads the foreword to *Garth, Man of Mystery*, a reprint of his first series of daily strips written and drawn by Steve Dowling for the London *Daily Mirror*. The still-continuing

saga began on July 24, 1943, with the body of the blond giant drifting on a raft. He is washed ashore and revived by Gala, the first of many girls to fall in love with this handsome giant. The amnesiac hero was frankly created as a British answer to *Superman*, but beyond his abnormal strength, Garth quickly evolved along more original lines (although for one story he did don a cloak to fly the sky in the best *Superman* manner.)

In his first adventure Garth, hailed as Son of Mor, thwarts an evil High Priest and sails off by barrage balloon to find his destiny! A dark girl, Ola, has become Gala's rival, a pattern which crystallized in the long-running feud that traversed many ages between Dawn, the bare-breasted cavegirl, and Karen, the dark sorceress. Garth's earthbound controller through his far-

"Garth," Steve Dowling. © Daily Mirror Newspapers Ltd.

ranging adventures is Professor Lumiere, the scientific genius of Carter Island, who calls everyone "mon ami"; Garth's key word for a safe return during a crisis is "Karma." In 1948, en route to the Olympic Games, he found himself running in the original games in the lost land of Olympia. In 1957 an encounter with Dr. Baal and his Black Magic brought Garth true love in the shape of Lady Astra, who turned out to be the goddess Venus! Perhaps his strangest metamorphosis occurred on December 7, 1971, when Garth was suddenly and utterly revitalized by a new artist: Frank Bellamy had taken over from John Allard (who had replaced Dowling in 1957).

The strip has been reprinted in several paperbacks: *Garth Man of Mystery*; *Garth in the Last Goddess* (1958); *Daily Mirror Book of Garth* (1974). There was also a *Garth* comic book published in Australia.

After a 54-year career, the longest in British newspaper strip history, *Garth* was suddenly discontinued on Saturday, February 8, 1997, at the end of an adventure entitled "Dam Drivers." The last cartoonist on the feature was Martin Asbury, a storyboard artist for cinema films.

D.G.

GASCARD, GILBERT (1931-   ) Belgian cartoonist born October 28, 1931, in Marseilles, France. Gilbert Gascard moved with his family to Brussels while a child, and exhibited a marked predilection for drawing and caricature during his high school studies. At age 18 he started his cartooning career in the Belgian magazine *Heroic-Albums*, in which he created (under the pseudonym "Tibet") *Dave O'Flynn*, an adventure strip, in 1950. The following year, Tibet transferred to the weekly *Tintin*, where he originated a string of short-lived series: *Yoyo*, *Jean-Jean et Gigi*, *Titi et Tutu*, *La Famille Petitou*, while creating his first continuity strip, *De Avonturen von Koenrad* ("The Adventures of Conrad") for the Flemish-language *Ons Volkske*. In April 1953, Tibet created his first successful comic strip, *Chick Bill*, a parodic Western starring the intrepid Federal Marshal Chick Bill and his faithful Indian boy-companion Petit-Caniche ("Little Poodle," a transparent allusion to Red Ryder's Little Beaver), and featuring the quick-tempered Dog Bull, the sheriff, and his inept deputy Kid Ordinn. The success of *Chick Bill* was such that it was transferred from *Ons Volkske* (where it had first appeared) to the more important *Tintin* a few years later.

In the wake of *Chick Bill*, Tibet followed (between 1953 and 1957) with a string of strips of varying merit: *Globul le Martien* ("Globul the Martian"), *Pat Rick*, *Alphonse* (with scripts by René Goscinny), and others.

His best-known feature appeared in March 1955 when he created, together with scriptwriter A. P. Duchateau, the detective strip *Ric Hochet* for *Tintin*. In 1958, Tibet tried his hand at another comic strip, *Junior*, with Duchateau and Greg as his writers, but it did not last, and since that date, he has been devoting most of his career to *Chick Bill* and *Ric Hochet*. Tibet has also contributed a number of covers to *Tintin*, as well as a series of caricatures spoofing celebrities, from Barbra Streisand to Chairman Mao. In 1992 he succeeded the late Bob de Moor as art director of the Belgian publishing firm Editions du Lombard.

Tibet has received a number of awards over the years, in his adopted Belgium as well as in his native France. His graphic style is loose and relaxed, with few innovations or flashes of brilliance, but well-suited to the youthful readers who make up the bulk of Tibet's public.

M.H.

GASOLINE ALLEY (U.S.) Frank King's *Gasoline Alley*, which first appeared on Sunday, November 24, 1918, in the *Chicago Tribune* (the daily strip commencing on August 23, 1919, in the *New York Daily News*), was the first comic strip to develop a self-serving realization of its open-ended temporal potential. By the close of the 1910s, it was as apparent to Frank King as anyone else that successful strips could go on almost forever—as *The Katzenjammer Kids* and *Happy Hooligan* had aptly demonstrated by that time—but only King saw that there was no reason why a comic strip character shouldn't have as long a *growing* life as an actual human, and age accordingly, day by day, on the comic page.

This is what Skeezix Wallet, adopted foundling son of *Gasoline Alley's* initial hero, bachelor Walt Wallet, did over the 21 years between 1921 and 1942, and later, in front of the amused eyes of fifty million plus American newspaper readers. His baby brother and sister, Corky and Judy (the first born to a married Walt Wallet in 1928; the second another foundling of 1935), did the same, as did all of Skeezix's childhood friends. Only the original adult characters of the strip in 1918, Walt, his married Alley buddies, Doc, Avery, and Bill, and their wives, remained relatively static as far as age.

The spectacle of first one, then three normal, typical American kids (by general prevailing standards of the time) going through all of the vicissitudes of growing up on a daily basis delighted the average newspaper reader, and the strip, which at first gained only limited if amused attention by its focus on a motley group of suburban car enthusiasts, soon riveted public involvement from the moment fat, bumbling Walt Wallet

"Gasoline Alley," Dick Moores. © Chicago Tribune-New York News Syndicate.

found a basketed Skeezix on his womanless doorstep in the daily *Gasoline Alley* episode of February 14, 1921. King and *Tribune* publisher Joe Patterson (who suggested the introduction of a child to enlarge the interest of woman readers for the strip) chose Valentine's Day for the memorable event, and this later became Skeezix's "birthday."

The story line in *Gasoline Alley* was as wandering and ramshackle as life itself: the characters had parties and spats, took trips and were sick, went to school and played hookey, but for the most part nothing out of the ordinary happened. King was not as inventive or comfortable with melodrama as his *Tribune* conferee, Sidney Smith, and his one major attempt at the lurid vein, when a mysterious Mme. Octave claims Skeezix as her child, is only mildly diverting as told in the strip between May 2, 1922 to June 17, 1924; in fact, it barely affects the continuingly slow meandering of the characters' lives. Realizing his indifferent ability in this area, King wisely returned afterward to his simple, realistic, day-to-day manner of storytelling, touching only occasionally on the Mme. Octave threat and letting the normal events of childhood life dictate the story and anecdote content.

There were a surprisingly large number of relatively memorable characters in *Gasoline Alley*, perhaps because King fashioned so many of them to be like someone the reader was likely to know. In addition to the original Alley gang and Skeezix's kid brother and sister, there was Rachel, the black cook Walt hires to keep house for him and Skeezix; Phyliss Blossom (Skeezix's "Auntie"), whom Walt marries on June 24, 1926; Squint the cowboy; Mr. Wicker; Nina Clock and Trixie, two of Skeezix's earliest girlfriends (he later married Nina, on June 28, 1944); Spud, Whimpy, and Gooch, Skeezix's boyhood pals; his Army buddies, Tops, Sissy, and Wilmer; Mrs. Nosey, and many more.

Since Skeezix was fortuitously 18 in 1939, he was among the first comic strip characters to serve in the Armed Forces, and his wartime experiences filled much of the strip's continuity between 1942 and 1945: like the strip itself, they were carefully low-keyed and routine, much of what the average GI encountered in England and Europe during the war. As an adult in the postwar years, he did the dutiful, expected things: went into business, had a child (Chipper), took vacations, etc. And so the strip continued until Frank King died in June 1969. Bill Perry, who took over the Sunday page in 1951, and Richard Moores, who worked carefully and closely with King in the 1960s on the daily strip, both kept *Gasoline Alley* a going concern after King's death, with Moores gradually guiding it away from close involvement with Skeezix, Walt, and the old characters, and into emphasis on a fresh batch of individuals, with whom the continuing strip is chiefly concerned today. After Moores died in 1986, the feature passed into the hands of his assistant, Jim Scancarelli.

Much of the popularity that *Gasoline Alley* earned derived from its commonplace presentation of life as it was for many middle-class Americans of this century, and it is accordingly an invaluable pictorial record of America's general way-of-life in our times. Its actual book republication record is poor, however: a single collection of early strips from Reilly & Lee in 1929; several picture-and-text children's books from the same publisher based loosely on the strip; a Big Little Book in 1934; and a few comic book reprints of the strip in the late 1930s and 1940s. (There were a wide variety of Gasoline Alley artifacts and toys, however; a Columbia film of 1951 named for the strip and starring Scotty Becket; and a short-lived radio show of the early 1940s.) It is evident, therefore, that *Gasoline Alley* is a neglected and important American work of art calling

"Gaston Lagaffe," André Franquin. © Editions Dupuis.

for republication in full to be made generally accessible for social study in institutions of learning.

B.B.

GASTON LAGAFFE (Belgium) *Gaston Lagaffe* was created by André Franquin as a panel feature in issue 985 of the Belgian weekly *Spirou* of February 28, 1957. *Gaston* became a full-fledged strip on December 5, 1957; it then appeared as a half-page from September 24, 1959, until 1966, when it finally graduated to full-page status, and has remained there ever since.

Gaston (who had previously appeared in Franquin's earlier strip *Spirou*) is an aggravating, bumbling, and incompetent newspaper office boy whose antics and flights of fancy are the despair of his boss Monsieur de Mesmaeker (in actuality the real name of Franquin's assistant Jidehem) and of his coworkers: Prunelle the harassed editor, Boulier the slightly dilapidated accountant, and Lebrac the resident artist. Even M'oiselle Jeanne, de Mesmaeker's secretary, whose love for Gaston is as hopeless as it is unrequited, does not escape the slings and arrows of mischievous fortune unleashed by the irrepressible object of her admiration.

Gaston's talents, moreover, are as varied as they are obnoxious. He is an inventor (whose experiments more often than not result in chaos and mayhem), an artist (his portraits of M'oiselle Jeanne are justly infamous), a sports enthusiast (who would not let such things as office routine stand in the way of his training as bicyclist or javelin thrower), a musician (he plays a variety of instruments, including the gaffophone, of his own invention). His greatest avocation, however, is that of animal lover, and he keeps a veritable menagerie around him, such as mice in file drawers, turtles in the paper basket, goldfish in the water cooler, not to mention a laughing seagull, a hedgehog, and several species of wildcats. All this contributes, of course, to the hectic pace and lunatic atmosphere for which the strip is famous. In the 1980s Gaston lent his goofy presence to a number of Spirou episodes. Franquin ended the series in 1996, shortly before his death.

Since 1960 Editions Dupuis in Belgium has reprinted a number of Gaston's adventures and misadventures. Since 1985 his adventures have been reprinted in their near-entirety by Rombaldi in hardcover, and in paperback form by J'Ai Lu BD.

M.H.

GEKKŌ KAMEN (Japan) Created by Jirō Kuwata (artist) and Yasunori Kawauchi (scriptwriter), *Gekkō Kamen* made its debut in the Japanese monthly *Shōnen Kurabu* (May 1958). When the *Gekkō Kamen* television series started the next year, the strip was also published as a newspaper feature.

Gekkō Kamen (the Moonlight Mask) is the secret identity of detective Jurō Iwai. Wearing a white cloak, white suit, yellow gloves, yellow boots, and a white mask with a moon symbol, Gekkō Kamen spreads terror in the hearts of his enemies, with the help of his trusted assistant Gorohachi. Mounted on his white motorcycle and firing from both his guns (which he never uses for killing) Gekkō Kamen seems to materialize from nowhere in his relentless pursuit of evildoers. Among the more picturesque villains against whom Gekkō has pitched his powers are Satan no Tsume, Yūreitō (the Ghostly Gang), Dragon no Kiba (Dragon's Fang) and the fittingly named Mammoth Kong.

The strip, filled with action, thrill, and speed, was one of the most popular ever to appear. Gekkō Kamen himself became the most famous superhero in Japan, as well-known there as Superman and Batman are in the United States. On October 1961 he made his last appearance in the pages of *Shōnen Kurabu*.

Gekkō Kamen was also the hero of a number of animated films and of a number of live-action movies. His adventures were collected in a series of seven hardbound volumes which rapidly became bestsellers. The theme song from the TV show *Gekkō Kamen wa Daredeshō?* ("Who is Gekkō Kamen?") also enjoyed great popularity in the heyday of the strip.

H.K.

GHOST RIDER (U.S.) The name *Ghost Rider* has appeared on three different U.S. comic book features, two of them westerns of a supernatural flavor.

1—In 1950, Magazine Enterprises introduced its *Ghost Rider*, about a Western avenger cloaked wholly in white to give a ghostly appearance and strike terror in the hearts of bandits. The identity of the strip's author is unknown, but Dick Ayers did all of the interior art. Some of the covers on the *Ghost Rider* comic book were by Frank Frazetta. The first issue of *Ghost Rider* was dated 1950 (no month given) and it—and all subsequent issues—were sub-numbered as issues of the company's *A-1* comic book. Each issue of *A-1* was actually an issue of a different comic book. (*Ghost Rider* number one was *A-1* number 27; number two was *A-1* number 29 and so forth.) There were 14 of these *Ghost Rider* issues in all, plus appearances of the strip in *Tim Holt Comics* (some with Frazetta covers), *Red Mask*, in all 12 issues of *The Best of the West*, and in *Bobby Benson's B-Bar-B Riders*.

2—In February 1967, the Marvel Comics Group issued a new number one of a new *Ghost Rider*, identical in appearance to the first one and also drawn by Dick Ayers. The book lasted only seven issues but was revived in reprints in 1974. The reprints were retitled *Night Rider* so as not to conflict with another *Ghost Rider* which Marvel had brought out in the interim.

"Ghost Rider," Dick Ayers. © Marvel Comics Group.

3—In 1972, Gary Friedrich (who had authored Marvel's Western hero of the same name) and artist Mike Ploog brought out a new *Ghost Rider*, this one about a motorcyclist set in the present. Otherwise known as Johnny Blaze, this Ghost Rider was a daring trick-cyclist who called upon Satan for a bargain to save the life of his longtime friend, Crash Simpson. In the deal, Johnny lost his soul and was later transformed into a creature with a flaming skull for a head. The character first appeared in *Marvel Spotlight* number five (August 1972) and, after six more issues, went into his own comic, beginning with number one (September 1973). Following Friedrich, stories were by Tony Isabella who moved the strip away from the supernatural angle, towards superheroics. Succeeding Ploog on the art were Tom Sutton, Jim Mooney, Sal Buscema, Frank Robbins, George Tuska, and Bob Brown.

M.E.

4—The third Ghost Rider series ended in 1983. In May 1990 Marvel revived the title character, giving him a new costume and persona and teaming him with many of the other superheroes (Spider-Man, Dr. Strange, Wolverine, et al.). Among the artists working on this latest series mention should be made of Al Williamson, Andy and Joe Kubert, and Jim Lee. A spin-off, *Ghost Rider 2099*, ran briefly from 1994 to 1996.

M.H.

GIARDINO, VITTORIO (1946-   ) Italian illustrator, scriptwriter, and cartoonist, born December 24, 1946, in Bologna. In 1978 his first short stories appeared in the weekly *La Citta Futura*. In 1979 Giardino quit his job as an electronic engineer to devote himself entirely to comics. In the same year he started to write and draw for the magazine *Il Mago* (1979-1980) the black-and-white adventures of the contemporary private investigator *Sam Pezzo*, which moved to the monthly *Orient Express* in 1982-1983. Pezzo's adventures are in the tradition of the *roman noir,* where the urban social environment and the troubled existence of the main characters is more important than solving the mystery.

In 1982 the same magazine published Giardino's first long, color spy story *Rapsodia ungherese* ("Hungarian Rhapsody"), followed in 1985 by *La Porta d'Oriente* ("Orient Gateway"), published in the monthly *Corto Maltese*. The protagonist of both adventures set in the late 1930s is the Jewish Frenchman, Max Friedman, who tries in vain to prevent the disaster of the impending war.

Little Ego is Giardino's series of dreamlike erotic short stories with humorous implications, which appeared in *Glamour International Magazine* in 1983 and 1985, and later in the monthly *Comic Art*. This magazine has also printed his series *Vacanze fatali* ("Fatal Holidays"), a crime story with a final humorous surprise at the end. Giardino has contributed cover illustrations to several comic magazines and has done illustrations for dailies such as *L'Unita, Il Messaggero, La Repubblica*, and the weekly *L'Espresso*.

Giardino is not a prolific author, but certainly one of the most learned, elegant, and sophisticated of the Italian cartoonists. His crime and spy stories are accurately plotted, the dialogues are literary and relevant, the characterization is accurate, and the settings are well documented. His main characters do not share the traits of conventional heroes; they are fallible, emotionally unstable, and have mood swings. His artwork offers rich and deep insights, thanks to its painstaking detail. In his black-and-white stories, the light and shade effects are stronger than in the color stories, where the narrative and rhythm are expressed through the combination and contrast of different colors.

Giardino's present work in progress is *Jonas Fink*, of which only the first of a three-volume set was published in 1994 in Belgium and France titled *L'Enfance* ("Childhood"). This trilogy narrates the life of a Czechoslovakian boy whose father has been accused of being an enemy of the people by the Communist regime.

Almost all of Giardino's works have been reprinted in book form by different publishers and have been translated in 18 countries. He has been awarded several prizes in Italy and abroad, including a Yellow Kid

Vittorio Giardino, "Sam Pezzo." © Vittorio Giardino.

in Lucca in 1982, and Alfred in Angouleme, and a Saint Michel in Brussels.

G.C.C.

GIBBS, CECILIA MAY (1876-1969) Author-cartoonist born in Surrey (England) in 1876. May Gibbs came to Australia aboard the *Hesperus* in 1880 and eventually settled near Harvey, W.A. She began drawing as a small child and was instructed and encouraged by her father, who was a gifted amateur artist. She soon developed her love for the Australian bush and its animals, and often invented stories about them to entertain younger children. After completing her education at the Church of England Grammar School, Perth, she journeyed to London around 1896 with her mother—the first of many such trips. She spent eight years studying art at Cope & Nichol School, Chelsea Polytechnic, and the Henry Blackburn School of Black and White Art. The poverty, cruelty, and richness of London made a deep impression on her, causing her to write and illustrate her first book, *About Us*, which was published in Bavaria about 1901.

On returning to Australia, she settled in Sydney and by 1914 was earning money by doing quick sketches of soldiers departing for WWI. In 1916, she produced her best-known book, *Gumnut Babies*, published by Angus and Robertson. This was followed by such books as *Snugglepot and Cuddlepie* (1918), *Little Ragged Blossom* (1920), *Little Obelia* (1921), and a host of others over the next 45 years. In 1925, she adapted *Gumnut Babies* to a Sunday comic page, which was titled *Bib and Bub*. The strip first appeared in the *Sydney Sunday News* and continued to run until September 1967—surviving three newspaper mergers in the process.

In her unique style, May Gibbs immortalized the Australian bush and its creatures, and recorded the faery lore of the continent. Her clean, crisp line drawings and soft watercolors were accurate and instructive and drawn for the juvenile reader. While her artwork generally tended to be charming and gentle, the lingering impressions of her London visits made her quite capable of producing some rather frightening characters (e.g., The Banksia Men).

She became Cecilia May Ossoli Gibbs Kelly when she married at the age of 40. She was quoted as once saying, "I think you can influence children through books. You can teach them to be thoughtful and kind to animals, and to love the bush." When she died on November 27, 1969, May Gibbs had no children of her own—but she had won the love of generations of children with her books, illustrations, and comics. And she remembered children in her will; leaving her estate to be auctioned with the proceeds going to UNICEF, The Spastic Centre, and Crippled Children. She was awarded an M.B.E. for her services to children's literature.

J.R.

GILLAIN, JOSEPH (1914-1980) Belgian cartoonist and illustrator born January 13, 1914 in Gedinne. After two years of studies at the Royal Academy of Fine Arts and a job painting church murals, Joseph Gillain started a career in comics in 1939 when he was asked to join the staff of *Spirou* magazine. That same year Joseph Gillain (using the pseudonym Jijé, under which he was to become famous) produced *Freddy et Fred*, a humorous adventure series strongly influenced by Herge's *Tintin*, and *Trinet et Trinette*, which depicted the tribu-

lations of two young children, a brother and a sister; also in 1939, Jijé created *Blondin et Cirage* ("Blondin and Shoe-Polish"), yet another humor-adventure strip, for the comic weekly *Petits Belges* (it was later tranferred to *Spirou*): This feature—Jijé's first popular success—retraced the adventures of a pair of bright-eyed young boys, one white, the other black.

By the early 1940s Jijé seemed to be producing the whole magazine almost single-handedly; not only did he continue to draw all the above-mentioned features, but he also assisted Rob Vel on the title strip, *Spirou*, and in 1941 he created (with the help of Jean Doisy as scriptwriter) *Jean Valhardi*, an adventure strip with an insurance investigator as hero (Jijé drew it straight). To top it all he also took complete control of the *Spirou* strip in 1944.

In 1950, tired and overworked, Jijé decided to leave on a long trip to the United States (as early as 1946 he had already begun to turn over his vast production to other artists), where he was later joined by fellow cartoonists Franquin and Morris. The trio wandered around the North American continent, from New York to California, and from Canada to Mexico. Coming home in 1954, Jijé, inspired by his travels, started a Western, *Jerry Spring*, for *Spirou* (it is now regarded as his masterwork). Difficulties with his publishers led Jijé to enter into a contract with the competing *Pilote* magazine: in 1966 he took over the drawing of the *Michel Tanguy* aviation strip from Albert Uderzo, and the next year he abandoned *Jerry Spring*. Jijé's love of the Western led him in 1970 to create (with his brother Philippe writing the scenario) *Le Specialiste* ("The Specialist"), another horse-opera, for the short-lived *Johnny* magazine; and in 1974 he finally rejoined *Spirou* where he revived *Jerry Spring*. In 1979 he also drew two stories for the swashbuckling strip *Barbe-Rouge*, in collaboration with his son Laurent (who signs "Lorg"). He died in Versailles, France, on June 20, 1980.

In addition to his comic strip work, Jijé has also illustrated the biographies of famous figures: Don Bosco, Christopher Columbus, Baden-Powell, and did a respectful treatment of the life of Christ. However, his name is forever connected with the European adventure strip, of which he is a pioneer and an innovator who has influenced a whole generation of cartoonists. In 1974 Jijé summed up his artistic credo in these words: "The main thing is to tell a story. One must be readable, understandable, simple. This is a tendency that I strive not to lose. . . ."

M.H.

GILLRAY, JAMES (1757-1815) The most eminent of English caricaturists was born 1757 in Chelsea, supposedly of Irish descent, the son of a church sexton. Like William Hogarth, James Gillray started his career as a letter engraver but soon escaped apprenticeship to join a company of strolling actors. Returning to London he became a student of the Royal Academy where he perfected his skills as a designer. He attained remarkable proficiency, as evidenced by a number of plates he engraved after his own designs, notably two subjects from Goldsmith's "Deserted Village" (1784), "The Wreck of the Nancy Packet" (1785), and two portraits of William Pitt.

It is as a caricaturist and cartoonist that Gillray is best known. The caricatures he turned out during his lifetime are said to number over 200, among which

Carlos Gimenez, "Bandolero." © *Carlos Gimenez.*

some are particularly famous. In 1792 he engraved a very funny illustration of "John Bull and his family landing at Boulogne," which is generally regarded as his first great work as a cartoonist. (The first cartoon attributed to him is the mediocre "Paddy on Horseback" of 1779.) Among his famous political cartoons are the "Anti-Saccharites" (1792), the "Fatigues of the Campaign in Flanders" (1793), a savage satire on the Duke of York and his way of conducting war from a safe distance, "The Consequences of a Successful French Invasion," in which the horrors to be expected are depicted with acerbic wit, and more significant "The King of Brobdingnag and Gulliver," published in 1803 and 1804 on the subject of an imaginary confrontation between King George III and Napoleon Bonaparte.

Gillray's nonpolitical cartoons (often having a social bite) include: "A Pic Nic Orchestra," "Blowing Up Pic

Nics," and the three remarkable series which he executed from 1800 to 1805: *Cookney Sportsman, Elements of Skating,* and *The Rake's Progress at the University,* a further takeoff on Hogarth's celebrated character and a bitter denunciation of the unsavory goings-on at England's most exalted seats of learning. The last known Gillray cartoon is dated 1811. Soon afterwards Gillray sank into a state of mingled delirium and early senility. He died in London in 1815.

Gillray's cartoons were highly popular and widely circulated not only in Britain, but also throughout Europe, and they have been credited with introducing the English style and format of the cartoon to the Continent. Gillray made ample (and often innovative) use of the balloon and pioneered in frame continuity, thus bringing his work up to the very threshold of the comic strip.

M.H.

GIMENEZ, CARLOS (1941-   ) Spanish cartoonist and writer born on March 6, 1941, in Madrid. After an apprenticeship at a porcelain factory, Carlos Gimenez started his art career in 1959 at the studio of illustrator Manuel Lopez Blanco. From there he went on to comics, at first only drawing, then, beginning in 1974, also writing the scripts. In the 1960s and early 1970s he drew comics on demand, many of them for the foreign market. His contributions in this period include *Drake & Drake, Gringo, Delta 99,* and *Dani Futuro,* an enjoyable science-fiction series by Victor Mora.

From 1974 on, his work took on a more original character. Taking his inspiration from a Brian Aldiss novel, he started work on a very personal story, *Hom.* The titular hero came first under the domination of a parasitic fungus, then fell prey to a pseudo-prophet, until the final annihilation of both dictators. Only after Fransisco Franco's death could this thinly veiled allegory be published in Spain.

Gimenez's autobiographical saga opened with *Paracuellos* ("Daredevils" 1976). The strip's different episodes, short and self-contained, refer directly to the author's childhood and include deeply lyrical sketches about an unusual juvenile world subjected to the cruelties of a dictatorial regime. The author continued his bitter reminiscences in *Auxillo social* ("Social Assistance"); in the meantime he had published recollections of his adult life in several interrelated series of short duration, *Barrio* (1977) and *La saga de los Menendez* (1978).

Gimenez used the same formula to retrace his career as an artist at Josep Toutain's art agency in his long-running series begun in 1982. In it there are many humorous allusions to Spanish artists and to Toutain himself. In addition to his more personal work, Gimenez has produced a number of stories dealing with sexual problems, including *Espana Una, Espana Grande,* and *Espana Libre!* He has also adapted the works of famous authors such as Stanislaw Lem and Jack London into comic-book form. In 1987 he started a new strip, *Bandolero,* based on the memoirs of the 19th century Spanish highwayman Juan Caballero.

Gimenez is better known in other European countries and known even better in the United States than in his homeland. Most of his creations during the 1990s, such as *Amor Amor!!* and *Coco, facho & co* ("Commie, Fascist and Co.") have been published first in France.

Unlike many of his Spanish colleagues, Gimenez does not display any spectacular grahpic abilities. The artist's style is based on a slightly cartoony line, with emphasis on the scripts first and foremost. There exists in the artist a burning desire to express his passionate conviction, which fully comes out in his work.

J.C.

GIMENEZ, JUAN (1943-   ) Spanish cartoonist and illustrator of Argentinean origin born on November 26, 1943, in Mendoza, Argentina. After studies at the Universidad Nacional de Cuyo in Mendoza, Juan Gimenez worked as an art director, and later, owner, of an advertising agency from 1966 to 1978. Since 1975, he has devoted most of his time to the creation of comics, although he is an illustrator and a designer for promotional and animated films. He worked on *Heavy Metal,* the 1981 animated feature, and on the live-action movie *El caballero y el dragon* ("The Knight and the Dragon" 1985). His clients have included many Spanish publishers and corporations, but it is for his highly original comic stories that he is best known.

Gimenez's most frequent scriptwriter has been Richard Barreiro, whose radical ideas regarding sociology and politics surface, though subdued, in his war and para-scientific stories. These collaborations first gained recognition with *As de Pike,* an aviation series published in the Argentine comic magazine *Skorpio* (1975-1979), followed by *La Estrella Negra* ("The Black Star") about a neutron star inhabited by zombies revived by magnetic storms and under the control of warrior-monks. Then came *Ciudad* (1982) also scripted by Barreiro and published in *Comix Internacional;* another Argentinean, Carlos Trillo, wrote the texts of *Basura* ("Garbage"), a science-fiction tale serialized in *Zona 84* (1985-1986), and published the following year in the U.S. magazine *Heavy Metal.* Barreiro, Trillo, and several other scriptwriters collaborated with Gimenez on a series of short stories, some of which were later compiled in the books *El extrano juicio a Roy Ely* ("The Strange Life of Roy Ely") and *La fabricas.* Gimenez himself wrote the tales that make up the volume *Cuestion de tiempo* ("A Matter of Time" in the United States, 1985).

In recent years Gimenez has written and illustrated two comic-strip series in the Sunday supplement of the Madrid daily *ABC,* titled respectively *Lem Dart* and *Leo Roa* (1986-1988). *Leo Roa* ran until the end of the decade. Gimenez also drew and scripted *El cuarto poder* ("The Fourth Power," 1988). In the 1990s he has divided his time between drawing illustrations and comic strips. Among the most notable has been *La caste des metabarons* ("The Caste of the Meta-Barons"), a long episode in the John Difool series (1992-1993), scripted by Alejandro Jodorowsky.

J.C.

GIMPEL BEINISH THE MATCHMAKER (U.S.) Samuel Zagat created *Gimpel Beinish the Matchmaker* for the Yiddish-language daily *Warheit* in 1912.

As his title indicates, Gimpel was in the business of arranging marriages (for a fee), a profession popularized in more recent times by one of the hit songs in *Fiddler on the Roof;* a bearded little man sloppily attired in black coat and striped pants, he went about his business unperturbed by the idiosyncrasies, pretensions, and foibles of his prospective customers. Scheming widows, self-deluded spinsters, and desperate mothers all found an attentive ear in Gimpel, who would attempt to match the most unlikely of twosomes with amiable but firm persistence. While admittedly not on a par with Sholem Aleichem, Samuel Zagat nevertheless paints a loving but truthful portrait of Jewish life in the New York of the 1910s. Unlike many other ethnic comic strip artists, he never tried to homogenize his characters and settings for general consumption, and his strip remains a sociological document virtually untainted by parochial self-consciousness.

Gimpel Beinish was dropped by *Warheit* in 1919 when Zagat left the paper to become the editorial cartoonist and illustrator of the *Jewish Daily Forward,* a position he retained until his death in 1964. Zagat was an artist of great, if unrecognized, comic talent and, like McManus, Opper, and a few others, had the knack of making his characters always look funny. *Gimpel Beinish* can thus be enjoyed even without any

Juan Gimenez, "Cuestion de Tiempo." © Juan Gimenez.

knowedge of Yiddish (the text was always printed in captions unobtrusively kept away from the pictures).

M.H.

GIM TORO (Italy) Very few of the comic strip characters created after World War II lasted more than five years; and even fewer have been reprinted or revived. Rarest of all are those characters still recalled with affection by other than comic fans: and of all of those none is more fondly remembered than *Gim Toro*.

The long saga of Gim Toro (literally "Jim Bull") started on May 12, 1946, and lasted for a total of 332 comic books published by Gino Casarotti, the last of which appeared on the newsstands on February 22, 1959.

Gim Toro—a name chosen by the publisher to symbolize the hero's strength—was a globe-girdling adventurer whose first exploits took him to the wilds of the Matto Grosso. Later Gim was confronted by his most deadly opponent: a Chinese gang, "the Hong of the Dragon," whose hideout was located in the subterranean depths of San Francisco. With the help of his companions, the muscular Greek Bourianakis, and the scrawny Kid, Gim Toro finally wipes out the sinister band, not, however, without plenty of fights and perils. In the course of his mortal struggle against the "yellow peril," our hero meets for the first time his most beautiful opponent, Lilyth Howard, nicknamed "the blonde viper," whom he would later convert to the good cause and who would become his faithful life-companion. After final victory over the Chinese gang, our heroes bring justice to other countries from Latin America to the Middle East.

The adventures of *Gim Toro* were written by Andrea Lavezzolo and most of its pages drawn by the painter Edgardo Dell'Acqua. A number of specials—"I Gimtorissimi"—were realized by other artists, among them Cappadonia, Cossio, Ferrari, Perego, and Canale. Very popular in Italy, the *Gim Toro* stories have also been translated in several European countries (especially in France, where the hero was depicted as French) and in South America.

G.B.

GINESITO (Spain) One of the rare Spanish features to be produced by a team, *Ginesito* came out in comic

"Gim Toro," Andrea Lavezzolo and Edgardo Dell'Acqua. © Editrice Dardo.

book format in 1944. The scripts were the product of various authors working under the supervision of playwright Adolfo Lopez Rubio, including Pipo, José Laffond, and Gordillo. The illustrations were done by a number of cartoonists who alternated and shared the work: some of them went on to become famous, like Victor de la Fuente, José Laffond, J. Fernandez, Lodial, and Perellon. At the start of the series, not anticipating the incredible success awaiting their creation, the authors had called their hero Satanas; when the feature became popular, however, the censorship authorities, ever vigilant, demanded that this diabolical name be changed, and thus the feature became *Ginesito* (which was the name of the real young boy who served as model to the cartoonists, and who later had a role in the movie *Lecciones de Buen Amor*).

Ginesito is probably the ugliest character in Spanish comics: his head is very big and he wears double-focus glasses, but each of his comic books, in which he goes through one complete episode, contains thrills galore. Ginesito has fought against the invisible man, against the Amazons, has traveled to the country of the dwarfs, and to the center of the earth. *Ginesito* was a typical product for consumption, without any pretense, and it enjoyed a tremendous success among young boys for a short period, superseding foreign comic books for a time. It inspired a movie, in which puppets were used alongside live actors, in the last year of its run (1946).

L.G.

GINGER MEGGS (Australia) Originally titled *Us Fellers, Ginger Meggs* was created for the Sydney *Sunday Sun* by Jimmy Bancks on November 13, 1921. *Ginger*, along with *Weary Willie and the Count de Main* by D. H. Souter, was Australia's first Sunday comic strip; the first major strip to occupy a full newspaper page printed in color; the first to be syndicated overseas and the most popular local strip ever published. Initially, Ginge (as he was affectionately known) was only a supporting character to the strip's star, Gladsome Gladys—but it wasn't long before the lovable, red-headed, eternal schoolboy became the lead character. Bancks had an instinctive feeling for his urchin and was able to capture all the warmth, charm, character, and innermost feelings of a small Australian boy, almost from the beginning; and it was these traits blended with Bancks' natural humor that allowed the strip to transcend the rather poor draftsmanship of the early years.

Whether winning or losing, Ginge's homespun philosophy and observations on life were a sheer delight.

"Ginesito," Adolfo López Rubio. © Editorial Rialto.

He exuded monumental self-confidence in his own abilities as a sportsman and all-around "good feller" and was almost devoid of modesty—yet, his bragging was done with such style that it was impossible not to admire his youthful swagger. Always the opportunist, *Ginge* was quick to take advantage of any given situation, even if it meant a complete reversal of his previously stated principles. For such a small boy, he was involved in a remarkable number of fights—many of them violent. His bitter enemy was Tiger Kelly, an uncouth ruffian some years older than Ginge, who took a constant delight in battering Ginge insensible on sight unless Ginge outsmarted him by splattering Tiger's face with a rotten tomato or rendering him unconscious with the assistance of some outside source.

He often crossed gloves with Eddie Coogan, his rival for the affections of the red-headed Minnie Peters—but generally, his encounters with this rival were based more on belittling than on mayhem. Minnie spent most of her life in the same dress, carrying a muff, and trying to lead Ginge to church or Sunday school and getting him to become a gentleman. His constant companions were his young brother, Dudley; a monkey, Tony; a dog, Mike; and his mate, Benny. Ginge lived with his parents who, despite their stern exterior, admired his spirit and often succumbed to his silver-tongued flattery. Next to Ginge, the down-to-earth, hard-working, plump Sarah Meggs was the most important character in the strip. Doomed to spend her entire life in the same dress, she was an excellent foil for Ginge and was responsible for her own subtle brand of humor. Nationalistic in flavor, the strip exhibited a resentment of authority which appealed to the Australian taste. When Bancks died, suddenly, in July 1952, the strip passed into the hands of Ron Vivian, who tried to be faithful to the original concept but never captured its unique flair. After Vivian's death in 1974, the strip was handled by a number of ghost artists who have only assisted in its decline. Lloyd Piper drew the strip for a while. It is now in the hands of James Kemsley, who marked the 75th anniversary of the venerable feature in November 1996.

J.R.

GINO E GIANNI (Italy) The Italian version of Lyman Young's *Tim Tyler's Luck* met with extraordinary success not only among the readers, but also among comic strip writers; and soon a whole host of youthful adventurers (all looking like Tim and Spud) were born. They always worked in pairs and helped each other out of various scrapes and perils: there were *Gianni e Luciano* by Fancelli and Guido Moroni-Celsi; *Marco e Andrea* by Sandro Cassone and Mario Tempesti, *Mario e Furio* by Federico Pedrocchi and Edgardo dell'Acqua, and so on.

Gino e Gianni, whose heroes were two young African colony settlers, were drawn by Rino Albertarelli. The strip first appeared on October 13, 1938 in the pages of the comic weekly *Topolino*; only later was the name of the scriptwriter revealed: Federico Pedrocchi (followed in 1942 by Amedeo Martini).

In the first episode titled "The Raiders of the Guardafui—Adventures in Somaliland, 1918," the two young friends were called in to put an end to the raids against Italian shipping off Cape Guardafui, perpetrated by Somali rebels led by the Greek adventurer Pandelidas. The story (now retitled *I Grande Caccie di Gino e Gianni*—"The Big Hunts of Gino and Giani") moved from there to more typical adventures in which Gino and Gianni, together with white hunter Bracchi, were hired by American millionaire Clink to capture a white lion. Albertarelli displayed his drawing abilities and pictorial sense to the fullest, making this the best period of *Gino e Gianni*, with beautifully laid-out pages rich in adventures. Unfortunately the strip was ruined early in 1942 by a heavily propagandistic text and did not survive the defeats suffered by Italy the following year.

G.B.

GIORDANO, RICHARD (1932-   ) American comic book artist and editor born July 20, 1932 in New York City. After studies at the School of Industrial Art, "Dick" Giordano began his comic book career in 1951, working on Fiction House's *Sheena* for the Jerry Iger Studio. In 1952, he began a 17-year relationship with Charlton, working on the group's complete range of comic titles, including Western, war, crime, science fiction, love, and horror. He was the group's assistant editor (1957-1959) and editor (1966-1967).

As a Charlton artist, Giordano's best strip was undoubtably his artwork on the adventure-oriented *Sarge Steel* strip. While his storytelling was weak—it was apparent he was not concerned with the story's flow—his draftsmanship and illustrations were superb. When Giordano assumed the group's editorship in 1966, he began a series of well-received superhero titles, among them Steve Ditko's *Blue Beetle* and *The Question* strips. While Charlton always had a deserved reputation for inferior material, Giordano's short tenure as editor allowed them to produce some of the finest material in the otherwise depressed late 1960s. Unfortunately, the line was not financially successful, and was cancelled, and the last titles appeared in summer 1968.

Giordano moved to National as an editor in 1968. Again he instituted a whole new line, among them the well-done but short-lived *Creeper, Hawk and Dove,* and the *Secret Six*. He also gave established books like *Aquaman* and *Blackhawk* notable, if short, creative boosts. He was also instrumental in bringing talents like writer/artist Steve Ditko, writer Denny O'Neil, and artists Jim Aparo and Pat Boyette to National. He resigned in 1970, after most of his titles—perhaps too advanced for the comic books' younger readership—had been cancelled.

After his resignation from National, Giordano resumed his art career, primarily as an inker. His style—which had become more lucid since his *Sarge Steel* days—made him one of the most respected and prolific inkers in the field, and he and Neal Adams eventually opened a studio to produce comic books and advertising work. During his career, Giordano has also worked for Dell (1964-1966), Archie (1974), Lev Gleason (1955), Marvel (1970-1975), and others. His brother-in-law, Sal Trapani, is also a comic book artist. Giordano came back to DC as managing editor in 1980. He had risen to the rank of vice-president and editorial director by the time he resigned in 1993 to resume a freelance career. (In 1994, for example, he illustrated an original *Modesty Blaise* graphic novel.)

J.B.

GIR *See* Giraud, Jean.

GIRAUD, JEAN (1938-   ) A French cartoonist and illustrator born 1938 in Paris, Jean Giraud—or "Gir" as he is better known—displayed a love of comics at the earliest age, copying comic features before he even went to school. Later he attended the Technical School of Applied Arts, where he studied home furnishing and decorating crafts. In 1954, while still at school, he produced his first comic strip, a Western called *Les Aventures de Franck et Jéremie* ("The Adventures of Franck and Jéremie") for *Far West*, one of the many comic magazines edited at one time or other by Marijac. That same year Gir met Jean-Claude Mézières, also a comic strip fan, who introduced him into the Catholic publication, *Coeurs Vaillants*; there Gir illustrated a number of realistic and didactic stories. After two years he was drafted into the army, but continued to draw for the military magazine *5/5*.

Discharged in 1960, Gir became assistant to Joseph Gillain (Jijé) on *Jerry Spring*; as he himself admitted, this proved to be the best art school he ever attended. In 1961 he left Jijé to work for Studio Hachette (again on an introduction by Mézières) until 1963, when he created (with scriptwriter Jean-Michel Charlier) a Western strip titled *Fort Navajo* (which became *Lieutenant Blueberry* the next year for the comic weekly *Pilote*.)

In addition to his work on *Blueberry*, Gir has produced a number of other comic strips under the pseudonym "Moebius" for such publications as the satirical monthly *Hara-Kiri* and the cartoonist-run *L'Echo des Savanes*; he has also done illustration work for science-fiction novels and stories published by Editions Opta.

Gir is widely—and justly—regarded as one of Europe's top comic strip artists; his *Lieutenant Blueberry* has been a popular, as well as a critical, success since 1964. And Gir himself has been the recipient of countless awards, including one as "best foreign artist" awarded him by the Academy of Comic Book Arts in the United States.

Since 1975 Giraud has led a double life. As Gir he has continued to turn out the *Blueberry* series, adding the writing to his drawing chores after Charlier's death in 1989. Along with supervising *La jeunesse de Blueberry* ("Blueberry's Youth") drawn by Colin Wilson, he has also been scripting since 1991 *Marshal Blueberry* on illustrations by William Vance.

At the same time, under his Moebius *nom-de-plume*, he was one of the founders of the trailblazing *Métal Hurlant* magazine: it was there that he published some of his most acclaimed creations, beginning with the fantasy tale of *Arzach* realized entirely with visuals, *sans* text or dialogue. Other notable stories to stumble out of his facile pen have been *Le garage hermétique* ("The Airtight Garage," 1976-77), midway between science fiction and tall tale; *The Long Tomorrow* (on a script by Dan O'Bannon, 1976); and an episode of *The Silver Surfer* written by Stan Lee (1988-89). Some of his more memorable narratives have been done in collaboration with *avant-garde* filmmaker Alejandro Jodorowsky, who supplied the scripts: *Les yeux du chat* ("The Eyes of the Cat," a 1977 exercise in terror); *John Difool* (the extraordinary adventures of a detective of the future) from 1981 to 1989; and *Le coeur couronné* ("The Crowned Heart," 1992).

In addition he has also been very active in the field of animation. In 1978 he drew the storyboards of René Laloux's *Les maitres du temps* ("Time Masters"); followed by his doing the storyboards and backgrounds for Disney's *Tron* (1982); and in 1985 he did the same

for the Japanese *Little Nemo*. He is currently working on animated versions of some of his works. Among the many distinctions and honors bestowed upon him, Giraud was made a Knight of Arts and Letters by the French Minister of Culture.

M.H.

"The Girl from the People's Commune," Ho Yu-chih.

GIRL FROM THE PEOPLE'S COMMUNE, THE (China) Adapted from an original short story by Li Chun, *The Girl From the People's Commune* was published in comic book form in 1965 by the People's Art Publications in Shanghai. The narrative was written by Lu Chung-chien, and drawn by Ho Yu-chih.

The Girl From the People's Commune is a good example of the didacticism and homespun philosophy often explicit in Chinese comic books. In this simple tale of a young, uneducated peasant girl, Li Shuang-shuang, who is able to reform not only her whole commune but also her non-reconstructed husband, the traditional values of Chinese life are subtly interwoven with the teachings of Chairman Mao (although his name is never mentioned). The pace in this tale of edification is slow, and nothing much happens. Actually the story is often boring and were it not for the unmistakeable Socialist message, one might easily confuse *Girl* with any number of *Treasure Chest* homilies about the rewards of hard work and clean living.

The artwork is not very distinguished, although it always remains craftsmanlike. As in most Chinese comic books, the layout is uninspired (four panels of equal size to a page), and speech balloons are only sparsely used (befitting peasant people, as the characters do not talk much). All in all, *The Girl From the People's Commune* is of interest only to historians, sociologists, and Sinologists.

The Girl From the People's Commune was reprinted (under the title "Li Shuang-shuang") in the collection of Chinese comics published by Doubleday (*The People's Comic Book*, 1973).

M.H.

GIRLS IN APARTMENT 3-G *See* Apartment 3-G.

GLASS, JACK (1890-1970) Although the artwork of Jack Glass was striking and recognizable immediatly to any young reader of the comics and boys' weeklies published by D.C. Thompson from the 1920s to the 1960s, he was another cartoonist who was refused the right to sign his own work. Among his credits is the first American-style superhero in British comics, *The Amazing Mr. X,* who first burst into action in *The Dandy Comic* on December 23, 1944.

John Glass was a Scotsman, born in Edinburgh in the late 1890s. He joined the art department of D.C. Thompson Company in the late 1920s. In the early years of his career he specialized in drawing what were known then as "the heading blocks," the title illustrations which decorated every story series and serial published in the Thompson "Big Five:" the boys' story papers *Adventure, Rover, Wizard, Hotspur,* and *Skipper.* Glass adapted his style to any story, from western to epics of the Empire, school stories, and early science-fiction sagas. He also drew many of the full-color covers, the best remembered of which was *Wilson the Wonder Man* (1943), a black-cloaked athlete around 100 years old who came out of nowhere to break every record at the Olympic games.

Glass's career as a picture story and serial artist began in 1937 with the first issue of *The Dandy Comic* (1937), Thompson's first weekly comic for children. His two-page strip, *The Daring Deeds of Buck Wilson,* starred a cowboy. The strip's format set Glass's style for the rest of his comic art life: no lettering or speech balloons, but lengthy captions teling the story in eleven or more lines under every panel.

Later characters included *Never Never Nelson, the Circus Scout Who Never Fails; Cracker Jack, the Wonder Whip Man* (both 1938); *Young Strongarm, the Axe Man* (*Beano,* 1939); *Wildfire, the War Horse* (*Dandy,* 1940); *The Prince on the Flying Horse* (*Beano*); and *Boomerang Burke, the No-Gun Mountie* (*Dandy,* 1941). He also adapted some of the story paper heroes into strip serials, including *The Iron Teacher,* a prewar serial, returned as a strip to *The Hotspur* in 1951, and in the same paper a masked cowboy called *Leatherface* had four adventures from 1951 to 1956. Among the fantasies drawn by Glass were *Little Master of the Swooping Monster* (*Dandy,* 1953), *The Iron Fish* (*Beano,* 1958), and *South with the Hover-car* (*Dandy,* 1967). His last serial was *Gunsmoke Jack* (*Dandy,* 1968), after which he drew several single episode items for *New Hotspur,* and the complete adventure, *Randall's Vandals* for the *Dandy Annual* (1969). He then retired, and died not long after in the early 1970s. His style, bold, harsh, some might say crude, but always action-packed and distinctly his own, died with him.

D.G.

GLOBI (Switzerland) *Globi,* created by J. K. Schiele and Robert Lips (1912-1975), is one of the few comic characters that grew out of an advertising campaign. When the Swiss department store Globus's 25th anniversary was to be celebrated in 1932, J. K. Schiele, head of the advertising department, invented the parrot Globi, who was to head a two-week children's festival in all of the five Globus stores in Zurich, Basel, St. Gallen, Chur, and Aarau. On August 24, 1932, Globi made his first newspaper appearance in a comic strip advertising campaign announcing the big event. Emerging from his egg clothed with checkerboard pants, Globi immediately left the Sahara to fly north, where he discovered all the festivities at hand and invited children to join him in the fun. The art was by Robert Lips, who hit the spot with his clean, witty style. The name "Globi" was given to the parrot by Heinrich Laser.

"Globi," Robert Lips. © Globi Verlag.

The festival, personal appearances of Globi included, was immensely successful. There were Globi ads in Swiss newspapers during its duration. The character was too good to be wasted in a one-time advertising campaign. Thus, J.K. Schiele started *Der Globi,* a children's magazine that featured Globi comics, poems, stories, puzzles, contests, etc. The magazine was available at the Globus stores and after specials in 1933 and 1934, was published monthly starting in January 1935. Also in 1935, J.K. Schiele had the first *Globi* book published, but it was not overly successful. It was decided that future books should be printed on other than slick paper so it would be easier for children to color the comic strips. It was also decided to add verses, and these were written by Alfred Bruggmann. They are now being written by Jakob Stäheli.

The second book, *Globi junior,* introducing the first of the Globi kids, was published in 1938, and this new format worked. Since then, a total of 42 *Globi* books have been published, the latest one drawn by Swiss cartoonist Werner Büchi. Total sales in Switzerland alone up to 1975 have totalled some four million books. Over the years there have been numerous foreign editions, in France, Belgium, Holland, Norway, Brazil, Japan, and in 1948 *Globi* came to the United States in the monthly *Story Parade. Globi* books were exported into Germany and Austria after World War II for some time. They have been introduced there in pocket book editions in 1973. There have been many Globi toys, and a television program is being prepared.

Renowned cartoonist Werner Büchi only produced two *Globi* books. His style did not mesh with the *Globi* universe. Since 1980 new stories have been written and drawn successfully by Swiss cartoonist Peter Heinzer. (Born in 1945, Heinzer is one of the few Swiss who did not get to read *Globi* as a child.) Heinzer's stories are put into verse by Guido Strebel. In 1988 a female version of Globi was introduced, *Globine,* drawn by Anne Christiansen. A baby Globi, *Globeli,* was introduced in 1992 by Brigitte Conte. In 1994 another relative was introduced, the Scot McGlobi. The McGlobi comic (with speech balloons instead of rhymed narrative) was written by Jan Marek and drawn by Heiri Schmidt. After more than 60 years, Globi is still a successful merchandising character and has appeared on a number of products as well as on television.

W.F.

GLOOPS (G.B.) Gloops is the original lisping cat, born years before Warner Brothers's cartoon cat, Sylvester. He first appeared in May 1928, in the *Sheffield Evening Telegraph,* a four-panel daily strip in the Children's Corner run by "Uncle Nick." His original artist signed himself "Ken," later "Cousin Ken," and then a remarkably

"Gloops." © Weekly Telegraph.

similar artist took over in 1934, "Cousin Toby." (Around the same time "Uncle Nick" gave way to "Aunt Edith.") The strip then appeared in the *Yorkshire Telegraph* and *Weekly Telegraph*, and in 1939 transferred to *The Star*, an evening paper. Dropped for some years, both the character and his Gloops Club were revived by *The Star* in November 1972, when the old strips were reprinted in a new weekly supplement for children, *Junior Star*. An actor in a specially made Gloops Suit made personal appearances and promoted the newspaper at children's hospital parties, etc.

Gloops ("Thummer time ith over, it'th my turn to get breakfatht!") is a large white cat who lives with twins Burford and Belinda, Granpa, and their maid, Emmer. There is the odd visit from Aunt Snork, and the odder visit from cat Ginger. The format is a daily joke, with occasional continuity, and Gloops's ability to speak is taken for granted by all.

The strip was reprinted in thirteen thick paper comic books between 1930 and 1939, beginning with *The Christmas Book of Gloops* (1930) and ending with *Gloops*

Christmas Annual (1939), including a special *Jubilee Number* (1935).

D.G.

GODWIN, FRANCIS (1889-1959) American cartoonist, illustrator, and painter born October 20, 1889, in Washington, D.C., Francis (Frank) Godwin's father, Harry R. Godwin, was city editor of the *Washington Star*, and the young Godwin started his art apprenticeship on that paper around 1905. He later went to study at the Art Students' League in New York, where he became friends with James Montgomery Flagg, with whom he shared a studio at one time. Thanks to Flagg's friendship, Godwin started contributing to the major humor magazines of the day (his earliest recorded work, a two-line cartoon, appeared in *Judge* in 1908). From then on, he became one of the most prolific cartoonists and illustrators of the time, whose work (signed and unsigned) appeared regularly in every major (and not so major) magazine in the country. His illustrations (notably for *Collier's*, *Liberty*, and *Cosmopolitan*) display a craftsmanship that few other illustrators could equal. He also did a great deal of advertising work (his ads for Prince Albert tobacco in *Life* are as good as anything he did in straight illustration) and in the 1930s he took up painting—the murals he did for the Kings County Hospital in Brooklyn show him as a vigorous and accomplished practitioner of the art.

By his own account, Godwin felt no special inclination toward the comic strip and, like Harold Foster, he entered the field at a relatively late age. In 1927 he started *Connie* for the Ledger Syndicate: a girl strip at the beginning (not unlike Charles Voight's contemporary *Betty*), *Connie* soon became a sophisticated action feature worthy of comparison with the best production of the period. Unheralded and almost unnoticed during the time it ran from 1927 to 1944, *Connie* is now regarded as one of the most vibrant, innovative, and lyrical creations ever to grace the comics page. (In the early to middle 1930s the Sunday *Connie* was accompanied by a bottom strip, *The Wet Blanket*, a weak gag feature saved only by Godwin's superlative penwork.)

Frank Godwin's talent was soon noticed by the *Ledger* editors and he found himself turning out most of the illustration strips distributed by this unfortunately obscure syndicate. Most of Godwin's prodigious output for the *Ledger* remained unsigned, but his mark (composed of a network of fine crosshatchings and a cursive line, as distinctive as a signature) can clearly be

"Rusty Riley," Frank Godwin. © King Features Syndicate.

seen on such disparate features as *Babe Bunting* (the adventures of a little girl, created by Fanny Cory and later credited to Roy L. Williams); *Eagle Scout Roy Powers* (a Boy Scout strip bylined by Paul Powell); and the anonymous *War on Crime* (a comic strip pictorialization of the careers of notorious criminals, on which each and every *Ledger* artist and writer seems to have taken turns). Just before and after *Connie* folded, Godwin worked sporadically in comic books (on *Wonder Woman* for National in 1943-45, and for various Lev Gleason publications from 1945-48). That same year he produced *Rusty Riley*, a luminous strip of youth and the outdoors, for King Features Syndicate. He died of a heart attack in his home in New Hope, Penn. on August 5, 1959. A few weeks earlier he had abandoned the drawing of *Rusty Riley*.

Frank Godwin has always received greater recognition as an illustrator than as a cartoonist (he was vice-president of the Society of Illustrators and a member of its Hall of Fame). Yet his work in the comics field, underrated as it is, deserves the higher praise. *Connie* is an undisputed masterpiece of draftsmanship, composition, and design, and *Rusty Riley* is not too far behind. Even *Babe Bunting* and *Roy Powers* are worthy of study. It has been Godwin's misfortune that the bulk of his work was carried by a syndicate so obscure as to be virtually invisible; and that his latter and better-known effort (*Rusty Riley*) was saddled with an inane story line and a restrictive editorial policy. Unlike Harold Foster's, Alex Raymond's and Burne Hogarth's, Frank Godwin's *oeuvre* is still waiting for a comprehensive, scholarly evaluation: when this study finally comes, he will be found to be one of the undisputed giants of the field.

M.H.

GOHS, ROLF (1933-   ) Rolf Gohs, born 1933 in Esthonia, lived and grew up during World War II in Poland, from there fleeing to Germany, then to Austria, and finally coming to live in Sweden in 1947. He finished school there and at the age of 16 started working for Centerförlaget, the first Swedish comics publisher. His earliest illustrations were destined for covers or as illustrations for cowboy novels. His first chance to do a comic feature came along when the artist of *Kilroy* died and the 19-year-old Gohs took over the strip, which was published in Sweden in *Seriemagasinet*. Later, the strip was continued by Spanish artist Francisco Cueto, while Gohs drew the science-fiction comic *Mannen från Claa* ("Man from Claa") and the mystery strips *Bomben* ("Bombs") and *Dödens fågel* ("Bird of Death"). These appeared in *Seriemagasinet* between 1956 and 1958. Also in 1958 he concentrated on illustration, photography, and film. For some time he even became chief illustrator for *Levande Livet* ("Live Life"). In 1958 he won a prize with *Statyetten* ("Statuettes"), one of his movie shorts. Another of his films shown on Swedish television was a short about war comics, *Pang, du ar dod* ("Bang, You're Dead").

While working mainly as a photographer and on movies, in the 1960s Gohs started working for Semic Press, another Swedish comic book publisher, doing covers for *Fantomen* ("Phantom") comic books. At the same time he also helped Börje Nilsson draw a daily strip version of *Pelle Svanslös* ("Pelle No-Tail"), a humor strip about an adventurous anthropomorphic cat without a tail.

In 1969, Rolf Gohs and comic editors Per Anders Jonsson and Janne Brydner started their own publishing house—Inter Art, which produced two comic books, *Kilroy*, a revival of the *Seriemagasinet* feature now written by Swedish writers and drawn by Spanish artists, and *Mystiska 2:an* ("The Mystic Two" or "Sacho and Stefan"), an original Gohs creation. When financial difficulties developed, the group sold out to Semic Press, and *Mystiska 2:an* was continued. Gohs himself is now largely out of the comics scene.

The Gohs style depends largely on sharp contrasts of light and dark. It is a photographic style influenced by Gohs's other career in photography and by Hal Foster, Burne Hogarth, and Alex Raymond, favorite comic artists.

W.F.

GOLDBERG, REUBEN LUCIUS (1883-1970) Born July 4, 1883, Reuben Lucius Goldberg was the second-born of three sons of Hannah and Max Goldberg. As the son of a well-to-do moneylender and land speculator, and possessed of a competent talent as an artist, the young "Rube" had a great time at the University of California at Berkeley, cartooning for the campus humor magazine and yearbook. Deciding to work on newspapers, Goldberg went to the *San Francisco Chronicle* after graduation in 1904, and made a fair hit with readers with a series of amusing sports cartoons. From there, he went to the *S. F. Bulletin*, covering the raucous boxing and football scene of the period. By then he felt ready to tackle the big city, and went to New York in October 1907, in the wake of a series of *Mike and Ike* Sunday half-pages (dealing with identical twin shrimps in slapstick situations) he had sold to the World Color Printing Co. comic section. But the company appears to have reported minimal reader response to the early, crude pages upon Rube's arrival, and he had to resort to considerable street-tramping to land a job as sports-page cartoonist on the *N.Y. Evening Mail*. Starting at $50.00 a week, Rube made some impact with his drawings on *Mail* readers, and shortly found his work appearing back in San Francisco (in the *Call*) and elsewhere on a semi-syndicated basis. The popularity of his sports cartoon work with the *Mail* made the paper give Goldberg a Sunday page in 1915, which he called *Boob McNutt*. Quickly syndicated by Hearst, this strip led to much of Rube's later national recognition (as did the nutty comic-strip string, pulley, and fire-bucket inventions with which the public credited him), and after a stint as creator of other, lesser strips, a job as political cartoonist for the *N.Y. Sun*, notable accomplishments as a comic sculptor, and acclaim as an after-dinner speaker, Goldberg died, full of fame and friendship, on December 7, 1970.

After *Boob McNutt* was launched, Goldberg revived his early Mike and Ike characters in his daily *Mail* strip in 1917 as occasional gag sequence figures. By then, his daily sports-page feature had developed such publicly popular running gag items as *Foolish Questions, I'm The Guy* (source of one of the first song hits based on newspaper cartoon work, in 1912), and *Boobs Abroad* (based on Rube's 1913 trip to Europe). Rube had found time to go into vaudeville in 1911 as a stand-up funnyman, cartoonist, and fortune-teller. It was not until 1928 that he finally gave up his daily miscellany strip (which never had a standard running title) and launched his first daily continuity strip (probably the best sustained work he ever did) called *Bobo Baxter*, about a middle-aged, balding man who stumbles in and out of fantastic adventures suited to the more stalwart kind of hero,

COOLING DEVICE FOR BUSY OFFICE-WORKER

IRANIAN PREMIER **MOHAMMED MOSSADEGH** (A) WEEPS AND FAINTS DURING SPEECH, FALLS ON PIANO (B) AND MUSIC STARTS **BARBARA HUTTON** AND **BARON GOTTFRIED VON CRAMM** (C) DANCING—

BARON KICKS OVER BOTTLE OF **GROMYKO'S** VODKA (D) WHICH DROPS IN **JOE E. BROWN'S** MOUTH (E) — HE PATS SELF ON BACK WITH HAND (F) TO STOP CHOKING—

LEVER (G) STARTS **EDDIE ARCARO** (H) TESTING NEW **CENTRAL PARK** MERRY-GO-ROUND (I), TURNING AUGER (J) WHICH BORES HOLE IN LARGE CAKE OF ICE (K)—

PIECES OF ICE DROP DOWN NECK OF OFFICE WORKER (L) GIVING REFRESHING COOLING EFFECT—HE **DRIES SELF WITH HANDY DESK BLOTTER.**

Rube Goldberg, gag cartoon.

which Goldberg unfortunately dropped in 1930 to return to the miscellany format. On January 28, 1934, he again tried continuity in a disastrous stab at a serious, soap-opera strip called *Doc Wright* (distributed, like all of his post-1918 work, by Hearst syndicates), which folded its story about a doctor and his troubled patients a year later. On September 20, 1936, he started a daily *and* Sunday comic strip narrative called *Lala Palooza* for the Frank Markey Syndicate, having left Hearst distribution with *Doc Wright* in 1935. This, too, had a mediocre public response—Rube's image of a Mae West-shaped, chocolate-munching heiress as heroine and her ne'er-do-well brother, an imitation of Segar's Wimpy, did little to spark reader fancy—and was dropped in 1939 with little notice and no regret. His last strip effort, a 1939 Sunday miscellany page called *Rube Goldberg's Sideshow*, distributed by the Register and Tribune Syndicate, featured one minor continuity strip, *Brad and Dad*, part of which was as amusing as anything Rube ever did, but was tucked away in 1941. (Unlike most cartoonists, his wealth, inherited from his father, permitted him to indulge his whims in this high-handed fashion with no financial worries.) After *Sideshow*, Rube turned to editorial cartooning (for which he won a Pulitzer prize in 1948), augmenting this work with the occasional magazine article and book writing which he had done throughout his career, and developed his skills as a sculptor. He also found time to do important work in organizing the National Cartoonists' Society in 1945, (becoming its first president the next year), and filled out his time with toastmaster stints and travels.

Goldberg's cartooning style, compared to that of his equally famed peers, was not attractive or memorable. It was sloppy and imprecise, and often betrayed his sometimes excellent conceptions, which were more than his faulty style could handle adequately. Striking comic notions and humorous narrative suspense were his real talents, yet when he hit his stride with a good strip concept, as he did with the later *Boob McNutt* and *Bobo Baxter*, he didn't seem to know it, and tired of these works as readily and abruptly as he did of his less

effective efforts. He engaged the public interest with simple gimmicky running features (such as the *Foolish Questions*) and reaped enormous general fame as a result (much as did the MCs of the *Professor Quiz* and *People Are Funny* radio shows at a later date). His foolishly complicated inventions, which gained him dictionary entry (for "Rube Goldberg contraption," etc.), appealed to the same broad audience base, even though it was not his unique idea. W. Heath Robinson had developed fanciful inventions of his own in various cartoon series for English magazines and newspapers in the 1910s, while the American strip cartoonist, Clare Victor Dwiggins, introduced devices very similar to those of Goldberg's in a *New York World* Sunday page called *School Days* of the 1900s, which Goldberg must have read before he ever drew any of his own comic contraptions, since his early *Mike and Ike* ran in the same comic section. A curious case of a strip cartoonist better known to the public than any of his characters (except possibly Mike and Ike), Goldberg did some memorable work in spite of all his defects, and is one of the major strip artists.

B.B.

GOLGO 13 (Japan) Golgo 13 was created by Takao Saitō for the monthly (later twice-monthly) *Big Comic* and made its debut in January 1969.

Golgo 13 is a super-efficient killer whose real name, race, nationality, and personal antecedents are all equally unknown. He has thick eyebrows, sharp eyes, a long nose, crew-cut hair, and steel-like muscles. He never expresses his feelings, laughs, or cries. He always accomplishes his murders with the utmost professionalism and detachment, whomever his clients may be (these have indifferently included the C.I.A., the K.G.B., the F.B.I., Arab guerrillas, and American gangsters). Golgo's victims have been equally eclectic, ranging from mafia chieftains to neo-Nazis to spies to highjackers, and none has ever escaped the implacable fire of his guns (his favorite one being a custom-crafted M-16 rifle). Golgo 13 has also been the target of other

わすことに全力を注げ。

"Golgo 13," Takao Saitō. © Big Comic.

killers, detectives, and sharp-shooters, none of whom could match his steely resolve and machine-like precision.

Golgo 13's name is a combination derived from "Golgotha" and the unlucky number 13. The protagonist himself is clearly beyond law and morality. His activities have taken place all over the world, in North and South America, Europe, Africa, the Middle East, etc.

Golgo 13's scriptwriters have been Takao Saitō himself, Kazuo Koike, K. Motomitsu, Kōtāro Mori, Tsutomu Miyazaki, Kyōta Kita, and Masaru Iwasawa. Soon after the strip's inception, Golgo 13 became the new kind of hero—cool, cruel, nihilistic—and widely imitated by other comic book artists. *Golgo 13* has also appeared in magazines and in book form. His books have been best-sellers and have been reprinted many times. *Golgo 13* was also adapted to television (but with considerable alterations) and was made into a movie. After a record 25 years of serialization, the series ended its run in 1994.

H.K.

GOMEZ, PABLO S. (1931-) Pablo Gomez is a Filipino cartoonist born on January 25, 1931, in Manila. He was the seventh child in a family of 14. His greatest ambition was to become a good writer and a publisher. Both his goals have long been fulfilled. His brother, Dominador, is also a comic book writer.

Pablo Gomez started out in 1950 as a proofreader for one of the comic companies in the Philippines. At that time he was also developing his craft as a writer. Eventually he was promoted to assistant editor, then editor, for *Pilipino Komiks* and *Hiwaga*, two of the foremost comic books in the country.

As a writer, his dramatic and moving portrayal of people trapped in the web of circumstances beyond their control was immensely popular. His graphic novels had solid plots and excellent characterizations. His sensitive handling of emotional scenes and his ability to create the proper mood and feeling in his comic strips made his work readily applicable to the performing arts of stage, motion pictures, and television. Many of his stories have been adapted into film.

Through the years Gomez has teamed up with many of the finest comic artists in the field to produce memorable graphic stories. Some of the artists he worked with were Nestor Redondo, Alfredo Alcala, Noly Panaligan, Jesse Santos, Alex Niño, Hal Santiago, and Tony Caravana.

In 1963 he formed his own company, P.S.G. Publications. Along with his art director, L. S. Martinez, Gomez produced a variety of movie and rock music magazines as well as songbooks. His line of comics included *United Continental, Kidlat* ("Lightning"), *Universal*, and *Planet*. Among the contributing writers and artists for his comics have been Francisco Coching, Jun Bordillo, Ruding Mesina, Frank Redondo, Jorge Peñamora, Alcabral, Steve Gan, Rico Rival, Abe Ocampo, Fred Carillo, Deo Gonzales, and Vir Aguirre.

Recently Gomez was the recipient of the highest award the Philippine publications industry has to offer. He has also been awarded by the film industry for his writing. His most popular works are *Gonzales, Kalik Sa Apoy* ("Kiss of Fire"), *Odinah, Pagbabalik Ng Lawin* ("Return of the Hawk"), *Santo Domingo, Esteban*, and *Biyak Na Bato* ("Broken Stone"). In the 1980s he went to work for Philippine television, notably with his own series, *Panohon*; he has also written well over 100 novels, many illustrated by Nestor Redondo.

O.J.

GONICK, LARRY (1946-) American cartoonist and author born on August 24, 1946, in San Francisco. Larry Gonick forsook an early love of drawing for a foray into mathematics at Harvard University, where he received both his B.A. and M.A. He later returned to drawing, however, and he later averred, "I dropped out of mathematics graduate school and into cartooning because I wanted to abandon the estoteric for the accessible and popular."

Gonick's efforts at enlightening the masses initially took the form of comic books, which he turned out for Rip Off Press from 1978 to 1985 under the general title *The Cartoon History of the Universe*. These proved reasonably successful and became best-sellers several years later. Encouraged by his success, Gonick followed up with *The Cartoon Guide to U.S. History* (1987-1988). In the meantime he had also penned *The Cartoon Guide to Genetics* (in collaboration with Mark Wheelis), *The Cartoon Guide to Computer Science,* and *The Cartoon Guide to Physics* (with Art Huffman). His latest venture in this vein has been *The Cartoon Guide to (Non) Communication* (1993), which is a revised version of an earlier work he turned out for a Belgian publisher, *New Babelonia*.

Gonick treats his serious subjects with a light, even facetious, touch. A chapter of U.S.history is titled "In which happiness is pursued, with a gun," while a chapter dealing with Julius Caesar is called "Caesarian Section." In his overview of the institution of slavery in the South, he writes, "Race mixing was illegal—which only proves that not all laws were enforced 100%." Compared to the writing, the drawing is primitive, even crude, and only serves as humorous counterpoint.

His works are more like comic treatises with doodles than *bona fide* comic books, but they are very entertaining, as well as highly informative in a light-hearted way. Gonnick may have found the key to every educator's dream—making learning fun.

M.H.

GOODWIN, ARCHIE (1937-   ) American comic book and comic strip writer born September 8, 1937, in Kansas City, Missouri. Goodwin's first comic art material began appearing in 1959 and 1960, when he assisted Leonard Starr on *On Stage*, drew a comic art page for *Fishing World*, and was an assistant art director and spot illustrator for *Redbook* magazine. Harvey's *Hermit* strip was his first comic book work, and it appeared in October, 1962's *Alarming Adventures* number one.

After another stint at *Redbook*, Goodwin became an associated editor/writer for Warren's black-and-white comic magazines, and it was there that he wrote for the landmark *Blazing Combat* title. At a time when the American citizenry was still supporting their country's involvement in Vietnam, *Blazing Combat* was an early, outspoken, consistent critic of all types of war; in this regard Goodwin's scripts surpassed even the Kurtzman stories from a decade before. This novel editorial stand doomed the book to a short, four-issue history (October 1965 to July 1966). Goodwin remained at Warren until 1970, scripting for the usually nonpolitical horror magazines.

In December 1966, Goodwin teamed up with Al Williamson to produce King's *Secret Agent Corrigan* syndicated strip. And while the contemporary spy features were heavily-influenced by the then-popular James Bond "gimmick" movies, Goodwin's material was more mature and intelligent than the standard fare. It might well have been the best adventure strip of the time, and he and Williamson still do the strip. Goodwin also ghosted King's *Captain Kate* feature from 1966 through 1969.

Goodwin made his first considerable foray into the comic book market in 1968, when he joined the Marvel group and began writing the whole range of Marvel superheroes, including *Iron Man, Sub-Mariner,* and *Dr. Strange.* While many of his contemporaries were indulging in gimmicks and campiness to bolster the faltering "Marvel Age of Comics," Goodwin emerged as the company's premier adventure writer. While Roy Thomas, Marvel's other young star of the period, concentrated on personalities and interaction, Goodwin wrote Marvel's most intelligent and believable action

"Sinner," art and story, Archie Goodwin. © Archie Goodwin.

stories. Rarely was there a lacklustre or skimpy Goodwin script. In 1972 he moved to National as an editor, and while his National war material fell short of his *Blazing Combat* work, he was responsible for helping *Batman* regain the aura of mystery and intrigue that was once its trademark. He and artist Walt Simonson created the unique *Manhunter* adventure feature, and it earned Goodwin two ACBA "Shazam" awards for best dramatic writer and best short story.

Goodwin also ghost-wrote, under the pseudonym "Robert Franklin," two of the era's most experimental features, both drawn by Gil Kane: *His Name is Savage* magazine (1968) and the *Blackmark* paperback (1971).

J.B.

In 1980 Goodwin took over the editorship of *Epic Illustrated*, a comics magazine published by Marvel. In addition to his considerable comic-book writing, he also continued to turn out scripts for newspaper strips; besides *Secret Agent Corrigan*, which he left in 1980, he also wrote again on illustrations by Al Williamson for the *Star Wars* strip from 1981 to 1984.

M.H.

GORDO (U.S.) Gus Arriola started *Gordo* for United Feature Syndicate on November 24, 1941; the strip was suspended from October 28, 1942, to June 24, 1946, as a daily but the Sunday page followed on May 2, 1943.

The Widow Gonzales is a very determined woman, and she has to be. For better than 30 years now she has schemed, stolen, defrauded, and all but murdered in order to obtain in marriage her conception of a small Mexican town's most eligible bachelor. The shrinking bachelor of Del Monte is a one-time local farmer (now the driver of a marginally profitable tourist bus that he owns himself) named Gordo, who is more interested in following his roving eye in pursuit of women in general than in settling down with one: marriage is a state he views with mortal terror. It would mean no more tippling at Pelon's grape juice lounge, no more batching around with such close buddies as Juan Pablo Jones or Poet Garcia (himself married now and only infrequently in view), no more driving young female tourists around in El Cometa Halley, no more lounging in bed with Senor Dog, Senor Pig, Popo the rooster, Poosey Cat, Senor Owl, and tousle-headed nephew Pepito, until all hours of the *mañana*.

So over the decades Gordo has valiantly warded off the most fiendish efforts of the determined Widow to wed him, avoiding her subterfuges of witchcraft, interstellar science, a mammoth carniverous plant called the Widow's Weed, a teleporter, a dormitutor, a double, etc., by hairbreadth degrees each time. In the long intervals between the wealthy Widow's onslaughts, however, Gordo has enjoyed himself immensely with his cronies, greedy or hapless American tourists, strange local characters, and various inanimate and/or animal aspects of the Del Monte scene. Poet Garcia's love affair and marriage with the American girl, Rusty Gates, occupied a long and amusing story, as did the visit by freckle-faced 12-year-old Mary Frances Sevier to Rusty and Garcia (followed by her amorous pursuit of Gordo's nephew, Pepito). The attempt (and failure) by an American tourist car collector to buy Gordo's 1912 Michigan Mateor for $70,000 or more is still a local legend around Del Monte. And the curious appearance and behavior of such local phenomena as Shocking Pedro, Goblin, and Little Coronado with his

"Gordo," Gus Arriola. © United Feature Syndicate.

bottomless bag of tricks enlivened the strip over the years. Among the inanimate characters featured were the philosophic crackpots of Del Monte; while the least visible but perhaps most noted creature of the city is Bug Rogers, the hip and hungry spider with his splendidly designed webs (not to mention the drunken earthworms who make whoopee in the wee smalls of the Mexican night).

Gus Arriola is a weaver of strip legend and a creator of comic characters in the best tradition of E. C. Segar, Billy De Beck, and Charles Schulz. Unfortunately, Arriola developed a tendency to neglect the narrative adventures that once sharpened and defined his characters so well, and too many of his Sunday episodes became little more than eye-pleasing designs built around a simple verbal gag. Following the last assault by the Widow Gonzales (it was a masterpiece!), there was no prolonged story of any worth in *Gordo*. But Arriola had, in any event, accomplished enough in over three decades of *Gordo* to do with the strip as he pleased: he created a classic among the best in his field. Eight paperback reprints of the *Gordo* comic strips were published by Nitty Gritty Productions in 1972. The strip ended in 1985, the Sunday in February, the dailies in March.

B.B.

GORDON FIFE AND THE BOY KING *See* Gordon, Soldier of Fortune.

GORDON, SOLDIER OF FORTUNE (U.S.) Created in October 1935 (under the title of *Gordon Fife and the Boy King*, later changed to *Gordon, Soldier of Fortune*) as a daily strip for the *Brooklyn Eagle* by Bob Moore (script) and John Hales (drawing). In December 1936, Carl Pfeufer (who was already doing *Don Dixon and the Hidden Empire*, also scripted by Bob Moore) took over the drawing of *Gordon* as well. In August 1940, *Gordon*

started as a Sunday feature (replacing *Tad of the Tanbark* and sharing the page with *Don Dixon*). Both daily and Sunday were discontinued a few months later, in July 1941.

Gordon Fife is an American adventurer who gets himself involved in the intrigues of the mythical Central European kingdom of Kovnia. In an atmosphere reminiscent of Anthony Hope's *The Prisoner of Zenda*, Gordon, with the help of his faithful Hindu partner Ali, foils assassination plots, coups d'etat, and other assorted conspiracies directed against young King Nicholas and his sister, regent of Kovnia and Gordon's light-of-love, Princess Caroline. His most constant adversaries are the scheming prince Karl of neighboring Livonia, and the subversive organization known as "the Markala."

Gordon was not by any means among the topmost adventure strips of the 1930s, but it was unpretentious and entertaining. Today it seems to reflect with great accuracy some of the fears, hopes, and concerns of the period.

M.H.

GOSCINNY, RENÉ (1926-1977) French writer and editor born in Paris in 1926. When René Goscinny was two, his parents emigrated to Argentina, where the young boy received his schooling; he also developed a love for cartooning in his schooldays. After his high school graduation he worked briefly as a bookkeeper, but in 1945 he left Argentina to join an uncle in the United States, with the secret ambition of becoming a cartoonist for Walt Disney. He never made it but instead worked in various jobs in New York; in the early 1950s he worked in the *Mad* magazine offices, where he was spotted by Morris, the creator of *Lucky Luke*, then on a trip around the United States.

In 1954 Goscinny went back to Europe with Morris, and in 1955 he became the scriptwriter on *Lucky Luke*. Under Goscinny's guidance, this parodic Western started incorporating real figures from the old West into its *dramatis personae*. While writing the continuity for *Lucky Luke*, Goscinny also contributed scripts for many other features then appearing in *Spirou* magazine: from *Blondin et Cirage* to *Jerry Spring*, rare is the series in which his name did not appear at one time or another. Not content with his work for *Spirou*, Goscinny produced a number of strips for other publications: *Le Docteur Gaudeamus* (drawn by Coq) for *Jours de France* in 1954; *Signor Spaghetti* (a gag strip illustrated by Dino Attanasio) for *Tintin* in 1958; and, also for *Tintin* in 1958, *Oumpah Pah le Peau-Rouge* ("Oumpah Pah the Redskin"), the comic tale of a gigantic Indian during the French and Indian War. *Oumpah Pah* was drawn by Albert Uderzo, who had already teamed up with Goscinny one year earlier on the short-lived *Benjamin et Benjamine*.

In 1959 Goscinny cofounded the comic weekly *Pilote* (later sold to Editions Dargaud). In the first issue of the new magazine, Goscinny and Uderzo created *Astérix*, about a diminutive Gaul in the time of Caesar's conquest. In a short while *Astérix* was so extravagantly successful that it made its authors millionaires several times over.

Along with *Astérix*, Goscinny has created a number of lesser-known series in recent years: *Le Petit Nicolas* ("Little Nicholas" with Sempé); *Haroun El Poussah* (with Jean Tabary), and *La Fée Aveline* ("Aveline the Fairy") with Coq.

René Goscinny is certainly the best-known, as well as the highest-paid, comic strip writer in recent history. With the income derived from *Astérix* he bought a large share of Editions Dargaud stock, and for a long time he guided the destinies of *Pilote*, a responsibility which he wisely relinquished in 1974. Goscinny has been the recipient of countless awards and honors; in 1967 he was made a Chevalier of Arts and Letters by the Minister of Culture, André Malraux. He died of a heart attack in Paris on November 6, 1977.

M.H.

GOTTFREDSON, FLOYD (1905-1986) Floyd Gottfredson, uncredited artist and interpretative author of the daily *Mickey Mouse* newspaper strip from its fourth month on, was born on May 5, 1905 in the railroad station of Kaysville, Utah, the grandson of the town station agent. As a youngster entranced by the comics (his early favorites were Walter Hoban's *Jerry on the Job*, *Krazy Kat*, *Barney Google*, and *Wash Tubbs*, among others), he took a number of correspondence courses in cartooning and won a prize in a cartooning contest. Then a projectionist in Utah, he saw no reason why he couldn't work as a projectionist in Hollywood and see what he could do about making a career out of his cartooning talent, so he went to Los Angeles in the late 1920s.

News that Walt Disney was about to go to New York to hire more animators for his burgeoning Hyperion studio prompted the young Gottfredson to try his luck at landing a job with Disney, with hopes that the experience might lead to strip work at a later date. Disney hired him at $18.00 a week as an apprentice animator (a considerable cut from his $65.00 a week salary as a projectionist, particularly since he was then married), but Gottfredson managed to survive by doing freelance cartooning on the side for an automotive trade journal. Within eight months, however, his salary had increased considerably, the freelancing was no longer necessary, and when an opening for an artist occurred in April, 1930, on the four-month-old *Mickey Mouse* daily strip then being drawn by studio personnel for King Features distribution, Gottfredson was tapped for a two-week fill-in stint, even though he had now gotten to like animation work and wasn't greatly interested in tackling a strip of any kind.

Comic strip work proved so swiftly engaging and rewarding to Gottfredson, however, that when Disney forgot about the two-week stint, the young artist did nothing to remind him. Originally grudgingly scripted by Disney in his spare time, the *Mickey Mouse* strip was quickly turned over to the eager Gottfredson for both art and story in mid-May of 1930, after which he drew and scripted it until late 1932. By then the strip was felt important enough to be handled by group discussion, with new plot ideas being threshed over by Gottfredson and several story men, after which one of the latter would be assigned to do a general action layout script, which would then be adapted panel by panel and balloon by balloon by Gottfredson in a pencilled strip, and turned over for inking to a number of artists, most notably Ted Thwaites (between late 1932 and 1940). In January, 1932, Gottfredson was also assigned to write and draw the *Sunday Mickey* page, which was then just being launched via King Features distribution, a welcome job which he continued (with the later aid of the same group of story outliners and inkers he had on the daily strip) until mid-1938, when the Sunday page was turned over to another artist to permit Gottfredson to undertake more elaborate illustrative techniques in the daily strip.

The *Mickey Mouse* strip which Gottfredson drew and effectively wrote between 1930 and 1950 remains as a two-decade monument to one man's graphic and narrative genius, and nothing which followed it can change that accomplishment. In terms of all the conceivable elements that go into the making of a great narrative comic strip: unforgettable characterization, sharp and apposite dialogue, graphic delineation enhancing character and action, inborn story sense, skillfully handled narrative pace, effectively maintained comedy, and an indefinable infusion of uniqueness that can come only from the personality of the artist himself (if it is there), Gottfredson's Mickey Mouse is an obvious masterpiece. Read today, it seems as fresh as if it were just published, a sure test of fundamental quality in any work a quarter-century or more old. The urge to keep reading, once begun, is irresistible. He retired in 1975 and died on July 22, 1986, at his South California home.

Whatever time and syndicate policy have imposed on Floyd Gottfredson's once free-flowing genius, or studio policy has tried to deny him by scrawling a "Walt Disney" signature upon every one of his 15,000-plus episodes for 45 years, then, is effectively negated by the living miracle of his unfettered work at the peak of his talent. One of the half-dozen finest strip talents of the 1930s, Floyd Gottfredson will always be mentioned in the same breath with Milton Caniff, Al Capp, Will Eisner, Walt Kelly, and Alex Raymond—now that he is at last known by name as well as accomplishment.

B.B.

GOULD, CHESTER (1900-1985) American artist born November 20, 1900 in Pawnee, Oklahoma. His father was publisher of the *Advance-Democrat*, a Stillwater, Oklahoma newspaper but wanted his son to become a lawyer. Gould went to Oklahoma A and M College for two years and at the same time worked as a sports cartoonist for the *Oklahoma City Daily Oklahoman*. From there he went to Northwestern University in Chicago and graduated in 1923.

Soon after graduation he started working for Hearst's *Chicago American*, where he created *Fillum Fables*, a takeoff on Hollywood movies, in 1924. In 1931 he sold one of his comic strip ideas about a hard-nosed plainclothes detective to Captain Joseph Patterson of the Chicago Tribune-New York News Syndicate. The strip, rechristened *Dick Tracy* by Patterson, started running as a Sunday page on October 4, 1931, and as a daily strip a week later.

Since 1931 Chester Gould has been devoting most of his life to *Dick Tracy*, in which can be found the author's personal views and philosophy. In this connection Gould's research into police rules and procedures has been painstaking. His "Crime Stoppers," small vignettes he inserts near the title of the Sunday page, are designed to draw the reader's attention to some small facet of police procedure or crime prevention. Gould still spends a great deal of time with the Chicago police as well as in the crime laboratories of Northwestern University, and he has received a number of awards and commendations from police departments and law enforcement agencies all over the country.

Chester Gould's position in the comic strip world was just as impressive. While he was never personally the kind of guiding influence on younger cartoonists that Milton Caniff or Alex Raymond were, his work permeated many aspects of the comic book as well as the newspaper strip. In recognition of his pioneering research in the field, Gould received a number of professional awards and citations, including the Reuben award.

Gould retired from the strip in 1977, and it was taken over by Rick Fletcher (art) and Max Alan Collins (writing), with the creator retaining a byline. Dissatisfied with the direction *Dick Tracy* was taking, Gould asked his name to be removed from the feature in 1981. He died a few years later, on May 11, 1985.

M.H.

GOULD, WILL (1911-1984) American cartoonist and illustrator born 1911 in the Bronx, New York. Will Gould (no relation to Chester Gould) started his cartooning career while still in high school. In 1929 he was sports cartoonist at the *Bronx Home News*, for which he also contributed a humor strip with a sports angle, *Felix O'Fan*. From there he went to the *New York Graphic*, again as a sports cartoonist, creating a racing strip along the way: *Asparagus Tipps* about a black waiter always ready with a tip for the morrow's races (along the lines of Ken Kling's *Joe* and *Asbestos*).

In 1930 Will Gould, along with his entire family, moved to California. He then freelanced as a sports and feature cartoonist variously for the McNaught Syndicate (whose outlet in New York was the *World Telegram*), Kay Features, and King Features (Gould's work appearing in the *New York Mirror*). In 1933 Gould competed (unsuccessfully) for the drawing job on the planned *Secret Agent X-9* strip, and then attracted the notice of the ever-vigilant W. R. Hearst. A few months later King Features approved a new police strip submitted by Gould, *Red Barry*, which started publication on March 19, 1934 as a daily (and on March 3, 1935 as a Sunday).

Almost from the start Gould had difficulties with the syndicate: his editors wanted (Will) Gould's *Red Barry* to compete with (Chester) Gould's *Dick Tracy* but could not abide the violence (a contradiction of purposes!). In 1940, after years of running arguments with his editors, Gould left *Red Barry* (which was dropped) and went on to a scriptwriting career for motion pictures and radio. Drafted in 1942 at Fort McArthur, Gould was given the task of creating the camp's paper, which he called *The Alert* and on which he worked as editor, reporter, and cartoonist. At the end of the war he went back to scriptwriting and also worked as reporter for various newspapers. After 1963 Gould was the cartoon editor of *Writer's Forum* and drew a cartoon series, *The Schnoox*, for the Writers' Guild's monthly newsletter. He died in 1984 in a Los Angeles home for senior citizens from burns sustained while smoking in bed.

Will Gould's career as a comic strip artist was brief, but his contribution to the art is undisputable. *Red Barry* had a pulsating, restless energy about it, a driving spontaneousness caused in great part by the artist's free-flowing, almost slapdash brush technique. "Pencilling was never in great detail," confided Will Gould in a 1974 interview, "The time was always fleeting. I knew what I wanted, looked at the clock and slapped it in." Will Gould has received increasing rec-

ognition (as usual, the movement started in Europe), and we can only hope, therefore, that some of the old *Red Barry* adventures will be reprinted in book form as they have already been in Europe.

M.H.

GRAFF, MEL (1907-1975) American cartoonist born 1907 in Cleveland, Ohio. Mel Graff's father was a small lumber mill operator who was wiped out by the Depression. As a child, Graff liked to draw, and while attending West Technical High School in Cleveland he became a cartoonist on the school paper, *The Tatler*. Dropping out of school in his teens, he worked at odd jobs in and around railyards and roamed the country on freight trains.

In the early 1930s, Graff got a small job in the commercial art department of NEA. Transferred to New York in 1933, he came under the influence of noted cartoonist George Clark, and in 1934 started drawing *The Adventures of Patsy* for Associated Press. A little girl strip in the beginning, *Patsy* turned more and more toward adventure. One of Mel Graff's strokes of luck came in 1939 when he got his former AP colleague Noel Sickles to ghost *Patsy* for him: the result was so eye-catching that King Features hired Graff the next year to succeed Austin Briggs on *Secret Agent X-9*.

Mel Graff's tenure on *X-9* proved disastrous. Not only was his drawing barely adequate but, following the departure of Max Trell (who had been writing the *X-9* scripts since 1936 under the pen name Robert Storm), he took up the writing chores as well, emasculating in no small measure the character of his G-man hero. In the 1950s Mel Graff, who was suffering from the strain of a weekly deadline, had a series of breakdowns and was finally eased out of the strip in 1960. He moved to Orlando, Florida, and lived in semi-retirement there, doing a variety of small illustration and advertising jobs.

Mel Graff was probably one of the most pathetic examples of the mindlessness of the King Features system. Despite a lackluster performance and a serious health problem, he was allowed to plod along in mediocrity and run the strip into the ground because of the editors' misguided sense of loyalty. He is only remembered today because of his 20-year-long association with the *X-9* strip and for his undisputed, if minor, contribution to *Patsy*. Graff died on November 2, 1975.

M.H.

GRAY, CLARENCE (1901-1957) American cartoonist and illustrator born in Toledo, Ohio, on November 14, 1901. During his grammar and high school days Clarence Gray (when he was not playing hooky) concentrated on art courses. After his high school graduation he was deciding what art school to attend when he was offered a job on the art staff of the *Toledo News-Bee*. Gray accepted the offer and throughout the 1920s he drew editorial and sports cartoons for the newspaper.

In addition to his newspaper career Gray had become a contributor to various national magazines, and he was spotted by Hearst in 1933. In August of that year he started *Brick Bradford* (on continuity by William Ritt) for the Hearst-owned Central Press Association of Cleveland. An adventure strip at the beginning, *Brick* soon veered toward science fiction (especially after the addition of a Sunday page in November 1934). For a brief period in 1935 Gray also drew a companion piece to *Brick, The Time Top* (again written by Ritt). When Ritt stopped writing for Brick in 1952, Gray abandoned the daily strip to Paul Norris to concentrate on the Sunday page, which he wrote and drew until his untimely death at 54 on January 7, 1957.

Gray's draftsmanship helped make *Brick Bradford* into one of the most exciting adventure and science-fiction strips of the 1930s and 1940s. His graphic style—elegant and unambiguous—radiated a warm poetry and a youthful élan often absent from other strips in the genre. *Brick Bradford* still continues in the hands of Paul Norris.

M.H.

GRAY, HAROLD (1894-1968) Unlike many strip cartoonists, who become bored in later years with the characters they once made famous and hire "ghosts" to do the bulk of the continuing strip work (usually with adverse results, which only the unperceptive general readership fail to notice), Harold Gray remained as vitally concerned with the creations of his imagination as a great novelist would from the day he began work on his *Little Orphan Annie* until the day he died. Gray was one of the few natural comic strip artists and authors: a man who took to the new strip medium as readily as a poet to verse, and who was as creatively fulfilled in it as Shaw was playwriting. He was also one of the most gifted storytellers of our time.

Born in Kankakee, Illinois on January 20, 1894, the young Gray got his first newspaper job in Lafayette, Indiana, in 1913, while he was attending Purdue University. Graduating in 1917, he enlisted in the army and served as a bayonet instructor, ending up as a second lieutenant. Always interested in cartooning, he got a job on the *Chicago Tribune* art department after his discharge, but left to do the lettering on Sidney Smith's *The Gumps* between 1921 and 1924. In mid-1924, Gray approached J. M. Patterson with an idea for a News-Tribune strip called *Little Orphan Otto*. Paterson thought the boy looked slightly effeminate, suggested to Gray that he make her a girl, and give her the name of the once-famous James Whitcomb Riley poem, *Little*

Harold Gray.

Orphan Annie, a *Tribune* property, which the paper was periodically reprinting. The first episode of the new *Annie* strip appeared on August 5, 1924, in the *New York Daily News*, where it was given a trial run. After making a hit with the *News* readers, the strip was added to the *Chicago Tribune* roster a short time later, and the first Sunday *Annie* page appeared in both papers on November 2, 1924.

The strip was a growing success in the mid-1920s, soon appearing in syndication from coast to coast. Gray moved to the east coast, residing in New York and Southport, Connecticut and eventually buying a California home at La Jolla. He added a long-lived Sunday gag strip named *Maw Green* to the *Annie* page on January 1, 1933 (Maw having been a character in *Annie*), after experimenting for two years (1931-32) with humorous social commentary in a Sunday quarter-page called *Private Lives* (*Private Life of a Hat, Private Life of a Doormat*, etc.). On Sunday, May 3, 1933, Gray's sole *Annie* assistant, a cousin, Ed Leffingwell, launched a weekly half-page strip in the *Tribune* and *News* featuring a youngster growing up in a part of the contemporary west that was still old-fashioned cattle ranch country, which was called *Little Joe*. Gray was always involved in shaping the narrative and characters of *Joe*, and by the mid-1930s was drawing the human figures in the strip, while Leffingwell concentrated on the western backgrounds: perhaps the only instance in strips where a major, successful cartoonist was vitally and regularly concerned with the minor strip of an aide over so many years. (Later, Ed's brother, Robert, took over *Little Joe* after Ed's death, and drew the entire strip, Gray returning full-time to *Annie*.)

Gray loved his strip work, preferring it to almost anything else. He spent long hours writing, drawing, and researching both *Annie* and *Joe*, and travelled little outside of the United States, where he enjoyed driving around back-country roads alone in the less populous states of the west and midwest.

With only minor flagging in his narrative invention toward the end, Harold Gray closed 45 years of continuous work on *Little Orphan Annie* and other strips with his death on May 10, 1968. Attempts to continue his strip by other hands have proven monumental failures, and the News-Tribune syndicate was finally forced to turn to direct reprinting of the old strip for current syndication.

B.B.

GREEN ARROW (U.S.) *Green Arrow* was created by writer Mort Weisinger and artist George Papp and made its first appearance in National's *More Fun* number 73 for November 1941. A rather pedestrian archery strip, the character's only innovations were a quiver's worth of trick arrows and the Arrow Car. His partner, Speedy, was added in the March, 1943 issue of *More Fun*.

The Green Arrow was really industrialist Oliver Quinn, another in National's long line of playboy heroes, and his partner's name was Roy Harper. Without a particularly fascinating storyline—most adventures consisting of a character being defeated by a barrage of Green Arrow's arrows—the feature was continually bouncing from book to book. After being dropped from *More Fun* after February 1946's 107th issue, he began a long run of more than 100 issues of *Adventure* and *World's Finest*. He also appeared in the

"Green Arrow," Bob Fujitani. © National Periodical Publications.

first 14 issues of *Leading* (Winter 1942 to Spring 1945) as a member of the ill-fated *Seven Soldiers of Victory* strip, a poor imitation of the *Justice Society.*

After his series in *Adventure* expired, Green Arrow did not have a regular feature, and his only appearances came as a member of the Justice League. The character was finally handed to artist Neal Adams who totally revamped him in the September 1969 issue of *The Brave and the Bold* (number 85). Stripping Oliver Quinn of his wealth, he gave the character a beard and a vicious, self-righteous disposition. He became the outspoken and impatient champion of the oppressed. When the *Green Lantern* strip was nearing extinction in 1970, editor Schwartz allowed writer Denny O'Neil and artist Adams to team up the two heroes in the now classic *Green Lantern/Green Arrow series.*

Given outstanding art and story for the first time, the character became a tireless—though often erratic, pompous, and ignorant—hero of the downtrodden. His bursts of self-righteous indignation became classic. Two highly acclaimed issues cast Speedy as a junkie, and both Green Arrow and Speedy's reactions became comic history. Unfortunately, due to flagging sales and artistic conflicts, the *Green Lantern/Green Arrow* book was discontinued after May 1972's 89th issue.

J.B.

In the 1980s DC starred Green Arrow in two miniseries: the first one, in 1983, was unsuccessful. The second one, however, *Green Arrow: The Longbow Hunters* (1987), scripted by Mike Grell, clicked with readers and led to an ongoing comic book series, starting in February 1988. Grell wrote the continuities for the first 80 issues and also did some of the artwork. Other artists of note on the revived title have included Denys Cowan and Frank Springer.

M.H.

GREENE, VERNON VAN ATTA (1908-1965) American artist born September 12, 1908 in Battle Ground, Washington. Vernon Greene grew up in Battle Ground, and attended the University of Toledo. He studied art with Dong Kingman and Henry G. Keller. His first work in cartooning was for the Port-

land, Oregon *Telegram* doing sports cartoons from 1927 to 1929; he also drew sports cartoons for the *Toledo Blade,* (1930 to 1932) and the *New York Mirror* (1934-1936).

Green drew editorial cartoons for Hearst's Central Press from 1932 to 1942, for the *New York Mirror* (1935 to 1937) and for the *Portland Oregonian* (1945 to 1950).

Greene broke into the pulp and comic book field in 1940, illustrating the *Shadow* and *Masked Lady* for Street and Smith; *Perry Mason* for McKay in 1946; various titles for Western in the 1940s and 1950s; and a good deal of freelance work from 1938 to 1954.

The versatile Green—he worked, at different times in his career, in every branch of cartooning except animation—from 1935 onward illustrated children's books, magazine stories, medical articles, and advertising comics, including Dentyne, Chiclets, Woolworth's, etc.

In the Air Force in World War II, he graduated from medical photography to cartooning; two service-related features were *Charlie Conscript* for *Pic Magazine,* 1941 to 1944, and *Mac the Med,* a comic strip. His first work in comic strips consisted of a few ghost panels for *Bringing Up Father* in 1935, six masterful years ghosting *Polly and Her Pals* (1935 to 1940), the *Shadow* from 1938 to 1942 for the Ledger Syndicate, and *Bible Bee,* a panel for the Register and Tribune Syndicate from 1946 to 1954.

Upon the death of George McManus in 1954, Greene was engaged by King Features to pick up *Bringing Up Father* when negotiations with McManus' assistant Zeke Zekely fell through. He continued with Jiggs and Maggie until his death in 1965.

Vern Greene was one of the warmest and friendliest men in the cartooning profession. His services to the NCS, other groups, and his young fans were remarkable. He did a creditable job with Jiggs, very conscious of McManus' style and conventions. He was an officer in the National Cartoonists Society, organized major comic strip exhibits in 1942 and at the 1964 World's Fair and won the prestigious Silver T-Square from the NCS in 1964. He was the host of the syndicated radio show, "The Cartoonist's Art," during which he proved to be a knowledgeable, sympathetic, and polished interviewer.

Greene adapted well to any genre he tackled; certainly the style of Sterrett's *Polly* and the *Shadow* were at the opposite ends of the artistic pole, but he handled both splendidly and simultaneously. The ever-active Greene seemed always engaged in half a dozen projects; in his last years he was drawing, attending to NCS duties, doing USO shows, hosting his radio program, and earning a degree in philosophy from Columbia University. He was a talented and unselfish lover of his profession and is sorely missed.

R.M.

GREEN HORNET (U.S.) 1—Like many radio heroes, pulp stars, and other media heavies, The Green Hornet's career in comic books was spotty and unimpressive. Shortly after the character made the successful transition from radio star to serial star—there were two Universal Green Hornet serials in 1940, both utilizing Keye Luke in the role of Kato—Holyoke introduced the first issue of *Green Hornet* in December, 1940. Like previous versions, the green avenger was really newspaper publisher Britt Reid who fought crime outside the law with the aid of his gas gun and his limousine, The

Black Beauty. Naturally, he was assisted by his Japanese assistant, Kato. When WWII erupted, Kato was hastily transformed into a Filipino, and his original Japanese heritage was never mentioned again. The stories in the comic version were hackneyed and pedestrian, saved only by the then-unique gimmick that the Green Hornet was wanted by the police because they frowned on his extra-legal crime fighting. Most of the stories were drawn by Irwin Hasen and Irv Novick, but the book died after August 1941's sixth issue.

2—The following year, Harvey (Family) comics began publishing the *Green Hornet* comic book beginning with the seventh issue (dated June 1942). The character was somewhat more successful here, however, and managed to survive until September, 1949's 47th issue. The writing continued in a facile vein, but the feature did have artwork by Art Cazeneuve (1942), Al Avison (1947), and Jerry Robinson (1946). The strip also appeared in two issues of Harvey's *All New* comics in 1946 and 1947.

3—Dell Publications issued a one-shot *Green Hornet* strip in 1953 as issue number 496 of their *Color* series.

4—When The Green Hornet made its move to television in 1966, Gold Key put out three issues of *Green Hornet* from November 1966 to August 1967.

J.B.

5—The character was revived once more by Now Comics. This was a politically correct version, in which Kato shared equal credit with his boss (he even briefly enjoyed his own comic book, *Kato of the Green Hornet*). Started in November 1989, *The Green Hornet* lasted until December 1994.

M.H.

GREEN LANTERN (U.S.) *Green Lantern* was created by artist Martin Nodell and writer Bill Finger and made its first appearance in National's *All American* number 16 for July 1940. Sporting a loud black, red, green, purple, brown, and yellow uniform, Alan Scott became Green Lantern by charging a "power ring" which gave him almost omnipotent qualities. Most *Green Lantern* stories were lighthearted, often concentrating on Doiby Dickles, an overweight, Brooklyn-born, tough cabbie. The more serious stories became predictable, however, because writers continually used the power ring's inefficiency against wood as the central theme of an adventure.

Like *Flash, Green Lantern* had a horde of interesting villains, the best being the Harlequin. Alan Scott's secretary in real-life, the Harlequin wore an equally outrageous costume and frequently fought the Green Lantern. She eventually became a government agent.

Artistically, *Green Lantern* wasn't particularly noteworthy. Literally dozens of artists, including Carmine Infantino (1948), Joe Kubert (1948), and Irwin Hazen (1941-1948), handled the strip in a relatively pedestrian manner. The character's best illustrator, Alex Toth, handled stories between 1947 and 1949 and was inventive with both layouts and pacing. Alfred Bester, a renowned and award-winning science fiction author, scripted stories between 1943 and 1945, aiding National staffers like John Broome and Bob Kanigher.

In all, *Green Lantern* appeared in *All-American* through October 1948's 102nd issue. A member of the legendary Justice Society of America, the character appeared in 48 stories in *All-Star Comics* between fall 1940 and March 1951. *Green Lantern* also appeared in *Comic Cavalcade* from winter 1943's number one through November 1948's number 29 and 38 issues of its own magazine from fall 1941 through June 1949.

When National made a general revival of superhero characters in the 1960s, Green Lantern was revived as a member of the Justice Society. Several months after National revived *The Flash*, they opted to revive *Green Lantern*, in October 1959, under the direction of editor Julius Schwartz, writer Gardner Fox, and artist Gil Kane. Introduced in *Showcase* number 22, this Green Lantern was test pilot Hal Jordan who had assumed the Green Lantern mantle from a dying, red-skinned alien. His powers, including the almost invincible power ring, were the same as the 1940 version, except that his ring was inoperative against yellow. This latest Green Lantern wore a more conservative green and black jumpsuit, which underwent only a modest change over the years. The feature was given its own book in August 1960.

Gardner Fox made the feature an amazing sample of scientific fantasy. This Green Lantern was cast as only one of hundreds, all from different planets, and all under the guidance of the blue-skinned Guardians of the Universe. Tomar Re, an orange, bird-faced Green Lantern, was the most often used alien, and the two Lanterns shared several interesting adventures. Fox also created a series of Green Lantern-in-the-future stories where the character became the leader of 58th century Earth, and a fascinating world-within-a-power-ring series. Along with these interesting, if far-fetched concepts, Fox also had strong supporting characters: Pieface, an Eskimo mechanic and Green Lantern's sidekick; and Carol Ferris. Hal Jordan loved her, but she loved Green Lantern, and the relationship developed into a Superman-Clark Kent-Lois Lane triangle. To complicate matters, she was Hal Jordan's boss and was often hypnotized into becoming Star Saffire, one of the character's toughest opponents. Sinestro, a fallen Green Lantern with red skin and a yellow power ring, was Green Lantern's most dangerous enemy and appeared often.

Artist Kane quickly made the strip into one of the best drawn in the 1960s. His style lent itself favorably to Fox's fast-paced material, and his work was always flawlessly rendered. Kane garnered a great deal of respect from *Green Lantern*, and it opened many new avenues for his unique abilities. He eventually became one of the most inventive and outspoken creators in the comic medium.

Green Lantern took a sharp downturn around the 50th issue—mainly due to the demise of the romantic menage-a-trois and Fox's and Kane's increasing boredom with the feature—and began a headlong artistic and financial decline.

Just before its cancellation, the feature was handed to artist Neal Adams and writer Denny O'Neil. What evolved is the already legendary Green Lantern/Green Arrow series. Starting in April 1970's 76th issue, the two superheroes made comic book's first significant excursion through the real world. Handling topics like racism, politics, religion, cultism, and contemporary social problems—including two highly publicized drug abuse stories—O'Neil and Adams and editor Schwartz revamped comic history. These dozen team-up issues are already collector's editions. Unfortunately, *Green Lantern* ended after the 89th issue (May 1972) amidst universal praise, discouraging

Green Lantern. © *DC Comics.*

sales, and increasingly antagonistic relationships between the creative trio.

A member of the Justice League of America, Green Lantern has appeared in the group's book since its inception. He was recently returned to his 1960s

science-fiction bent, and now appears as a strictly adventure-oriented character in *Flash*.

J.B.

DC brought back the title with issue number 90 (August–September 1976), picking up where it had left off four years earlier. Mike Grell's gritty writing and graceful artwork ensured the success of the revived series. After Grell's departure a number of talented artists worked on the feature, including George Perez, Gil Kane, and George Tuska; the writing, however, was not on par with the drawing, and after turning into *The Green Lantern Corps*, the series was cancelled in 1986. A fourth series began in 1990 and is ongoing.

M.H.

GREG *see* Régnier, Michel.

GRIFFITH, BILL (1944-   ) American cartoonist Bill Griffith was born in Brooklyn, New York, on January 20, 1944. He attended the Pratt Institute of Technology in New York in the hopes of becoming a fine artist. He turned to cartooning in 1967, and in 1970 moved to San Francisco, which was then the Mecca of underground artists. There he contributed to a number of "comix" publications, including *Yellow Dog, Real Pulp,* and *Yow.*

"My first character," Griffith told an interviewer, "was Mr. ('The') Toad, a rather mean-spirited amphibian dressed in a tight-fitting tweed suit." Mr. Toad was a tough customer, always spoiling for a fight with neighbors, coworkers, and the world at large. Among his hangers-on were the Toadettes, a bad-girl trio of singing (or croaking) batrachians. The artist's first hit came with *Young Lust,* a hilarious parody of 1950s romance comics, in which his fondness for bringing real-life figures into his plots initially surfaced. In its pages he created the modern couple of Randy and Cherisse who were patrons of shopping malls and after-hours bars, and spend a great deal of time in therapy.

Zippy the Pinhead, Griffith's most famous character, was created almost as an afterthought, in a story characteristically titled "I Gave My Heart to a Pinhead and He Made a Fool Out of Me." Originally known as Danny, the character evolved into his Zippy persona in 1971 as a sidekick to Mr. Toad. Dressed in a polka-dot clown suit, wearing an idiotic grin, and uttering his famous catchphrase, "Are we having fun yet?", he soon gained a loyal following among college students and amateurs of the bizarre. In the early 1980s, King Features started syndicating a daily and Sunday *Zippy* comic strip to a small but growing list of newspapers. While considerably toning down his creation for general consumption, Griffith still indulges his penchant for raucous humor and biting satire, best evidenced in his devastating attacks on our media-saturated and celebrity-obsessed society.

Zippy has been reprinted in numerous anthologies and has been the subject of serious analysis in *People* magazine, the *New York Times,* and the *San Francisco Examiner,* among other publications. Asked to comment on his creation's popularity, Griffith replied, "Possibly, Zippy provides a kind of release valve for all the pressure, all the information we're bombarded with every hour of the day." As the tempo of modern life accelerates, Zippy's brand of wise foolishness appears more timely than ever.

GRINGO (Spain) A Western created in 1963 by Carlos Giménez, *Gringo* was the literary brainchild of scriptwriter Manuel Medina, although a few episodes were authored by Miguel Gonzalez Casquel and Carlos Echeverria.

Under the nickname of Gringo, Syd Viking is a young, fair-haired American who devotes his life to the defense of oppressed people, whether Mexican or Indian. A foreman on the ranch where he has lived most of his years, he turned the pejorative-appellation of "gringo" from a term of contempt into a synonym of justice and chivalry. A man with a nervous trigger-finger, but never one to shoot first, he has become a homeless wanderer since taking up the cause of justice. He is a misogynist, and women have only played minor roles in his adventures, while Conchita, his original girlfriend, did not come back later. In turn, Gringo can on occasion be seen in the company of a pig-headed and ridiculous young girl with whom he sings *rancheras* accompanying himself on the banjo.

The seeds of Giménez's later graphic excellence can already be found in *Gringo,* such as his love for whimsical compositions, his taste for twisted trees and branches, and his frequent touches of humor. His work was later continued by Domingo Alvarez Gomez, and

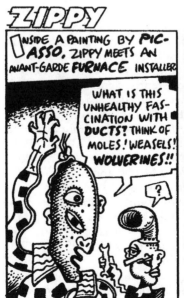   

Bill Griffith, "Zippy." © Bill Griffith.

by "Suso" (pseudonym of Jesus Pena Rego) who has been the cartoonist best able to understand and follow the trail blazed by Giménez. Like many comics of the Franco era, *Gringo* was terminated in the 1980s, but it lives on in countless reprints.

L.G.

GROSS, MILTON (1895-1953) Milton (Milt) Gross, born above the Bronx pushcarts in New York City in 1895, was one of the best things to ever happen to the comic strip. He began drawing in the sixth grade at the age of 12 (while attending classes with a kid who grew up to be Dutch Schultz, the gangster famed for his Joycean deathbed babble). He did little but draw throughout his single year of high school in Kearney, New Jersey, from which he fled to get his first job—a position that gave him more time to cartoon than school did. After about 16 other menial jobs, he took his first newspaper stint as copy boy on the *New York American* while still in his teens. Here the editors paid attention to his cartooning ability, and by the time he was 20, Milt was not only assisting the famed Tad Dorgan as sports cartoonist for the *American's* companion afternoon paper, the *New York Journal*, but was also turning out his first comic strip (in May 1915): a sports-page feature about a sporting fanatic named George Phan called *Phool Phan Phables* (initially spelled with "F's"). This was followed by other brief strips and features, such as *Izzy Human* (1915), *Amateur Night* (1915), *Kinney B. Alive* (1916), *Sportograms* (1916), and *And Then The Fun Began* (1916). In early 1917, Gross quit Hearst to try animation work at New York's Bray Studios, and from there enlisted and served with the U.S. Seventh Division in France in 1918. After his return, he worked for Hearst again, doing a short-lived daily continuity strip called *Frenchy*, then took a better-paying job with the *New York World*, where he did such occasional strips and panels as *Banana Oil* and *Help Wanted* in the early 1920s, but made his big hit with a weekly column of prose and cartoons called *Gross Exaggerations*.

It was in this column that Milt first introduced the Yiddish-dialect humor, distilled from the accents of first-generation Jewish immigrants, which made his initial fame. A book collection of 1926 based on some of these columns, *Nize Baby*, was a best-seller. In the same year, Gross and the *World* decided he was ready for a sustained Sunday page effort, and *Nize Baby* was launched across the country on January 7, 1927. Gross' *Banana Oil* gag strip ran in an untitled single row of panels across the top of the *Nize Baby* Sunday page.

More books appeared in short order from Gross' facile pen: *Hiawatta Witt No Odder Poems* in 1926, *De Night In De Front From Chreesmas* (1927), *Dunt Esk* (1927), *Famous Fimmales Witt Odder Ewents From Heestory* (1928), and above all, his superb parody of woodcut narratives in pictures masterfully undertaken in a 1930 volume titled *He Done Her Wrong* (Dell paperback reprint, 1971).

Gross, like his brother cartoonist Rube Goldberg, was rarely content with one idea or set of characters for long: on February 17, 1929, he replaced *Nize Baby* with a new Sunday page, *Count Screwloose of Tooloose*, but continued the *Banana Oil* strip until he was hired away from the *World* by Hearst in 1931; continuing *Count Screwloose* for the Hearst papers, but replacing *Banana Oil* with a quarter-page top strip, *Babbling Brooks*. By June 1931, *Babbling Brooks* was gone,

replaced by *Count Screwloose* at the top of the Sunday page, while Gross introduced a new feature in the primary space: *Dave's Delicatessen*, which also appeared daily. In June 1934, Gross usurped the *Count Screwloose* Sunday space for a pair of penguins named *Otto and Blotto*, while Screwloose dropped down to join Dave in the main Sunday strip. In January 1935, the penguins were replaced by *That's My Pop!* while *Dave's Delicatessen* was retitled *Count Screwloose*, with Dave and the Count featured together. In mid-1935, *That's My Pop!* became the primary feature, and in 1936, the two Sunday strips were altered in format to a half-page each, and ran in this form until the late 1940s, with ghost Bob Dunn taking over much of the work from Gross.

In the meantime, Gross himself continued with his books, with film scripting in Hollywood, with a new prose column and art for the *New York Mirror* called *Grossly Exaggerated* (which also ran as *Grossly Xaggerated*), another feature titled *Joe Runt*, and ultimately a daily news cartoon—all in the first half of the 1930s. *Pasha the Persian* (1936), *What's This?* (1936), and other books appeared, while Gross supervised a radio show based on *That's My Pop!* in the early 1940s. Also in the 1940s, Gross—by now a nationally acclaimed personality, famed magazine writer, scriptwriter, radio show guest, master of ceremonies, etc.—authored a new illustrated prose narrative feature for the Hearst papers called *Dear Dollink*, which appeared in book form in 1944. All this activity took its toll, unfortunately, and in 1945, Gross suffered a heart attack, after which he was forced to cut down his workload. Another, last book appeared: *I Shoulda Ate the Eclair* (1946), about a family named the Figgits, together with a short-lived cartoon feature for a curious comic book of 1946 called *Picture News*. Milt Gross did little of public note after that, and he died suddenly of a second heart attack at 58 while he was returning from a Hawaiian vacation aboard the liner *Lurline* on November 28, 1953.

B.B.

GUARDINEER, FREDERIC (1913-) American comic book artist and writer born October 3, 1913, in Albany, New York. After acquiring his fine arts degree from Syracuse University in 1935, Guardineer came to New York and drew for several pulp magazines before joining the Harry "A" Chesler Shop in 1936. There he drew adventure features for the Chesler books, including *Lobo* and *Dan Hastings*, before beginning his freelance comic book career in 1938. Over the years, Guardineer became one of the most recognized names in the fledgling comic book business, as he was one of the few artists who consistently signed his work. His appealing and unique art style was also easily recognizable and the artist's ability to turn out great amounts of work made his material readily available.

After a stint with Centaur between 1937 and 1939, Guardineer moved to National (1937-1940, working mainly on the *Zatara*, *Pep Morgan*, and *Speed Saunders* strips and covers), then Marvel (1941), New Friday (1941), Quality (1941-1944, working primarily on the *Tor*, *Merlin*, *Quicksilver*, and *Marksman* strips), Hillman (1946-1947), Eastern, Pines, Gleason (1946-1953, mostly on crime stories), and finally Me (1952-1955, on *Durango Kid*) before retiring at 42.

Of all his work, however, Guardineer's three magical strips made him most important to comic book history. While they were all heavily reliant on the *Mandrake* formula developed in the newspaper strips by Falk and Davis, they were all original in their own right. Consistently, *Zatara*, Guardineer's magical character for National, and *Merlin* and *Tor*, his Quality features, all spoke their mystical spells backwards. Even the simplest of tasks required the reversing of English, a gimmick which made the Guardineer strips fun to read.

About his art, much has been said in several comic art histories, but little of it is clear. Unlike many of his "golden" age contemporaries, Guardineer never illustrated with flashy design or spectacular drawings. His material was always presented in as straightforward a manner as possible. Drawings and narration were simple, backgrounds and foregrounds were divided by sharp contrasting uses of colors, and his anatomy was not realistic. On the other hand, all the individual panels in the artist's work, although they were drawn with an extremely heavy line and a self-styled technique, were the scenes one could have portrayed with a photograph. If nothing else, Guardineer was literal; he drew what the caption and dialogue called for. His characters may have been uniformly rounded and designed, but they followed the script explicitly. Many of his followers attempted to copy Guardineer's literal style, but his work always excelled beyond any imitators.

Guardineer left the comic book industry in 1955 to work as a government employee, but continued to draw for many publications generating from around his Long Island home.

J.B.

GUERILLEROS, LES (Belgium) Created in 1968 by Spanish cartoonist Jesus Blasco, *Les Guerilleros* ("the Guerilla-fighters") was produced for publication in the Belgian comic magazine *Spirou*. The initial idea came from the scriptwriter, illustrator, and movie director, José Larraz, who also wrote one of the episodes (others were written by Miguel Gusso and Blasco himself). In this work, Blasco tried to elaborate on a theme that was dear to him. His very personal vision of the American West had already inspired him to do one of his masterworks: *En los Dominios de los Sioux* ("In the Domains of the Sioux"), as well as a number of striking watercolors. The protagonists are: the American, younger than his companions and endowed with all the virtues found in Blasco's heroes, from Ta' Tanka to Wild Batson and Smiley O'Hara; Yuma the second guerillero, an Apache Indian integrated into the little group; and the colorful character of Pedro de Guzman. The latter (much beloved by the readers) is a coarse, shabby, cheating, gambling, and thieving little man; his major defect also turns out to be his greatest virtue: he is an inveterate liar. His lying, while often landing him and his friends in trouble, also just as often gets them out of delicate situations. Pedro adds a touch of humor and common humanity to the strip, in contrast to the earnestness of Yuma and the chivalry of Ray, both of whom are afflicted with all the virtues of conventional heroes.

L.G.

GUERRE À LA TERRE (France) The second science-fiction strip to appear after the end of World War II, *Guerre à la Terre* ("War to Earth") debuted in issue number 10 of the comic magazine *Coq Hardi* (April 1946); the illustrations were by Pierre Liquois and the continuity was supplied by the magazine's inexhaustible editor, Marijac.

The starting point of the series is as old as H. G. Wells's *War of the Worlds*: the inhabitants of the planet Mars, after having subjugated the other peoples of the solar system, plot to invade and conquer Earth. They find a willing Fifth Column in the Japanese, still seething with dreams of revenge (World War II was not far away), and start on their plan of conquest. In their strange, spherical spaceships they take over Siberia, then move on to Europe, before being crushed by the forces of the United Nations and their ace special agent, the Frenchman, Veyrac.

Moving at such a fast pace, the story left the readers breathless. There was no time for characterization, but the images were genuinely gripping (such as the Martian warships landing in the serene landscapes of Southern France, or the UN defenders checking the Martian advance along the tracks of the Paris subway). Of course, *Guerre à la Terre* ended in victory for the people of Earth (in July 1947).

In November 1947 a sequel was tacked on. This second round of the duel between Mars-Earth, no longer illustrated by Liquois, was taken over by Marijac's protégé, Duteurtre, a capable cartoonist who lacked in brilliance. *Guerre à la Terre* ended finally in July 1948.

Seemingly naïve by today's standards, *Guerre à la Terre* was a worthwhile series, strongly plotted and well written; had Marijac not changed illustrators in midstream, it would probably have gone on to a longer run than it enjoyed.

M.H.

GUERRERO DEL ANTIFAZ, EL (Spain) The most popular Spanish adventure strip of the postwar period was typical of a time when there was only scant competition from other mass media: radio had not yet conquered the imaginations of young people with *Diego Valor*, television did not exist, while, on the other hand, a publication like *El Guerrero del Antifaz* ("The Warrior with the Mask") offered, at a small cost, adventures galore to be continued each and every week. The feature debuted in October 1944; when it was finally discontinued in 1966, the *Guerrero* weekly comic book had reached number 668. Text and illustrations were the work of Manuel Gago, who achieved success with the feature.

The Masked Warrior was a noble son of the Count of Roca, whose adventures took place in the Spain of the Catholic Kings, before the conquest of Granada. The ferocious Ali Khan, who was later the Warrior's most deadly enemy, had abducted his pregnant mother and kept her in his harem. The child was born there, believing he was the son of the abductor; when he learned the truth he fled the palace, wearing a mask so as not be be recognized. He then devoted his life to fighting Ali Khan and his assassins, and later found a family and had a son.

If one was to define the author's style in one word, it would be action. Each page was filled with roaring fights and drawn sabers, the narrative unfolding its multiple plots and counterplots without a break. Gago was later succeeded by Matias Alonso (as illustrator) and Pedro Quesada and Vicente Tortajada (as scriptwriters), but his was the definitive version of the strip.

The value of the formula devised by Gago proved once again irresistible, when a new edition of the Warrior's adventures—this time in color—started success-

"El Guerrero del Antifaz," Manuel Gago. © Editorial Valenciana.

ful publication in 1974. The series ended with its creator's death in 1980.

L.G.

GUMPS, THE (U.S.) Sidney Smith's *The Gumps* (which first appeared daily on February 12, 1917, and Sunday on June 29, 1919, on both occasions only in the *Chicago Tribune*) was certainly the most famed and widely read comic strip of the 1920s, and its author was the F. Scott Fitzgerald of the newspaper reader. Like Fitzgerald, Smith mirrored the ambitions and appetites of his readers, accepting them himself as natural and rational elements of life; and like Fitzgerald, he died when the halcyon time he loved was over, from excessive indulgence in the good things of that lost age.

Yet *The Gumps* was intended only to chronicle the doings of a typical lower middle class family in Chicago when *Tribune* publisher Joe Patterson assigned the strip art and story to Sidney Smith in 1917, at a time when the *Tribune* was publishing no regular daily comic strip. The first episode, in which the Gump menage was introduced, portrayed Andrew (Andy) Gump (then with a round, stubby nose and a general James Finlayson appearance) as paterfamilias with cane and derby; Minerva (Min) Gump as "family brains" and an obviously dedicated housewife with purse and umbrella; Chester Gump, their son, about seven, with hoop and stick, described as a hellion; and two family pets: a cat named Hope, and a dog named Buck. Mentioned in a box on the main panel is the data that "the Gumps have a daughter in college and a son in the navy."

A good part of that information was probably Patterson's idea, to make the Gumps patently average and typical. Smith, however, was concerned almost entirely with the principal family trio: Andy, Min, and

Chester: the dog and cat were seldom seen in the following months, and then disappeared completely; the grown son and daughter were never mentioned again. Moreover, Smith was fascinated with money and cars, and communicated these desires to his characters early in the strip, giving Andy and Min the hopes of riches through the grace of an Australian billionaire relative, Uncle Bim Gump.

Aside from his compelling subject matter of imminent riches, Smith possessed a remarkable storytelling ability, with a love for the soap-opera frills of melodrama which the public, then as now, adored. With the gifted wit of Chicago jeweler Sol Hess to aid him with dialogue for a time, and the graphic skill and imagination of Stanley Link at the helm in the Sunday page continuity (which sent Chester Gump into one exotic adventure after another) through the early 1930s, Smith managed an unbeatable team for the time, and fielded what was certainly the most attractive strip in existence for the general reader.

Smith was not, oddly enough, a great creator of characters (aside from his central figure, Andy Gump himself). His comic and melodramatic actors, such as the Widow Zander, Mama De Stross and her daughter Millie, Carlos, Old-Timer, etc., etc., were superbly adequate for the parts they played in the Gump epic, but did not loom as fascinating and memorable figures in themselves. Uncle Benjamin (Bim) Gump is probably the strip's most sizable character after Andy, but he is only a richer physical and psychological duplicate of Andy himself. (Ching Chow, a Chinese adventurer, who achieved some popularity beyond *The Gumps* itself, was a Sunday strip creation who never took part in the principal daily narrative.)

Smith's Gump figures were everywhere: on lamp shades, penny banks, playing cards, games, curtain material, dolls of all sizes, mechanical toys: the list is almost endless. Screen comedies and animated films were made of the characters, while reprint comic books of *The Gumps* were large sellers (Smith even wrote and illustrated an autobiography of his hero, in *Andy Gump: His Life Story*, Reilly & Lee, 1924).

Some of the steam went out of the public identification with *The Gumps* as the Great Depression of the early 1930s deepened, but readers were still fascinated with the dramatic complications of the daily strip, and the Sunday page continued on the front pages of hundreds of comic sections. Then, abruptly in 1935, it all ended with the automobile crash which killed Sidney Smith after he had just signed the biggest contract of his life for the continuation of *The Gumps*. The syndicate panicked; after desperately trying to find someone (Link, Rube Goldberg, etc.) to continue the strip at its Smith level of humor and invention, they finally settled on a man who proved to be one of the worst choices possible: Gus Edson. Edson's strip became dull and predictable, and after coasting a number of years on the afterglow of Smith's stunning work, it was folded in 1959, with a bare dozen newspapers in its roster.

In 1974, Scribner's published a collection of Sidney Smith's *The Gumps*.

B.B.

GUNNIS, LOUIS (1864-1940) Louis Gunnis, who began his art career as a painter and illustrator, became one of the first comic artists in England to work in the picture story field, later known as adventure strips, although his work was limited to the more straightfor-

"The Gumps," Sidney Smith. © The Tribune Company.

ward serials published in the "Nursery School" comics, such as *Tiger Tim's Weekly* and *My Favorite Comic*.

Gunnis was born in Windsor in 1864 of a professional family. His father was Musician-in-Ordinary to Queen Victoria, and his grandfather was a musician in the Royal Marines Band. At age fifteen Gunnis was apprenticed to an engraver. He continued his art studies at Lambeth Art College where, in 1888, he won the Cressy Prize for his painting, 'Tilting at the Ring.' He exhibited his paintings at the Royal Academy from 1887 to 1897, while contributing black-and-white and color illustrations to monthly magazines including the famous *Strand*. His illustrations for the series, *How the Other Half Lives* for the *English Illustrated Magazine* were donated to the Victoria and Albert Museum, where they were exhibited.

When his wife died in 1905, leaving him with three young daughters, Gunnis decided to concentrate on more commercial illustration work for the popular but cheaper magazines. He had already contributed the occasional cartoon to the adult comic weekly, *Scraps*, and the publisher Edward Hulton hired him as a staff artist for his magazine chain.

In 1914, Gunnis joined the staff of the Amalgamated Press and developed the idea of picture stories in weekly episodes, and in 1920 his earliest-traced story appeared in *Tiger Tim's Weekly*. It followed the adventures of a young boy, *Bobby Dare*, and was followed by

The Baby and *Poor Peggy* in 1921, and a serial for *Bubbles* comic in 1922, *The Adventures of Matt. Our Bobbie* began in *Tiger Tim's* in 1924, followed by the more adventurous *School on the Island* (1925), *Mystery Wood* in *Puck* (1927), and *Little Jim from Nowhere* (1929). He moved to the new weekly, *My Favourite Comic*, in 1929 with *The Ivory Elephant*. Then came *Uncle Jonathan's Will* (1930), *Poor Little Lone Girl* (1932), *Children of the Mayflower* (1933), and *Chums of the Circus* (1934).

When *My Favourite Comic* folded, so did much of Gunnis' regular work, now considered old-fashioned by younger editors. He returned to painting, and his oversized painting of the 1937 Coronation was accepted by the Royal Academy. Disappointingly, the picture was too large for exhibition. He died, it is said, brush in hand as a bomb from a German airplane scored a direct hit on his house in August 1940.

D.G.

GURNEY, ALEXANDER GEORGE (1902-1955)

Born at Portsmouth (England) in 1902, Alex Gurney was the son of a Naval Petty Officer, who died when Gurney was 5 months old. His Australian mother brought the boy back to Hobart, Tasmania. Completing his education at Macquarie Street State School at the age of 13, he worked for a short period as an ironmonger. He then joined the Hydro Electric Commission and served a seven-year apprenticeship as an electrician. During this period he commenced art training by attending night classes at the Hobart Technical School and started selling cartoons to the *Tasmanian Mail, Melbourne Punch, The Bulletin,* and *Smith's Weekly.*

In 1926, he published a book, *Tasmanians Today,* comprised of caricatures of notables. This brought Gurney to the attention of mainland newspapers, and he was given a position with the *Melbourne Morning Post.* When this paper disappeared down the maw of the *Herald,* Gurney went to Sydney. Here he freelanced for *The Bulletin* and developed Australia's first strip based on actual personalities. The strip, *Stiffy & Mo,* was based on the exploits of the well-known vaudeville team of the same name, created by Nat Phillips (*Stiffy*) and Roy Rene (*Mo*), and appeared in *Beckett's Budget* in 1927. During 1928-29 he worked for the *Sunday Times,* and in 1931 he joined first *The Guardian* and then the short-lived Labour paper, *The World.* When that paper folded in 1932, he went to the *Adelaide News* and in 1933 found a permanent position with the *Melbourne Herald* as a sporting cartoonist.

In October 1933 Alex Gurney was asked to design a daily strip based on the *Gunn's Gully* letters written by C. J. Dennis. These letters presented a countryman's humorous views, particularly on city life. Gurney created *Ben Bowyang* (called *Gunn's Gully* in some States), which later passed on to such artists as Mick Armstrong, Keith Martin, and the very competent Alex McRae. That same year, Sam Wells elected to go to England, and Gurney took his place as leader page cartoonist.

On Wells' return, in 1940, Gurney set about creating his delightful humor strip about army life, *Bluey and Curley.* The strip, which was to make Gurney famous, first appeared in the magazine, *Picture News,* and then transferred to the Melbourne *Sun* as a daily. To get an authentic view of army life and humor, Gurney visited many army camps all over Australia and, in 1944, took his sketchbook to Port Moresby, Ramu Valley, Lae, and other points in New Guinea where Australian troops were fighting. A legacy of this visit was a bout of malaria in August 1944, resulting in *Bluey and Curley* being published only 3 times per week, until Gurney returned from the hospital.

His outstanding sense of humor was backed-up by very detailed panels, which contained a great variety of angles and well-balanced figures. Acknowledged as one of Australia's finest cartoonists, his particular strength was his ability to capture the flavor of the Australian character, as seen by the Australian. Alex Gurney died of a heart attack on December 4, 1955.

J.R.

GUSTAFSON, PAUL (1916-1977) American comic book artist born in Aland, Finland on August 16, 1916. He moved with his family to America in 1921, and "Gustavson" eventually studied surveying and engineering at New York City's Cooper Union. Using the pen-name "Paul Earrol" as well as his own, he joined the Harry "A" Chesler and Funnies, Inc. comic shops in the late 1930s and proceeded to unleash a torrent of comic strips. Always a clean and meticulous worker, Gustavson rarely attempted to stylize his work. It was straightforward and fast-paced, certainly competent, and never too frilly or gimmicky. His forte was volume. At the comic shops, he produced material for several companies. For Centaur he drew or helped create superheroes like *The Arrow* (1938-1941), *Black Panther* (1941), and *A-Man;* he created and drew *The Angel* for Timely in 1939, and it was probably the only superhero strip to feature a mustache-wearing hero; and he helped create Novelty Press' *Twister* character in 1941.

But Gustavson produced his best material as a member of Busy Arnold's Quality comics stable. Working side-by-side with the likes of Lou Fine, Jack Cole, Reed Crandall, and other greats, Gustavson drew *Quicksilver* (1941-1942), *Magno* (1941), *The Human Bomb* (1941-1946), and *Midnight* (1942-1946), all superheroes of one sort or another. *The Jester,* a strip he invented in 1941, probably contains his best work.

Gustavson spent most of 1942-1945 in the Air Force, but returned to Quality after his discharge. After the war, however, Gustavson began concentrating on Quality's ever-expanding humor line, especially *Will Bragg,* a well-drawn feature about a perennially poverty-stricken braggart. He remained with Quality until owner Arnold sold the company to National in 1956. After a short stay at the ACG group, again drawing humor features, Gustavson left the field entirely to begin a career as a surveyor and engineer. His brother, Nils, also worked in the comic book industry during the 1940s. Paul Gustafson died in 1977 in upstate New York, where he had been working as a surveyor for the state.

J.B.

Alex Gurney, "Bluey and Curley." © The Herald and Weekly Times Ltd.

HAENIGSEN, HARRY (1900-1990?) American cartoonist born 1900 in New York City. After brilliant studies in high school, where he developed a flair for drawing and caricature, Harry Haenigsen was contemplating a career in engineering—he even applied for, and was granted, a scholarship at Rutgers University—but his love for drawing prevailed and in 1918 he joined the Bray animation studio as an assistant. In 1919 Haenigsen enrolled at the Art Students League while supporting himself on a weekly salary of $7 as an art assistant on the *New York World*.

Haenigsen's first comic strip, created for the *World* in 1922, was *Simeon Batts*. It was about the zany doings of a radio buff and the havoc he caused with his attempts at building crystal sets out of kitchen utensils and office furniture. In 1929 Haenigsen developed a cartoon panel commenting on the day's news which the *World* ran until its demise in 1931. Transferring to the *Journal*, Haenigsen revived his panel (which he then called *News and Views*). Along with his career as a cartoonist, Haenigsen pursued a successful occupation as an illustrator, doing numerous drawings for magazines, books, and advertising (his illustrations for *Collier's* won him special notice).

In 1937 Haenigsen left the newspaper field briefly for a short stint as story editor for Max Fleischer Studios. Returning a year later to the comic strip, Haenigsen created *Our Bill* on March 6, 1939, for the Herald-Tribune Syndicate. This was a teenage strip with more energy than charm which ran until 1966. Haenigsen's most memorable creation came a few years later, on June 20, 1943, when he originated *Penny* as a replacement for Charles Voight's *Betty*, which the *Tribune* had just dropped. *Penny* was one of the first bobby-soxer strips. Penelope Mildred Pringle (Penny), her best friend Judy, and the members of the Pringle family were well-characterized, the plots reasonably funny, and the language up to date. But Haenigsen's graphic treatment was too elaborate, and his close-ups, angle shots, and scale distortions were too much of a distraction for what was essentially a simple premise. In 1970 Haenigsen discontinued *Penny* and went into semiretirement. He died at his home in Lambertville, New Jersey, in late 1990 or early 1991.

Harry Haenigsen's undisputed talents never found a satisfactory outlet. His creations, likable though they were, never caught the public's fancy or the critics' eye. Haenigsen will be remembered chiefly for his elegance of line and his understated and warm humor.

M.H.

HÄGAR THE HORRIBLE (U.S.) The creation of Dik Browne, who somehow resembled the title character, *Hägar the Horrible* invaded comic pages in February of 1973 and achieved the most notable success of a new comic in the art form's history: within two years it was carried in more than 600 papers worldwide—a rank near the top among a field of veterans.

Both critically and commercially *Hägar* has been a success. Browne almost instantly achieved a comfortable mix of "bigfoot" art and sophisticated design; slapstick gags and social commentary; broad humor and sympathetic characterizations.

The hero is a plunderer, sacker, and looter by profession, but not very far below the Viking exterior is a softie akin to Jackie Gleason's Ralph Kramden—or even Browne himself. Hägar may invade Gaul, but he takes a Paris shopping list from his wife. In one revealing Sunday page, Hägar tried on crowns on the sly—fantasizing like a little boy.

The family of this ninth-century Viking is cut from a different pattern as well. Wife Helga is more the warrior. Physically she is as ample as Hägar and is more consistently ferocious. Hamlet is the young son who continually embarrasses his parents: he refuses to grow his hair long, go without baths, or lust after conquest—he even reads books and aspires to dentistry! Daughter Honi is a 16-year-old beauty, almost an old maid, who, as a protean women's libber, dreams of accompanying her father on raids. Her major suitor, Lute, is a minstrel as sappy and unkempt as Honi is assertive and pretty.

One of the most inspired characters is Lucky Eddie, Hägar's amazingly chinless sidekick. He has a justifiable persecution complex, bungles the most simple tasks, and provides great slapstick relief in the strip.

Hägar's name was inspired by an incident in Browne's household: his sons Chris and Bob were having an animated debate one afternoon when the elder Browne came bounding down the stairs, lobbying for an atmosphere conducive to napping. "Well, if it isn't Hägar the Horrible," said one of the boys in a wisecrack out of the blue that later named this great comic figure.

"Hägar the Horrible," Dik Browne. © King Features Syndicate.

Dik Browne was named "Cartoonist of the Year" by NCS in 1974 for his work on Hägar. After his death in 1989, his son Chris, who gained a name as an underground comic book artist and also assisted his father on *Hägar* for many years, took over the strip.

R.M.

HAGIO, MOTO (1949-   ) The second of four children born to a white-collar mine worker in Fukuoka Prefecture, Japan, Moto Hagio began to show artistic talent at a very young age (one drawing assignment she submitted led her first-grade teacher to believe an adult had drawn it for her), and became an avid reader of both literature and comics. In her second year of high school, inspired by Osamu Tezuka's relatively unknown *Shinsengumi* (1963), Hagio decided to become a *manga* ("comic") artist.

In 1969, shortly after graduating from fashion design school, Hagio made her professional debut in *Nakayoshi*, Kodansha Publishing's popular comics magazine for girls, with the short story *Ruru to Mimi* ("Lulu and Mimi"). Lured to Shogakukan Publishing by innovative girls' comics editor Junya Yamamoto, she produced a string of short stories for the magazines *Bessatsu Shōjo Komikku* ("Special Edition Girls' Comic") and *Shūkan Shōjo Komikku* ("Weekly Girls' Comic"), culminating in 1971 with the groundbreaking *Jūichigatsu no gimunajiumu* ("November Gymnasium"), the first girls' comic to feature only boys and the first to overtly suggest same-sex love, thereby giving birth to a genre of girls' comics—stories of love between boys or young men—that remains popular to this day. In 1974, Hagio developed this story into the longer *Tōma no shinzō* ("The Heart of Thomas"), a work widely recognized as a classic of Japanese comics.

Hagio is a prominent member of a loosely defined group of women artists known as the *Hana no nijūyonen gumi* ("Magnificent 24-Year Group") because many were born in the year Showa 24, or 1949. Before these "Forty-niners," *shōjo manga* ("girls' comics") were generally dismissed by male comics fans as sappy melodramas and romances, but this group, which includes Yumiko Ōshima, Keiko Takemiya, and Ryōko Yamagishi, helped create a boom in girls' comics in the 1970s and brought the genre critical attention it had never enjoyed before.

In 1976, Hagio was awarded the Shogakukan Comics Award (Girls) for her science fiction classic *Jūichinin iru!* ("They Were Eleven," 1975), and her epic tale of two adolescent vampires, *Pō no ichizoku* ("The Poe Clan," 1972-76). The two-part *Hagio Moto sakuhinshū* ("Collected Works of Moto Hagio") spans 34 volumes, and since its publication she has produced more than 20 additional volumes, including the four-volume sci-fi masterpiece *Marginal* (1985-87) and her critically acclaimed drama of child sexual abuse, *Zankoku na kami ga shihai suru* ("A Cruel God Reigns," 1992 to present, nine volumes as of this writing).

M.A.T.

HAIRBREADTH HARRY (U.S.) In 1906 C. W. Kahles, already a veteran cartoonist at 28 with over a half-dozen comic strip creations to his credit, produced the feature that was to make him justly famous. Named *Hairbreadth Harry, the Boy Hero* (later simply *Hairbreadth Harry*) it was published as a Sunday half page (and later as a full page) first by the *Philadelphia Press*, then by T. C. McClure, and finally by the Philadelphia Ledger Syndicate.

Harold Hollingsworth (alias "Hairbreadth Harry") was forever outwitting villain Rudolph Rassendale and rescuing Belinda Blinks the beautiful boilermaker from his clutches in this witty cartoon burlesque of dime novels and movie melodramas of the period. In the beginning, Belinda was a head taller than the "boy hero" and although described as "a ravishing creature of dazzling loveliness," Kahles made her look pretty homely in his drawings, which made the whole thing all the funnier. Harry however, kept growing and sometime around 1916, he assumed a normal man's size, when he and Belinda became true sweethearts.

In relentless pursuit was Rudolph, the typical storybook villain, complete with black dress suit, top hat, handlebar mustache, and flashing teeth. He regularly concocted wild plots which Harry foiled no less regularly. Thwarted at every turn, Rudolph would shake his fist, exclaiming: "Curses on you, Harold Hollingsworth!" and vow terrible vengeance—and the triangle chase would resume, as funny and furious as before.

In 1923 the Philadelphia Ledger Syndicate acquired the distribution rights to *Hairbreadth Harry* and immediately asked Kahles to add a daily strip to his Sunday feature. Kahles carried both the *Hairbreadth Harry* daily and Sunday, practically unassisted, until his death in January 1931. The feature then passed to F. O. Alexander, who tried his best to maintain the strip's original flavor while attempting at the same time to accommodate it to the changing tastes of the 1930s, but the readership kept dwindling and *Hairbreadth Harry* was finally discontinued in 1939.

Hairbreadth Harry was the first strip to make systematic use of week-to-week suspense in order to hold the reader's attention, and as such it spawned a multitude of imitators (*Desperate Desmond* is probably the best-known of these). It was very popular in the 1910s and 1920s, and around 1925 six movie comedies were produced by West Brothers Happiness Comedies for Artclass Pictures Corporation in Long Island City. Some of these two-reelers were later released for television. Several attempts were made to revive *Hairbreadth Harry* in the 1940s and 1950s for radio, television, and newspapers, but none of these were very successful.

M.H.

HAKABA NO KITARŌ (Japan) Hakaba no Kitarō ("Kitarō of the Graveyard") was created by Shigeru Mizuki and made its first appearance in a comic book titled *Yurei Ikka* ("The Ghost Family") in 1959. Mizuki did a number of *Kitarō* stories, but the books were not widely circulated. Only in August 1965, when *Hakaba no Kitarō* started appearing in *Shōnen*, the most famous boys' weekly magazine in Japan, did the strip attain popular acceptance.

Kitarō was not a human being but a ghost with a grotesque face. He had use of only his right eye; his left eye, concealed behind a lock of hair, was the dwelling of his ghostly father. Kitarō was friendly to man and wore the traditional *chanchanko*, the Japanese vest, filled with the spirits of his ancestors. Kitarō could disembody his hands and project them on independent missions; he also had antennas concealed in his hair.

The storyline mainly related Kitarō's many battles against a host of monsters: La Seine, a vampire; Hangyojin, the sea monster; Gyūki, half-bull, half-spider monster; Ungaikyō, the mirror monster; as well as

"Hakaba no Kitarō," Shigeru Mizuki. © Shōnen.

assorted witches, werewolves, and demons. At one time or another, Kitarō took on every monster made famous by literature or film, from Dracula to Frankenstein. In his adventures, he had two assistants: his father and a mischievous and dirty old ghoul called Nezumi-Otoko. Kitarō also held sway over toads, spiders, lizards, and scorpions, and they would join in a song of praise (the *Ge-ge-ge no Uta* or "ge-ge-ge song") at the end of each story.

The prototype of *Hakaba no Kitarō* was *Hakaba Kitarō* (1933-1935, by Masami Ito), a story of horror and revenge. This was one of the most famous *kamishibai,* a kind of picture-show with drawings presented in sequence to the audience.

Kitarō was one of the weirdest Japanese comic strip heroes. His stories are imaginative, fantastic, and tinted with irony.

Hakaba no Kitarō inspired a series of animated TV cartoons before being discontinued in March 1969.

H.K.

HALF-HITCH (U.S.) Hank Ketcham's *Half-Hitch*, distributed by King Features as a daily and Sunday comic, began in early February 1970. It was originally intended to be a panel, but Ketcham disagreed with his own syndicate and went to King with a strip that gave the naval locale a more appropriate showcase. Ketcham designed all the characters and sought out Dick Hodgins, Jr., then an Associated Press staff artist (and later an editorial cartoonist for the *New York News*). Hodgins was engaged for the artwork and Bob Saylor

(no pun), a gagman on *Dennis the Menace*, worked on the story line. The characters, sailors on the aircraft carrier *Clagmire*, formed a little community on what was practically a floating city. In addition, shore leaves took the crew to all parts of the world.

The title character was based on the *Collier's Magazine* panel of the same name (although he was much changed in appearance and was no longer a mime) from Ketcham's gag days. He was, naturally, short; a fairly successful wolf; and was journalist third class on the ship's newspaper. Poopsy, a talking sea gull, was a major character who offered commentary, advice, and gibes to the crew. His speech was in lowercase lettering. Fluke was a country boy, new to big-city and foreign-port ways, but not as dumb as he looked.

Other major characters included: Zawiki, Hitch's big, dumb pal who worked in the sick bay; Flip Feeney, a hip disk jockey on the ship's radio station; Marji, his women's lib companion; gruff and lantern-jawed Capt. Carrick; Ensign Sweet, a prissy and inept foil of Poopsy; wise guy Haw Haw McGraw; the gourmet Chinese chef Ding Chow, who managed to raise exotic foods in every part of the ship; and a bevy of pretty females assigned to the *Clagmire*.

The combination of talent and research made the artwork in *Half-Hitch* something to behold; silhouettes, stylized shading, and panel experimentation made the strip, especially in Sunday format, a handsome piece of work. Unfortunately, the gags scored much less often and the strip, clever in conception and beautiful in visual execution, often lacked the narrative punch that could have lifted it to greater heights. *Half-Hitch* was discontinued in 1975.

R.M.

HAMLIN, VINCENT T. (1900-1993) American cartoonist born 1900 in Perry, Iowa. V. T. Hamlin, like so many other cartoonists, displayed an early flair for caricature which he put to use by lampooning his high school teachers. When World War I came, he enlisted in the Army at the age of 17 and was sent to France with the American Expeditionary Force. Returning to Perry in 1918, he finished high school, and then studied journalism at the University of Missouri. Out of the university, Hamlin worked as a reporter in Des Moines, Iowa, for the *Register and Tribune*, and later for the *News*.

In the early 1920s Hamlin moved to Texas, where he held jobs as photographer, reporter, and cartoonist at the *Fort Worth Record* and the *Fort Worth Star Telegram*. In 1927 he quit newspapering and went to work in the oil fields as layout man, poster designer, and mapmaker. It was then that the idea of a prehistoric comic strip developed in Hamlin's fertile mind, according to his own account. He started developing his idea upon his return to the art department of the *Register and Tribune* in 1929. The process was slow and painstaking, as Hamlin later recalled: "I first put a modern rough family into the cave-dwelling days. I worked on that idea for a year, then destroyed the strips. I tried another idea in caveman style for another six months and dropped that. Then I got the idea for *Alley Oop*."

Hamlin sold his new strip to NEA, which brought it out on August 7, 1933, as a daily (and on September 9, 1934, as a Sunday). Hamlin worked on *Alley Oop*— while pursuing his hobbies of playing football, fishing, and driving race cars—until his retirement in 1971

(Dave Graue and Jack Bender are now turning out the strip). He died in Brookville, Florida, on June 14, 1993.

Hamlin's career was unobtrusive, but fecund and rewarding. He was never self-assertive and was therefore passed over for cartooning awards in favor of lesser but pushier artists. Yet his stature as a fine humor strip artist and a master of the absurd has quietly grown among comic art critics, and it is likely that V. T. Hamlin's career will be reevaluated in light of his achievements as a comic innovator and storyteller.

M.H.

HAMPSON, FRANK (1918-1985) British cartoonist and illustrator, born at Audenshaw, Manchester, on December 21, 1918. He was educated at King George V School in Southport, leaving in 1932 to become a telegraph boy for the post office. His first cartoon was published in *Meccano Magazine* and he became its joke illustrator (1932-1935). He then became a civil servant and attended Southport School of Arts in the evenings, studying life drawing. He freelanced his first strips to the post office magazine, *The Post* (1937), but resigned from the post office in 1938 to become a full-time art student, then joined the Territorial Army in 1939. During the war he served as a driver in the Royal Army Service Corps, being commissioned in 1944. Despite passing the test for RAF aircrew training, he was refused a transfer. He was demobilized in 1946 with a grant to continue his art studies.

Hampson freelanced illustrations for *The Anvil* (1947), a religious monthly published by a local Anglican, the Rev. Marcus Morris. With Morris he designed and planned an ambitious new comic weekly for boys, which was christened *Eagle* by Mrs. Hampson. His dummy was accepted by Hulton Press, and the new paper, the most important landmark in postwar British comics, was launched on April 14, 1950. Hampson wrote and drew *Rob Conway, Tommy Walls, The Great Adventure*, and the two-page cover feature that became nationally famous, *Dan Dare, Pilot of the Future*. To cope with the weekly output, he set up a studio, with writers, art assistants, and models, both human (for the characters) and artificial (for the space ships, cities, etc.). Hampson acted as chief artist and designer for *Eagle* until 1960, when Hulton sold out to Odhams Press, and Marcus Morris resigned editorship to join National Magazines. Although Hampson had not drawn *Dan Dare* for some time, his style stamped the strip, the *Eagle*, and the companion comics that he and Morris had created: *Girl, Swift*, and *Robin*. Eventually all the titles were killed, but Hampson's influence remains, particularly in science fiction strips and the work of Frank Bellamy.

After a period of illustrating the educational color books for young children published by Ladybird, Hampson contracted cancer of the trachea in 1970. Recovering after treatment, he joined Ewell County Technical College as a graphics technician. His work on *Eagle* remains ahead of its time, and it is still unequalled in British comics. He died in Epsom on July 8, 1985.

D.G.

HANGMAN, THE (U.S.) MLJ comics did something rare in the July 1941 issue of *Pep* (number 17)—writer Cliff Campbell engineered the death of a minor superhero called the Comet. The Comet's brother, Bob Dickering, swore to avenge his death and adopted the role of the Hangman. He also inherited the Comet's spot in *Pep* as well as his brother's girlfriend, reporter Thelma Gordon. Garbing himself in a darkly colored costume with a ropelike belt, the Hangman was appearing in his own book by the winter of 1941. (The book had started as *Special* comics and the Hangman didn't have the book named after him until the second issue.)

Throughout its tenure, *The Hangman* had superior stories, mostly scripted by comic veterans Bill Woolfolk (1941-1942) and Otto Binder (1943-1944). Both writers kept the mood dark and ominous, and the Hangman apparently had no qualms about actually hanging transgressors. He also had an array of interesting villains. One of them, Mother Goose, committed all her crimes using nursery rhymes as clues; another, Captain Swastika, actually overpowered the Hangman. When he lost one of his many battles it was because of stupidity or carelessness, and he didn't die until he was inadvertantly stabbed with an ice pick by one of his own henchmen.

Artistically, the feature began poorly because George Storm, an excellent humor artist, simply couldn't handle adventure strips properly. In later years, however, Irv Novick (1941-1943) and Bob Fujitani (1942-1944) both handled *The Hangman* with the necessary verve and style.

The Hangman strip lasted in *Pep* through March 1944's 47th issue. The last issue of *Hangman* (number eight) was published in the fall of 1943. The Hangman was unsuccessfully revived as a villain in 1965 by MLJ.

J.B.

HANS AND FRITZ *see* Captain and the Kids, The.

HAPPY HOOLIGAN (U.S.) Fred Opper's classic Irish tramp with the tin-can hat, Happy Hooligan, made his first comic-page appearance in a single row of four colored panels in Hearst's Sunday comic sections in New York and San Francisco on March 26, 1900. This began a series of Sunday episodes called *The Doings of Happy Hooligan*, the first of several running titles under which the Hooligan strip would appear between 1900 and 1932.

Hooligan, first portrayed with a distinctly ruddy nose and a blue can for a hat (later changed to a permanent red, sometimes with a blank label), was the simple innocent whose impulsive undertakings nearly always landed him in the hands of the law (played, in these early years, by a heavily mustached policeman with a stout club and a Keystone Cop hat). Despite this continual bad luck, Hooligan lived up to his name by remaining always optimistic, and his enormous smile became a quick symbol of the new comic strip art form to millions of readers.

Soon a half page, then frequently a full front or back page feature in the four-page Hearst Sunday comics, Opper's *Doings of Happy Hooligan* often dropped its running title for a one-time episode caption, like "The Unfortunate Gallantry of Happy Hooligan." Originally short and rotund, Hooligan was already his leaner, taller self of later years when he met the first of several continuing characters in the *Hooligan* strip: his "long-lost" brother, Gloomy Gus, on April 20, 1902. Gus, as long-faced as Happy was jolly, experienced exactly the reverse of Happy's bad luck—whenever Happy ran afoul of the law, his disaster almost inevitably left Gus with a fine meal, a sack of diamonds, or some other

"Happy Hooligan," F. B. Opper. © King Features Syndicate.

such windfall. A bit later, Gus (of the ankle-length brown or yellow coat and battered top hat) was with Happy when the strip's hero acquired his pet dog, the black-spotted white mongrel, Flip, on March 15, 1903. (In an unusual episode of June 22, 1902, Happy and Gus dine with their parents, a brother-in-law, and Happy's three young nephews, of whom only the nephews are seen again in the strip.) Before long, on February 14, 1904, Happy meets a third brother, a monocled, Anglophilic tramp in ragged cutaway, spats, and tails, named Montmorency, with whom he eventually makes a very funny trip to England.

By 1914, the Hooligan strip was a full page running every Sunday under the fixed title of *Happy Hooligan*. By mid-1916, however, reflecting events in the strip, the regular title had become *Happy Hooligan's Honeymoon*, changing back in late 1918 to *Happy Hooligan* once more. In early 1919, however, Happy had joined forces with a scraggly mustached little fellow in a plaid hat named Mr. Dubb, for whom Opper renamed the Sunday page *Mr. Dubb*. In the spring of 1921, Dubb left the strip, and the locale changed to the farm home of Si, Mirandy, and Maud the mule together with a strip title switch to *Down on the Farm*.

After a period of rural adventures with Happy and (of all people) Alphonse and Gaston, the strip name was changed back, with the beginning of a world tour by Happy and Gloomy, to *Happy Hooligan* again in mid-1923. In the summer of 1925, however, Happy was dropped altogether for a time, the focus of the Sunday strip was switched to Mr. Dubb once more, and the title altered again to *Mr. Dough and Mr. Dubb*. (Mr. Dough, seen in the strip briefly in 1920, was Mr. Dubb's portly employer.) Happy reentered the strip by December 1925 as a night watchman (then a janitor) for Mr. Dough, and he and Dubb were a team for the remainder of the titular sequence until the strip name returned permanently to *Happy Hooligan* in January of 1927.

By the end of 1910 and thereafter, *Happy Hooligan* had become an involved continuity strip, with narratives running for many weeks and frequently involving cliffhanger episode breaks, with the simple weekly theme of Happy's bad luck long since dropped. In the early 1920s, a daily *Hooligan* strip, called both *Mr. Dough and Mr. Dubb* and *Happy Hooligan* ran rather obscurely and erratically in some Hearst papers at various times; it seems to have been short-lived, however, since Opper's weekday efforts were almost always political cartoons done for the Hearst chain of papers,

and *Hooligan* remained an essentially weekly strip from start to finish.

In the mid-1920s, when all Sunday Hearst strips were adding second weekly features at the top of the page, Opper first revived an old strip of his from the 1900s called *Our Antediluvian Ancestors* to run above *Mr. Dough and Mr. Dubb* as a single row of panels on January 17, 1926. He changed this for one week to a two-row, eight-panel strip called *The Optimist* on May 16, 1926, then reanimated *Maud* the following week for his permanent Sunday cofeature with *Hooligan*.

Hooligan was a popular figure in a number of fields beyond the comic page: he appeared in several stage productions in the 1900s, was featured in a song by Stillman and Vogel in 1902, starred in a number of animated cartoons released through Hearst's International Film Service circa 1917 (*Happy Hooligan at the Zoo*, etc.), and was reprinted in several books from the turn of the century on. These included *Happy Hooligan, Handy Happy Hooligan, Happy Hooligan's Travels, Happy Hooligan Home Again, The Story of Happy Hooligan*, etc. Most were published by Frederick Stokes & Co. before 1910, although the last work dates from 1932.

Drawn by Opper until he was in his mid-70s, *Happy Hooligan* finally had to be abandoned by its creator in 1932 (the strip last appeared in most papers on August 14, 1932) because of his failing eyesight. It deserves extensive reprinting, preferably in full, as a major classic work of the American comic strip.

B.B.

HARGREAVES, HARRY (1922-   ) British cartoonist, animator, and illustrator, born in Manchester in 1922. Educated at Chorlton High School, he then trained as an architect and engineer. In 1939 he joined the art staff of Kayebon Press, a Manchester agency, and assisted Hugh McNeill with his strips for D. C. Thomson. His first comic work was *Pansy Potter* in *Beano*, "ghosting" for McNeill. He turned down an offer from Thomson to do full-time freelance work on their comics, preferring a job with Rolls Royce working on the Merlin engine. He volunteered for the Royal Air Force Signals branch in 1942 and served four years in the Far East. During this time, he drew the Christmas airgraphs for RAF Ceylon and illustrated unit magazines. In 1946, he returned to engineering at Simon's of Stockport, then applied for an aptitude test with Gaumont British Animation, a new unit set up by David Hand, a Disney director. Taken on as trainee, he became an animator on the *Animaland* and *Musical Paintbox* series, until the unit was disbanded in 1949.

The Disney-style training both inspired and aided Hargreaves, and his new style quickly found strip work in children's comics: *Scamp*, a dog in *Comet* (1950); *Harold Hare* (1950) and *Ollie the Alley Cat* (1951) in *Sun*; *Don Quickshot* (1952) in *Knockout Fun Book*; *Terry the Troubadour* (1954) in *TV Comic*. He then joined the "Dutch Walt Disney," Marten Toonder, in Amsterdam to draw the newspaper strip version of his film character *Panda*, syndicated to 150 European papers and the *London Evening News*. Returning home in 1959, he settled in the West Country, where his love for animals combined with his animator's technique and interest in the strip form to originate a series of pictorial narratives featuring a small bird. This *Punch* series (1958) quickly caught on, and the reprinted episodes filled four books: *The Bird*; *The Bird and Others*; *It's a Bird's Life*; and *Bird for All Seasons*. From 1962 he drew cartoons for a local television series, *Discs a Go Go*, and then the weekly strip *Budge & Co* for Reveille (1966), and the advertising strip *Sammy Squirrel* (1968). His daily strip *Hayseeds* started in the *Evening News* in 1969 and ran until the mid-1980s. His other cartoon books include *How's That*; *Not Out*; *Googlies* (all about crickets); and two reprints of *Hayseeds*. After his strip was discontinued, Hargreaves went into retirement.

D.G.

HARISU NO KAZE (Japan) Created by Tetsuya Chiba, *Harisu no Kaze* ("The Whirlwind of Harisu") made its first appearance in the weekly *Shōnen* magazine in April 1965. *Harisu no Kaze* was a Gakuen Manga (the equivalent of the English public school story) and it soon rose to the top position in that genre.

Kunimatsu Ishida, the strip's diminutive hero, had been transferred to Harisu Gakuen (Harisu High School) from another school. As soon as he arrived at Harisu, he started acting like a whirlwind. Ishida was small, but bold, fearless, and a hater of injustice. He excelled in all sports, and was a friendly sort of fellow, but he was weak in his academic studies and his fondness for girls often landed him in trouble. Ishida soon established himself as a sports winner: he led the Harisu team to victory in the interscholastic baseball tournament, won the national fencing title, and insured his team's victory in the Tokyo soccer tournament by scoring the decisive goal. Ishida was also a peppery fighter, winning against all comers in fencing, boxing, and judo. Soon after he entered the school, Ishida became the hero of Harisu, as well as a very popular character in the history of Japanese comics.

Aside from Ishida, the main characters in the strip were: Yōko Asai, alias Ochara, the hero's classmate and the editor of the school paper; his teacher Gōzō Iwanami; A-bō, Ishido's younger brother; and Koyama, the captain of the new boxing club.

Harisu no Kaze was a very human story, full of laughter, emotion, friendship, and vitality. It was very popular with the readers and inspired a series of animated cartoons. The strip made its last appearance in November 1967.

H.K.

HARMAN, FRED (1902-1982) American artist born February 9, 1902, in St. Joseph, Missouri. Fred Harman, while still an infant, was taken by his parents to Pagosa Springs in Colorado, near the New Mexico border, where his father owned a ranch. There he grew up in the wilds of Colorado and northern New Mexico, learning the hard life of a ranch hand. In 1915 the Harmans moved to Kansas City, where Fred started a short-lived cartooning career on the *Star* in 1920. In 1921 he worked at the Kansas City Film Ad Company, a small animation outfit, alongside two other fledgling cartoonists, Walt Disney and Ub Iwerks.

In 1924 Harman shuffled around the country, doing illustrations in his native St. Joseph and trying different ventures in California, Minnesota, and Iowa, before settling in Hollywood in 1930. In 1934 he produced his first comic strip, a Western called *Bronc Peeler* which he syndicated himself, but the returns were meager and he abandoned it early in 1938.

Harman then went to New York, where he tried unsuccessfully to succeed Allen Dean on *King of the Royal Mounted*. (His agent, Stephen Slesinger, also represented Dean and *King's* creator, Zane Grey). Discouraged, he was about to leave when, through his agent, he met Fred Ferguson, president of the Newspaper Enterprise Association, who asked him to do another western strip for NEA. On November 6, 1938, *Red Ryder* was born.

In 1940 Fred Harman returned to Pagosa Springs where he developed the "Red Ryder Ranch" and could be seen parading around dressed-up as his comic strip hero. He became a painter of western scenes and one of the founders of Cowboy Artists of America. In the 1960s Harman moved to Albuquerque, New Mexico. He died in Phoenix, Arizona, on January 2, 1982.

Fred Harman received a number of distinctions over the years, but as a western artist rather than as a cartoonist. He was made Man of the Year in Colorado and an honorary citizen of Texas, and he received many other awards and trophies. A number of Fred Harman's works were reproduced in Ed Ainsworth's excellent study *The Cowboy in Art* (World, 1968) and an anthology of his pictures was published in 1969 by Sage Books under the title *The Great West in Paintings*.

M.H.

HAROLD TEEN (U.S.) One of the additions to the *Chicago Tribune's* new comic section of May 4, 1919, was Carl Ed's *The Love Life of Harold Teen*. A bright page of nine panels, it presented its dark-haired juvenile hero in a straw skimmer and red jacket, learning from a teenage crony named Buck that there is a new "queen" in town. The queen (1919 teen slang for girl) was named Mae Preston, and she was to be Harold's love interest for several months to come. (His longer-lived love, Lillums Lovewell, first appearing on March 28, 1920, was still in the future.) A weekly gag strip without continuity—aside from the love affair—*The Love Life of Harold Teen* was an invention of the Tribune's copublisher, Joseph Patterson, who felt that the public would like a teenage comic, in view of the success of Booth Tarkington's *Seventeen* two years before. Ed did a fast, amusing job with the Patterson character, and within five months was asked to start a daily version for Patterson's new tabloid, the *New York Daily News*. The first daily episode, still bearing the long title, appeared in the *News* on Thursday, September 25, 1919, and was an introductory panel listing the early characters of the strip—none of whom were retained in the later, 30-year cast of the comic, except for Harold's "Moms," his "Pa" (Thomas Teen), and his kid sister, Josie (here given her full name of Josephine). Immedi-

"Harold Teen," Carl Ed. © Chicago Tribune.

ately after the introduction, the daily strip (not introduced into the *Tribune* for some time) continued with the Sunday page story of Harold's difficult romance with Mae Preston. (We also learn Harold's exact age here for the first time—it is, of course, 17.)

The teenage populace of America took to the *Harold Teen* strip (its long title was quickly trimmed) because of Ed's awareness of the current teen vogues in speech and dress. Harold's use of popular terms like "Sheba" (for a girl), and "lamb's lettuce" (as an endearment) wowed the juvenile set of the time, and the strip served as a bridge to carry the latest city slang and doings to the laggard countryside. Given his head by Patterson, Ed now developed and introduced his own characters, such as Lillums Lovewell; her father Lemuel Lovewell; the shrimpish Shadow Smart; Pop Jenks and the Sugar Bowl soda parlor gang, Horace, Beezie, and the others; the swinging Aunt Pruny, and many more characters relished by the comic readers of the 1920s and 1930s.

By the wartime 1940s, however, Ed assumed his readers would be out of sympathy with a self-indulgent teen set and moved Harold into the service of his country as an espionage agent. Ed was not particularly good at the melodrama this entailed, however, and his dramatics were more often ludicrous than effective. An attempt to return to the old Sugar Bowl ways after the war didn't work well, either, and the once-large circulation of *Harold Teen* began to dwindle, until by Ed's death in 1959 the strip was appearing primarily in its original newspaper birthplace. The strip was folded after Ed's death—the era that it represented so memorably was then as long gone as F. Scott Fitzgerald and Texas Guinan.

Several Harold Teen strip collections were published, and two film versions were made of the strip: the silent

one of 1928 starring Arthur Lake (later of *Blondie* fame), and the sound film of 1933 featuring Rochelle Hudson as Lillums.

B.B.

HART, JOHNNY (1931-   ) American cartoonist born in Endicott, N.Y., on February 18, 1931. Graduating from Union-Endicott High School in 1949, Johnny Hart joined the U.S. Air Force one year later and was sent to Korea, where he drew cartoons for the Pacific *Stars and Stripes.* Discharged in 1953, Johnny Hart and his wife, Mary (whom he had married two years before), went to live at her mother's farm in Georgia.

In 1954 Hart sold his first cartoon to the *Saturday Evening Post* and gradually established himself as a cartoonist, contributing regularly to the *Post, Collier's,* and *Bluebook.* In 1956 the Harts moved to New York City, and Johnny went to work for two years in the art department of General Electric. After several unsuccessful attempts, Hart finally persuaded the Herald-Tribune Syndicate to accept his first comic strip creation, *B.C.,* a far-out feature about a weird assortment of cavemen, talking plants, and animals. The first *B.C.* daily strip appeared on February 17, 1958.

In 1964 Hart developed a new strip idea and teamed up with cartoonist Brant Parker (whom Hart had known since the time they were both residents in Endicott) to produce *The Wizard of Id*, the hilarious saga of a ludicrous monarch and his equally grotesque subjects.

Johnny Hart is capable of dazzling humor and hilarious originality, and is also a thoughtful author who tries to impart his vision of the modern world, seen through the reducing lens of faraway (and purely imagined) historical periods. He has been the recipient of a great number of prizes for his work, including the

Reuben Award, which he received in 1968 in a tie vote with the editorial cartoonist Pat Oliphant. Other honors have included the NCS's Elzie Segar Award in 1981 and the Silver Plaque for best newspaper comic strip in 1989.

M.H.

HARTOG VAN BANDA, LO (1916-   ) Lo Hartog van Banda, one of the busiest and most prolific of Dutch comic writers, was born November 11, 1916, in Den Haag, Netherlands. Hartog van Banda did not emerge as a comic writer until after World War II. He wrote *Fabulus de klokkendokter* ("Fabulus, Clock Doctor") for a clockmakers' trade journal in 1947. In 1952 he was hired as a staff writer in the Marten Toonder Studios. He wrote some of the episodes of *Panda*, the first of the *Kappie* episodes for Toonder, *Kappie en het drijvende eiland* ("Cappie and the Floating Island"), and *De ondergang van Ur* ("The Destruction of Ur"), an episode for the strip *Aram*, normally written by Waling Dijkstra and drawn by Piet Wijn.

Most importantly, however, he plotted and wrote all of the *Tom Poes* episodes for the weekly version of that strip which appeared in *Week in beeld, De Avrobode, Revue,* and *Donald Duck*. Apart from the weekly version of *Tom Poes*, which incorporated speech balloons, he also suggested some of the plots used in the daily *Tom Poes* strip, talking them over and developing them with Marten Toonder, who always wrote the finalized version to be put under the strips. He also created some of the characters to appear in the strips plus new comic features. For several years he even added Toonder's *Koning Hollewijn* to the strips he was writing. In 1966, after 14 years with the Toonder Studios, Hartog van Banda left the world of comics to enter that of advertising. It was only two years later that he returned to writing comics, this time casting off the cloak of anonymity, working under his own name on eight different series.

Working with The Tjong Khing, he wrote *Iris* in 1968. That same year he also started writing scenarios for *De Argonautjes* ("The Little Argonauts"), drawn by the very talented Dick Matena, expanding this collaboration the following year by writing *Ridder Roodhart* ("Knight Redheart"). In 1969 he started working with several other artists: with Gideon Brugman on *Ambrosius*, a strip about the wild adventures of elderly Professor Ambrosius; with John Bakker on the superhero parody *Blook*; and with artist The Tjong Khing on *Arman en Ilva* ("Arman and Ilva"). In 1970, among other things, he started writing the semifunny science fiction series *Arad en Maya* ("Arad and Maya") for artist Jan Steeman. With the discontinuance of most of his strips in the mid-1980s, he went into retirement.

W.F.

HASELDEN, W. K. (1872-1953) Regarded as the father of the British newspaper strip, William Kerridge Haselden was born in Seville. As a 30-year-old insurance clerk, he walked into the office of the newly revamped *Daily Illustrated Mirror* on Tuesday, January 5, 1904, a portfolio of sample cartoons under his arm. Editor Hamilton Fyfe was so impressed that he published one the very next morning: *Only Waiting for the Torch*. Haselden did not leave the Mirror until 1940, for 36 years their staff cartoonist. Very soon his daily panel evolved from a single joke to a series of small comments on a single topic, not a new idea in itself but

W. K. Haselden, "Big and Little Willie." © *Daily Mirror Newspapers Ltd.*

new to newspapers. His first cartoon in this prototype strip style was published January 15, 1904: *The Bourchier-Walkeley Episode in Four Scenes*. Gradually characters began to recur and by the summer of 1908 a form of serial developed: *Mr Simkins On His Holiday*, which ran for 16 days. Other running characters he included from time to time were Burlington Bertie the Knut with a K; Miss Joy Flapperton, the sweet young thing; and Colonel Dugout, departmental beureaucrat.

His most famous creations first appeared on Friday October 2, 1914, under the title *The Sad Experiences of Big and Little Willie*. These were caricatures of Kaiser Wilhelm of Germany and his son, the Crown Prince. The public so loved these ludicrous representations of England's enemy that they became running characters and were reprinted in a sumptuous art paper book by Chatto & Windus (1915). When a *Daily Mirror* reporter interviewed the captured Kaiser at the end of the Great War, he confessed that the cartoons were "damnably effective."

Haselden's 100 best cartoons were collated each year into annual paperbacks titled *Daily Mirror Reflections*, the first being dated 1908, the last (Vol. 31) 1937. Other books illustrated by Haselden included: *Accidents Will Happen* (1907), *The Globe 'By The Way' Book* (1908), and *America As I Saw It* (1913). He also illustrated drama reviews for *Punch*. He died in 1953 at the age of 81.

D.G.

HASEN, IRWIN (1918-   ) American cartoonist born July 8, 1918, in New York City. Irwin Hasen attended the National Academy and the Art Students League. He started his cartooning career in the late 1930s by drawing sports cartoons and doing advertising artwork. In 1940 he went into comic books, working for various publishers on such features as *The Green Hornet* (1940), *The Fox* (1940-42), *Green Lantern* (1941), *The Flash* (1943), and creating the short-lived *Citizen Smith, Son of the Unknown Soldier* for Holyoke in 1941.

Drafted into the Army, Hasen became the editor of the Fort Dix Reception Center newspaper. Discharged in 1946, he went back to more comic book work, almost exclusively for National Periodicals, where he drew, among other features, *Johnny Thunder*, *The Justice League of America*, and reprised both *The Flash* and *Green Lantern*. He also tried his hand at his first newspaper strip (for the *New York Post*); this was *The Goldbergs*, based on a top-rated radio program of the time, but it folded after a few months.

In the 1950s Hasen became active in the National Cartoonists Society and while on a NCS tour in Europe he met Gus Edson; this resulted in their collaboration (with Edson writing and Hasen drawing) on a new comic strip, *Dondi*, which first appeared in September of 1955. After Edison's death in 1966 Hasen also took over the writing of the strip. In 1986 *Dondi* was discontinued, and Hasen has been occasionally working in comic books again.

A competent and solid craftsman, Irwin Hasen is one of the many unsung cartoonists who have managed to carry on the best traditions of comic art in an unobtrusive and yet praiseworthy way.

M.H.

HATANOSUKE HINOMARU (Japan) *Hatanosuke Hinomaru*, created by Kikuo Nakajima, made its first appearance in 1935 in the comic monthly *Shōnen Kurabu*.

Hatanosuke was a boy samurai: he wore a sun-crested kimono (*hinomaru* means "sun" in Japanese) and a striped hakama. He was brave and witty; as a lord's squire he was adviser to the lord's son. His activities were boundless—not only did he give wise advice, he took part in its implementation, arresting thieves and thwarting conspiracies. Hatanosuke was a master at swordplay (which he learned from Musahi Miyamoto, Japan's most famous swordsman) and a skilled practitioner of lasso throwing. He was a brilliant warrior and a loyal vassal to his lord.

Hatanosuke Hinomaru was created in answer to Japanese militarism; it faithfully toed the official line, stressing loyalty, obedience, duty, and military prowess. Very nationalistic and bellicose, it did not resist Japan's defeats in the Pacific and was discontinued in 1943. (After World War II it was revived, but lasted only four more years.)

The strip's artistic style and story line were equally simple and did not display any great inventiveness. It was fairly popular, however, and presumably served its purpose of psychologically preparing Japanese youths for war. When the war did come, *Hatanosuke Hinomaru* inspired a song (with words by the author himself) that was sung by children in school. A record of Hatanosuke's adventures was also made at about the same time.

H.K.

HATLO, JAMES (1898-1963) The madcap cartoonist who tipped his hat in thanks to the thousands of readers who suggested theme after theme for his daily panel, *They'll Do It Every Time*, James "Jimmy" Hatlo, was born in Providence, Rhode Island, in 1898, the son of a printer. Moving with his family to California the following year, Hatlo attended school in Los Angeles, developing a natural aptitude for cartooning. But he approached his later newspaper fame as a cartoonist through an odd back door: his first press job, following

a trek to San Francisco in 1918, was with the old *San Francisco Bulletin* as automobile news editor at a time when newspapers were just beginning to devote considerable Sunday sections to autoing events and advertising. Leaving the *Bulletin* for the *Call* a few years later, Hatlo (an inveterate sports fan and game attendee) whipped up a football cartoon for the *Call* sporting section. Delighted, the editor demanded more and soon Hatlo became the new *Call* sports cartoonist. Hatlo quickly developed a mythic setting for the local football players in an annual seasonal series which ran under the title of *Swineskin Gulch* for many years.

Early in 1929, in response to a *Call* feature editor's request for a small filler panel gag on the comic page, Hatlo drew his first *They'll Do It Every Time* cartoon. He never stopped drawing it. The public guffawed and wrote letters agreeing with Hatlos points and suggesting their own. The *Call*, sensing a hot property, switched the panel to the sports page, where it garnered an even more enthusiastic following and a King Features syndication a few years later (1936).

Aside from a year-long series of advertising panel cartoons for Standard Oil in 1933 and 1934 called *Give It a Whirl*, and a 1943 Sunday half-page titled *Little Iodine* (from a character developed in the daily panel), *They'll Do It Every Time* remained Hatlo's prime outlet for almost 40 years. Married in May 1937 to Eleanor Dollard, who met him while asking for an autograph, the Hatlos lived in San Francisco and New York (the latter for four months a year "so as not to stagnate"). He gave the last tip of the Hatlo hat to his millions of

Jimmy Hatlo, "They'll Do It Every Time." © King Features Sydicate.

readers on December 1, 1963, when he died in New York City, mourned by more devoted readers than any other sports page cartoonist since Tad Dorgan, whose mantle Hatlo had inarguably acquired.

B.B.

HAWKMAN (U.S.) *Hawkman* was created for National Comics by writer Gardner Fox and was first drawn by Dennis Neville. Making its first appearance in January 1940s *Flash* number one, *Hawkman* was one of the earliest comic book strips to utilize the old flying-man legends. The character sported a massive hawk headgear and a huge pair of furry, birdlike wings. Through the years, the headgear underwent constant change and there were over a dozen variations.

In reality, Hawkman was Carter Hall, a reincarnation of the Egyptian Prince Khufu. His flying powers came from an antigravity belt made from a substance known as "ninth metal." He was also able to communicate with birds, and eventually added a partner, Hawkgirl, in *Flash* number 24. As the strip matured, the team became more deeply involved in pseudo-Egyptian culture, and their fighting arsenal included crossbows, maces, axes, shields, spears, and anything vaguely resembling ancient weaponry. The feature also showcased an array of colorful villains, the most notable one being the Ghost, an exotically attired apparition.

During the strip's career, Fox handled most of the scripts, although Bob Kanigher contributed several outstanding tales during the 1947-1949 period. Artistically, *Hawkman* was graced with two outstanding illustrators. The first was Sheldon Moldoff, who assumed the strip from Neville and drew it from late 1940 to early 1945. He was an excellent draftsman and his work showed the influences of Alex Raymond and Hal Foster. In late 1944, the young Joe Kubert began taking control and he used unique layouts and heavy blacks to give the strip a pleasing and appropriately moody look. He handled the strip until its demise in 1949.

Hawkman was one of National's major supporting features and lasted through all 104 issues of *Flash*, the last published in February 1949. The character also appeared in *All-Star Comics* from the first issue (Summer 1940) through the last, March 1951's 57th issue. He was a member of the Justice Society of America.

When the superhero feature began to sell again, *Hawkman* was revived in March 1961's *Brave and Bold* number 34. Hawkman was still Carter Hall, but this time he was cast as a visiting policeman from the planet Thanagar. Much of the ancient weaponry was returned, even though this Hawkman had his headquarters in an orbiting spaceship. *Hawkgirl* was also revived and the artist was once again Joe Kubert. After several more tryout issues of *Brave and Bold*, the character was given a regular feature in *Mystery In Space*, starting with the 87th issue (November 1963). He lasted there through the 91st issue, and began his own title beginning in April 1964. By this time, however, Kubert had been replaced by Murphy Anderson. And, as had happened in the 1940s, *Hawkman* again developed two outstanding artists. Anderson's slicker, more pristine renditions also suited the character well.

As the second superhero era faded, however, *Hawkman* folded after September 1968's 27th issue, and the feature lasted several final months in a hybrid book entitled *Atom and Hawkman*. The character still appears, however, as a member of the Justice League of

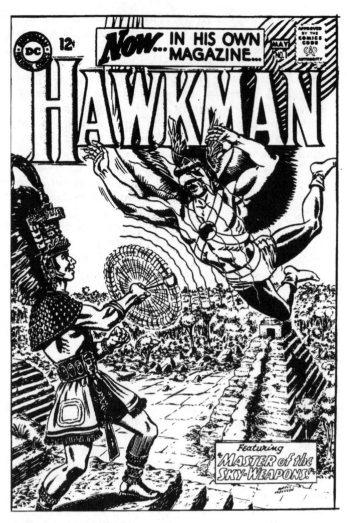

"Hawkman." © DC Comics.

America, a group which he joined in the 31st issue of *Justice League of America*.

The post-1970s history of *Hawkman* gets a bit complicated. A second *Hawkman* series came about in August 1986, but it lasted only to December 1987. In 1989 a miniseries titled *Hawkworld*, retracing the history of Thanagar, Hawkman's home planet, enjoyed sufficient success to warrant the issuance of a *Hawkworld* monthly series in June 1990; this in turn led to a third (and still ongoing) *Hawkman* series, starting in September 1993.

J.B.

HAWKSHAW THE DETECTIVE (U.S.) In 1913, when Gus Mager, who had just taken his *Sherlocko the Monk* to the *New York World*, was threatened with a lawsuit by A. Conan Doyle's representatives in the United States, he decided to turn for inspiration to a 19th-century detective play, *The Ticket-of-Leave Man*, by Tom Taylor, with its famed sleuth, Hawkshaw (a detecting name as widely known as Sherlock, but safely out of copyright). Accordingly, the new feature appeared in bright colors on the first page of the *New York World* Sunday comic section for February 23, 1913, (with obvious corrections in the dialogue balloons to eliminate the "Sherlocko" and "Watso" references and replace them with new names) as *Hawkshaw the Detective*. Hawkshaw and his aide, the Colonel, had now lost all "monk" resemblances, although they still encountered their old associates, Groucho, Nervo, Bookkeepo, et al. (A curious daily strip Mager now undertook for the *World*, called *Millionbucks and Kandykiddo*, featured a team which looked exactly like Sherlocko/Hawkshaw and Watso/the Colonel, but who were presented as eccentric millionaires in slapstick situations.)

The strip folded in time, and Mager concentrated on the Sunday page. This continued until mid-1922, when Mager dropped *Hawkshaw* as a full page and replaced it with a new small town life strip called *Main Street*, ghosted by someone in close mimicry of George McManus' style. Mager himself devoted his talents to developing a semiserious continuing daily strip once more called *Sherlocko*, which he distributed to a number of papers in 1924 on his own. The venture was unfortunately short-lived, since the Doyle representatives did indeed move against the strip and closed it down in 1925.

Mager's detective surfaced one last time, however, on December 13, 1931, again as *Hawkshaw the Detective* for United Feature Syndicate, as a top for Dirks' *Captain and the Kids*. Mager, who had left the *World* and had been working for Dirks, drew the first five months of the new feature himself, then turned it over to Bernard Dibble for a year and a half (as Dirks did his kid strip), taking it up again, under the pseudonym "Watso," after 1933. Mager continued with it as a companion piece to *The Captain and the Kids* until the late 1940s, when he retired to paint on his estate in Newark, New Jersey. Only two collections of Mager's strip work appeared: *The Monk Joke Book* (N.Y. American, 1912), and *Hawkshaw the Detective* (Press Publishing Co., 1916).

B.B.

HAXTUR (Spain) With a name perhaps derived from that of Ambrose Bierce's shepherd-god, and also utilized by Chambers and Lovecraft, *Haxtur* was created by Victor de la Fuente for the Spanish magazine *Trinca*. It lasted 14 episodes, the first of which saw publication on May 15, 1971, and the last appeared on January 1, 1972.

Haxtur was a character of heroic fantasy, but with a difference. He was a guerrilla fighter, not unlike Che Guevara, whose exploits also took place in the jungle; fighting against the forces sent to defeat him by the government he had only his anachronistic medieval sword as a weapon. The four horsemen of the Apocalypse had condemned him to wander through space and time in search of his destiny, until death brought him ultimate liberation in the last episode: this end adds an epic dimension to the feature, the first in the history of comics in which the principal hero dies.

The place of the action is a neverland where everything is possible, where we do not know whether the protagonist dreams or remembers, or whether his memories are recalled by his slow agony. Haxtur rides along the road, meeting beings and people who wander in and out of his life. The comic was rendered with a fascinating technique: the action took place on three different time levels, which were presented to the reader by means of flashbacks all coming together at the same time. The reading is not easy, and one must discover (or imagine) the time frame for himself, as in an Alain Resnais movie or in Carlos Saura's *La Prima Angelica*. The colors, masterfully overlaid, do not help comprehension, but do fulfill an aesthetic function. A

difficult work of great merit, *Haxtur* was widely translated abroad.

L.G.

"The Hayseeds," Harry Hargreaves. © *Daily Mirror Newspapers Ltd.*

HAYSEEDS (G.B.) The Hayseeds were an amiable crowd of country-dwellers who happened to be animals. They talked and occasionally walked like humans, but despite these characteristics they were amazingly close to the real creatures they represented. Harry Hargreaves, their creator, is an animal artist and lover, and was careful to keep his cartoons, animated as they are, as similar to nature as he could. Inspired by the American animal strip *Pogo*, but lacking even Walt Kelly's scraps of clothing, *Hayseeds* soon developed along its own line, reflecting human behavior in the animal world. Toby the Badger, the nearest thing *Hayseeds* had to a regular hero, was central to the strip. But even he left the stage for days at a time while Hargreaves pursued stories with another of the strip's cast. This included, in no pecking order, Braithwaite the water-wading Bird, Homer the Snail, Ern the Owl, Entwistle the Mole, Lizzy Lizard, a pair of shrews called the O'Toofs, and a Frog, a Squirrel, a Hedgehog, a Worm, a Rabbit, a Snake, a Bat, a religious Bird and on occasion, a Great Spotted Twit.

The strip commenced July 1, 1968. A paperback reprint, *Hayseeds*, was published in 1971. It was dropped September 14, 1974, when the *Evening News* changed from broadsheet to tabloid, but restored by readership demand on November 20, 1974. *Hayseeds* was dropped again in the 1980s.

D.G.

HE YOUZHI (1922-) From 1952 to 1980, He Youzhi created more than 30 comic books. The best-known stories and plays were *Chao Yang Gou* (the name of a village), *Li Shuangshuang* (a woman's name), *Lou Ah Shu* (a classical drama named after the main figure in it), *Shan Gou le de Nu Xiou Cai* ("A Woman Scholar in the Remote Mountains"), *Hua Tuo* (name for a medical doctor in ancient China), *Lian Sheng San Ji* ("Promoted Successfully Three Times"), and *Shan Xiang Ju Bian* ("Great Changes in a Mountain Village," which is based on a long novel). Some of his works are made in traditional Chinese painting style with brush and color ink, others are drawings with full-page backgrounds, and some have a blank background. He tries to make vivid drawings that reflect the original stories. "Every figure drawn should be of a live person, but not the illustration of an autopsy," He Youzhi believes.

In *Chao Yang Gou,* when the city girl Yin Huan is traveling to the countryside to visit the family of her fianceé, Shuan Bao, for the first time, Shuan Bao's younger sister rushes into the house to tell her mother, "Ma, she is here! My sister-in-law! Ma, this time she has really come!" The artist purposefully let Shuan Bao's father forget to take the hoe from his shoulder, which creates an expression of the excitement from this simple, honest old peasant.

In *Li Shuangshuang,* after Shuangshuang and her husband, Xi Wang, had a big fight, Xi Wang left home. Soon, he realized he was wrong but he was ashamed to return home, so Shuangshuang came to him to make peace. She whispers, "This family will never dismiss you," and in order to represent the love expression of a typical Chinese wife in such a circumstance, the artist depicts the couple's young daughter handing Xi Wang the key to the family home. *Lian Sheng San Ji* is color-inked with brush. Both paintings and text are humorous. The story is about a rich, stupid young man of ancient times who gets a high-ranking position by tricks and sheer luck.

He Youzhi is a self-taught comic artist; he learned to draw in 1952 at age 30 when he was assigned to work in the Shanghai New Art Publishing House. His comic book *Shan Xiang Ju Bian* won the first award in the National Comics Contest in the 1960s.

H.Y.L.L.

HEAP, THE (U.S.) The Heap character was created in December 1942 by writer Harry Stein and artist Mort Leav for an appearance in the *Sky Wolf* feature in Hillman's *Air Fighters* number three. Originally introduced as a villain, the Heap was once World War I flying ace Baron Eric von Emmelman. And though his origin was retold and revised constantly over the years, the most often cited "facts" claimed that von Emmelman had been shot down in a dogfight over Poland, survived the ensuing crash into a swamp, and somehow evolved into the hairy, brownish-green brute called the Heap.

After two additional appearances as a foe of Sky Wolf (February 1945 and May 1946), the Heap was awarded his own feature beginning in the October 1946 *Airboy* number 32. And, as the emphasis of *The Heap* series evolved from airfights and Nazis to sociology and almost religious allegories, the Heap was given a young sidekick, Rickie Wood. Ironically, *The Heap* outlasted *Sky Wolf* and was not discontinued until *Airboy* number 111 (May 1953). Over the years, many outstanding artists like Leonard Starr, Carmine Infantino, Bernard Sachs, and Dan Barry produced stories, but none handled it with the grace and style of Mort Leav. His visualization of Stein's character, which was drawn while he was employed by the Jerry Iger shop, remains the definitive version, even though Leav drew only the character's first story.

On the other hand, writers Bill Woolfolk and creator Harry Stein made *The Heap* the most perplexing

"The Heap," Mort Leav. © Hillman Periodicals.

feature of the era. As the strip continued to grow in popularity and respect, Woolfolk transformed the Heap from a snarling, raging behemoth into a puzzling and misunderstood paradox. Created by Stein strictly as a wartime villain, the character was revamped by Woolfolk who used concepts from classic horror creatures such as Frankenstein and Dracula. By the end of the strip's run, the Heap was cast as a victim of our insane and corrupt society. He became more a symbol of man's inhumanity to man than a hulking, crime-combatting hero-villain. He even developed many of the traits later found in the cinematic antiheroes of the late 1960s.

A new *Heap* feature began in *Psycho* number two (March 1970), a black-and-white comic magazine published by Skywald. Greatly inferior to his namesake, this Heap was also a pilot—a test pilot who fell into a vat of chemicals and emerged as a gelatin-like mass of glop. Although the stories were generally vapid, artist Tom Sutton produced one outstanding story in *The Heap* number one (a one-shot, standard-sized color comic published in September 1971). Drawing heavily on the hero-as-victim-of-society motif of the original *Heap,* this singular story displayed both emotion and sensitivity—rare qualities for this second *Heap* series.

J.B.

HEART OF JULIET JONES, THE (U.S.) One of the few outstanding strips of its genre, *The Heart of Juliet Jones* was the happy collaboration of Stan Drake's desire to draw a strip, Eliot Caplin's desire to write a romantic strip, and King Features's desire to develop high-quality competition to *Mary Worth*, the leading soap-opera strip of the time. The strip began in dailies in March 1953 and in Sundays a year later.

Bob Lubbers had suggested strip work to the commercial artist Drake, and Gill Fox had introduced him to Eliot Caplin. Ironically, in a conference between comics editor Sylvan Byck and Caplin, each insisted he had the perfect artist—and eventually realized they were both talking about Drake.

Margaret Mitchell, of *Gone with the Wind* fame, had been developing a love strip for King at the time of her death, so when *Juliet Jones* came along the syndicate was satisfied that it could enter the field. An advance sales push sold *Juliet Jones* to almost 90 papers before the start of the strip, a record at that time.

"The Heart of Juliet Jones," Stan Drake. © King Features Syndicate.

The major characters live in Devon, a small town. Juliet Jones, originally a girl in her early 30s, is a smart, attractive, and conservatively stylish woman who served a term as mayor of her town. In the course of the strip—how long could an attractive young lady have romance after romance without A) getting married or B) being suspected of one of several character defects?—Juliet married Owen Cantrell, a major criminal lawyer, and they lived in an apartment in a New York-type city while Eve, Juliet's vivacious blonde sister, in her early 20s, carried the romance of the strip. However, Cantrell was murdered in the 1970s and Juliet and Eve now live at home with their father, wise old Howard "Pop" Jones, a retired lumber company executive. He counsels and scolds as the perfect story strip father should. Other characters are recurring rather than major (people of the town) and new episodes bring temporary casts.

Drake and Caplin combined to make *Juliet Jones* an exciting strip with one of the most sophisticated story lines and outstanding artwork. The scripts ran the gamut from ethereal happiness to intense loneliness to profound tension. And Drake's art attempted great things and achieved them; there was frequent experimentation in visual techniques, shading, and mood. Where other straight artists use models and photographs to work from, Drake far surpassed his fellows in utilizing bold angles and cinematic blocking. Only Leonard Starr is perhaps his equal in their particular branch of strip art: romantic, breezy, and sophisticated.

At its peak, Juliet Jones had over 600 papers—a major showing. The strip was the recipient of the NCS Best Story Strip award in 1969, 1970, and 1972. Drake left *Juliet Jones* in 1989 to devote his full time to drawing *Blondie*, and he was replaced on the strip by Frank Bolle.

R.M.

HEATH, GEORGE (1900-1968) British cartoonist and illustrator, born 1900 in Tonbridge, Kent. Considerable aptitude at drawing while at school led him to study art at the Goldsmith College, then to train as an art teacher at the Regent Street Polytechnic in London. He taught art at the Teddington Art School in Middlesex until it closed down in the early 1930s. He then abandoned teaching for commercial art, entering an agency in London. His work interested Stanley J. Gooch, controlling editor of a comics group at Amalgamated Press, and a few story illustrations led to a picture story assignment for the back page of a penny comic. He quickly became the top artist for these full-page serials, drawing with a firm line, attention to setting and detail, and dramatic action. These serials were a new departure for the penny comics, which up to the 1930s featured nothing but humor strips. They reflected the trend to adventure strips begun in the American newspaper funnies a few years earlier and were more dynamic than the picture serials already running in the twopenny comics, such as *Rob the Rover* (q.v.). Later, Heath introduced the American style of speech balloon and caption to replace the typeset narrative that ran underneath his panels.

His first serial strips were *Forest of Fear* in *Funny Wonder* and *Young Adventurers* in *Larks* (both 1932), changing to *Sacred Eye of Satpura* (*Funny Wonder*) and *Two Little Wanderers* (*Larks*) in 1934. That year he added a third serial, *Red Man's Gold*, in *Jester*. In 1935 he introduced *Fortune in the Desert* (*Funny Wonder*), and in 1936 *Call of the West* (*Jester*). Also in 1936 came a new departure, the depiction of famous film stars in adventure strips: *Tim McCoy* (*Funny Wonder*), and *James Cagney* (*Larks*). This trend continued in 1938 with *Clark Gable* in *Radio Fun*, followed by radio stars *The Western Brothers,* and *Bebe Daniels* and *Ben Lyon*, his first attempts at humorous strips (1941); *Felix Mendelssohn and his Hawaiian Serenaders* (1946); *Stewart McPherson* (1947); and *Anne Shelton* (1949). Moving to *TV Fun*, he drew *Jack Warner* (1953). His other serials were *Two True Friends* (1938) in *Crackers*; *Happy Bob Harriday* (1947) and *Rivals of the Spanish Main* (1948) in *Tip Top*; *Outlaw Trail* (1949), *Land of Silent Perils* (1951), and *Cowboy Charlie* (1952) in *Jingles*; *I Vow Vengeance* (1954) and *Family Theatre* (1958) in *TV Fun*. But his best remembered character is *The Falcon*, a detective character whom he converted into a flying superhero. *The Falcon* ran in *Radio Fun* from 1947 to 1960.

Despite an enormous body of excellent work, Heath never signed a single strip, and it is said by his son, cartoonist Michael Heath, that he disliked his job. He died in Brighton in 1968.

D.G.

HEATH, RUSSELL (1926-   ) American comic book and comic strip artist born September 29, 1926, in New York City. Russ Heath's first work came at 16 on Holyoke's *Hammerhead Hawley* strip in 1942, and in 1946 he moved to Timely and began drawing a full range of strips. His best work was on Westerns, however, and his material for *Arizona Kid* and *Kid Colt Outlaw* stands as some of the finest Western work ever done in comic books. It was amazingly realistic and Heath's ability to draw the "nuts and bolts" aspects of costumes, scenery, and weapons was unsurpassed. Comic writer Archie Goodwin once commented that his work was "filled with convincing grit."

Also during this time, Heath was working for Lev Gleason (love), St. John, Quality (*Plastic Man*), Avon (science fiction), E.C. (*Mad* and *Frontline Combat*) and National. Joining the latter in 1950, he became a mainstay and drew the full range of comic book features. His *Silent Knight* and *Golden Gladiator* stories, which ran in *Brave and Bold* in the late 1950s and early 1960s, are among the best ever produced in the sword-and-sorcery genre. Again, it was Heath's flair for accuracy and realism that excelled. His storytelling style was straightforward and direct, never stooping to gimmicks or frills.

After some dazzling work on National's *Sea Devils* adventure book, Heath assumed the *Sgt. Rock* strip from editor Joe Kubert. Although he had already done outstanding war material for Warren's *Blazing Combat* book in 1965 and 1966, it went generally unnoticed. But Heath outdid himself on *Sgt. Rock*, and utilizing Goodwin's "convincing grit," turned the feature into a war comics clinic. His chronicles of the adventures of Rock and his Easy Company was always as good or better than the finest cinematic interpretation.

In addition to his comic book work, Heath assisted George Wunder on *Terry and the Pirates*, Dan Barry on *Flash Gordon*, and Kurtzman and Will Elder on *Playboy* magazine's *Little Annie Fanny* feature.

Heath finally got to sign a newspaper strip when he was asked by the New York Times Syndicate in 1981 to draw the revived version of *The Lone Ranger* on texts by Carey Bates; the venture unfortunately lasted only until 1984. Aside from a few comic book assignments, he has devoted most of his time to animated cartoons.

J.B.

HECKLE AND JECKLE (U.S.) Heckle and Jeckle debuted in a cartoon produced by Paul Terry in 1946, "The Talking Magpies." The two identical, zany birds were created by Terry's story department and the first film was written chiefly by Tom Morrison, although in later years Terry was known to claim credit for the characters' inception. Whatever their origin, Heckle and Jeckle appeared in a series of cartoons and quickly joined the other Paul Terry characters in *Terry-Toons Comics*, published by Timely (later known as Marvel).

When the license on the Terry properties passed to the St. John company, *Heckle and Jeckle* went along. The feature was never an overwhelming success and its future was linked to the more popular Terry strip *Mighty Mouse*. The two magpies appeared frequently in the *Mighty Mouse* book and, beginning in 1949, in a *Heckle and Jeckle* comic, the first issue named *Blue Ribbon Comics*. The magazine lasted ten years and 34 issues, well into the period when the Terry license was assumed by the Pines company.

The St. John and Pines issues were amusing, though never outstanding. Both companies drew upon New York animation studios (especially Terry's) for their writers and artists and so the Terry strips passed through many hands, often adapting the cartoons into comic book format. Many of the stories were surrealistic in their humor, paralleling the animated films' format of having Heckle and Jeckle defying all laws of science. The two were completely unrestrained, not even by what is considered "possible" and "impossible." Some of the comic book stories had Heckle and Jeckle discussing the fact that they were comic book characters; other tales had them playing strange—and often cruel—tricks on a variety of opponents, including Dimwit Dog.

Heckle and Jeckle appeared in a number of Pines's *Mighty Mouse* giant specials before Western Publishing Company assumed the licence and featured them in three issues of *New Terrytoons* (1960-1961) and two issues of a new *Heckle and Jeckle* comic (1962). These were under the Dell Comics banner. When Western shifted its book to the Gold Key company name, it issued four issues of *Heckle and Jeckle*, beginning again with number one in 1963. They also began anew with *New Terrytoons*, which was published intermittently from May 1963 on, starting and stopping but always featuring *Heckle and Jeckle* in the lead position. The new version of the strip lacked the surreal brand of humor but was rather successful nonetheless. Although companies had always bought the rights to the Paul Terry characters to acquire *Mighty Mouse*, at Western the *Heckle and Jeckle* feature outlived the *Mighty Mouse* comics. A *Heckle and Jeckle 3-D* comic book was issued by Spotlight Comics in 1987.

M.E.

HELD, JOHN JR. (1889-1958) An American illustrator and cartoonist born on January 10, 1889, in Salt Lake City, John Held sold his first cartoon to *Life* magazine in 1904. Encouraged by this initial success, the young boy sold more cartoons to various national magazines. After dropping out of school in 1905 he became sports cartoonist on the *Salt Lake City Tribune* and received his only art training from sculptor Mahonri Young. He moved to New York in 1910 and took a job with the *Collier's* agency. In the years preceding World War I he contributed his first cartoons to *Vanity Fair* under the pseudonym "Myrtle Held."

In 1918 John Held started drawing the flat-chested, angular girls that became the flappers of the 1920s. His full talent flowered in the pages of the *New Yorker,* where he depicted with a caustic, if indulgent, pen the ludicrous goings-on of America's silliest decade. It was inevitable that Held would attract the attention of William Randolph Hearst. In the late 1920s, Held did a panel, *Oh! Margy!,* which blossomed in 1930 into a full-fledged comic feature called *Merely Margy*, with *Joe Prep* as a companion piece. The flapper era was over by then, however, and John Held's complacent depictions of the fatuous antics of racoon-coated, hare-brained college boys and their vacuous girl friends did not quite fit the mood of the Depression. By 1935 *Margy* was gone. John Held tried again with *Rah! Rah! Rosalie*, about a pompom girl, but it flopped instantly.

Discouraged, Held went back to illustration, turned to sculpting in 1939, and later became artist-in-residence at Harvard University and the University of Georgia. He died on March 2, 1958.

M.H.

HENRY (U.S.) Carl Anderson's *Henry* started on March 19, 1932, as a series of weekly cartoons for the *Saturday Evening Post*. At first the bald-headed little hero spoke a few lines of dialogue, but later Anderson had him express himself strictly in pantomime. The cartoon series was so popular that it was often reprinted abroad; a German version drew the attention of the ever-vigilant William Randolph Hearst, who decided there and then that it should be distributed by his own syndicate, King Features. *Henry* started its career as a full-fledged daily strip on December 17, 1934, and was followed by a Sunday version on March 10, 1935.

Drawn in a sketchy, "cartoony" style, Henry is neither a Katzie-like childish demon nor a "reg'lar feller" like most other comic strip kids of the time, from Perry Winkle to Mush Stebbins. He is a loner, and his muteness (its cause is never explained) keeps him all the more estranged from the society around him. This estrangement is reflected in Henry's almost unlimited freedom: he does not seem to have strict parents or a real home or to go to school often. He is a creature of impulse who does whatever strikes his fancy; when his whims are challenged he is quite capable of hitting back at his tormentors. There are no memorable characters in the strip besides Henry himself—the secondary figures who recur from time to time are only there as foils to this diminutive hero of the absurd.

In 1942 Anderson was forced by ill health to turn *Henry* over to assistants Don Trachte, who drew the Sundays, and John Liney, who did the dailies. Trachte and Liney were reasonably successful in preserving the feature's flavor, and *Henry* remained the most popular strip of the dying pantomime genre. At Liney's death in 1979 the dailies devolved to Jack Tippit, who drew them until his own death in 1983. From that time, Dick Hodgins has been turning out the daily strip, while the Sundays are still done by Trachte.

M.H.

HERB & JAMAAL (U.S.) The very existence of *Herb & Jamaal*, by African-American cartoonist Stephen R. Bentley, was prompted by a letter sent in the late 1980s to cartoonists and syndicates from the *Detroit Free Press*. This newspaper, in a city with an African-American majority population, wanted to see more blacks in newspaper comics. It is not conicidence, therefore, that the start dates for King Features's *Curtis*, Tribune Media Services's *Herb & Jamaal*, and United Feature Syndicates's *Jump Start* are, respectively, 1988, 1989, and 1990.

Stephen Bentley is a cartoonist who paid his dues prior to the success of *Herb & Jamaal*. Born in Los Angeles, California, in 1954, Bentley joined the U.S. Navy after graduating high school. During his military service, he drew a panel titled *Navy Life* for his base newspaper. After leaving the navy, Bentley attended Pasadena City College in California and began a freelance career. He drew artwork for the Los Angeles Dodgers baseball team, including the feature *The Tenth Player*.

Bentley's freelance cartoon career prospered. In 1983, his comic strip *Squirt*, about a female firefighter (then a radical concept), was briefly distributed by Weekly Features Syndicate. His cartoon *Hey Coach* was a regular feature in Swimming World magazine. For three years prior to *Herb & Jamaal*, he drew weekly humorous ad layouts for Quinn's Natural Food Centers that appeared in the *Los Angeles Times*.

After hearing about the *Detroit Free Press* letter from fellow cartoonist Ed McGeean, Bentley was introduced to *Motley's Crew* creators Ben Templeton and the late Tom Forman, who were trying to collaborate with an African-American cartoonist on a feature for Tribune Media Services (TMS). Ultimately, *Herb & Jamaal* was created, and TMS quickly decided it should be written and drawn exclusively by Bentley.

Herb & Jamaal centers on two high-school pals who meet at a reunion and decide to go into business together, opening what was first an ice cream parlor and has become a soul food restaurant. The lanky bachelor Jamaal, a former pro basketball player, finances the business. Herb had previously worked for the gas company. He's married to Sarah Louise, and the couple has a son, Ezekiel, and a daughter, Uhuru, named in honor of the Nichelle Nichols' character in the original *Star Trek* television series. Herb's mother-in-law, Eula, is a Trekkie.

This is family humor done in a style distinctive to Bentley. His theory is that a cartoonist must entertain but can still get a message into the start of a daily if he has a good punch line for the last panel. The charac-

ters are also involved in their community, although this aspect of the strip is not as hard-edged as the inner-city life shown in *Curtis*. Both *Herb & Jamaal* and *Jump Start* focus more on pure family humor.

B.C.

HERCULES (U.S.) 1—The first comic book character to capitalize on the mythological name "Hercules" was Timely's *Hercules* which made only two appearances, in issues three and four of *Mystic* (January 1940 to August 1940). Known only as the "son of Dr. David," the character and premise were as short on imagination as on longevity.

2—The second comic book *Hercules* appeared in MLJ's *Blue Ribbon* comics from June 1940 to January 1941 (issues four through eight). Probably created by writer Joe Blair, this Hercules was sent back to earth by Zeus to rid the planet of gangsters, mobs, and the like. Alternately costumed in a blue business suit or white trunks with red boots, this Hercules occasionally returned to Olympus for advice.

3—The next use of the Hercules name came in Quality's *Hit* number one. Created by artist Dan Zolnerowich and writer Gregg Powers in July 1940, this strip featured Joe Hercules, a blond and superpowered character who wore a relatively standard superhero suit and cape. But despite the hackneyed plots and villains, *Hercules* managed to be handled by a few of Quality's fine artistic stable, including Reed Crandall, Lou Fine, Matt Baker, and George Tuska. The feature last appeared in the April 1942 issue of *Hit* number 21.

4—Marvel introduced their version of Hercules in a 1967 issue of *The Avengers*. Still a man-god from Olym-

"Hercules," Lou Fine. © *Comic Magazines, Inc.*

pus, this Hercules was also saddled with the stereo-typic superhero-with-problems theme plaguing every Marvel character, but he only appeared sporadically.

5—In 1963, Gold Key produced two issues each of the *Adventures of Hercules* and *Mighty Hercules*. The first was a serious comic book, the second a funny adaptation, but neither were financially or artistically successful.

6—Charlton Comics produced the only serious adaptation of the Hercules mythology in 13 issues of *Hercules* produced between October 1967 and September 1969. Written by Joe Gill, the stories were only adequate and suffered from poor research. A black and white reprint of the eighth issue was produced, but its almost invisible distribution has made it somewhat of a collector's item.

7—Additionally, Dell Comics produced two comic versions of *Hercules* movies in their *Color* series and they were numbered 1006 and 1121. The latter contains art by Reed Crandall.

Naturally, over the years, the name Hercules has been used in various comic books as a moniker for both hero and villain, but any complete listing of its uses would clearly be impossible. Mention should be made, however, of the *Hercules Unbound* comic book series published by National in 1975-77, and of the two *Hercules* miniseries (1982 and 1984) released by Marvel.

J.B.

HERGÉ *see* Rémi, Georges.

HERLOCK SHOLMES (Yugoslavia) *Herlock Sholmes, the Master of Disguise*, later simply called *Herlock Sholmes*, was created in 1957 by Jules Radilović and Zvonimir Furtinger, but appeared ten years later in the Yugoslav comic weekly *Plavi Vjesnik*.

If Sir Arthur Conan Doyle had been alive he would have read with great pleasure the adventures of Herlock Sholmes, an obvious adaptation of his popular detective, because in this series the detective is presented in an entirely new kind of adventure. He finds no difficulty in transforming himself into a horse, a stove, a dog, a palm, or even into a signpost if need be, if only he has his indispensable makeup case at his side. The indefatigable Sholmes jumps from one incredible adventure to another, always in the company of his good-natured and faithful friend, Doctor Waston. The strip is a fascinating creation, full of delightful humor, suspense, and hilarity.

With this series Furtinger and Radilović presented themselves as masters of the many sides of any subject which could be used in comics. In his adventures Herlock Sholmes often met Pinkerton agents or Scotland Yard detectives, who frequently asked him for help. In the first episode Sholmes searched for the gorilla-thief Anastasia; in the third episode he was in the Wild West saving a kidnapped girl; and the fourth episode, which bore the title "The Ghost of Baskervil," abounded in humor and strange events in a Scottish castle. In the fifth episode, Sholmes met his rival in the art of disguise—Prince Nana—and in the sixth episode he was a guest at the court of King Arthus. In the seventh he journeyed into the wilderness of the African jungle and there met the real Tarzan.

Radilović suspended the series in the late 1970s after he began working for several foreign publications.

E.R.

"Herlock Sholmes," Julio Radilović. © Strip Art Features.

HERMANN *see* Huppen, Hermann.

HERNAN EL CORSARIO (Argentina) Argentine cartoonist José Luis Salinas created the adventure strip *Hernan el Corsario* ("Hernan the Privateer") in one of the first issues of the comic magazine *Patoruzú* (November 1936). The strip's historic value is notable because it represents the first attempt by an Argentine cartoonist to produce a nonhumor feature of quality. Considering that this was Salinas's first work of this type and that he was then learning the rudiments of his art, one must concede that *Hernan el Corsario* was a memorable creation. With this strip, one of the author's masterworks, Salinas gave birth to his unforgettable graphic style, and many of the qualities that can be found in the later *Cisco Kid* are already present in these pages. Each panel could be compared to a film frame, never static, but full of motion.

When Salinas's publisher decided to launch a new comic magazine called *Patoruzito*, he again selected *Hernan el Corsario* for the first issue (October 11, 1945). The new version was smaller in format and Salinas made use of speech balloons where previously he had used only captions; it retained, however, all its flavor and its masterly quality. It was discontinued on August 20, 1946, with Salinas going on to greater triumphs.

L.G.

HERRIMAN, GEORGE (1880-1944) Born 1880, in New Orleans of African heritage, George "Garge" Herriman, creator of *Krazy Kat* and the foremost comic strip artist, was the son of a baker who moved to Los Angeles while he was growing up. While in high school, Herriman drove the family bread wagon and helped with the baking. Never happy with his parents, he played pranks on them, such as salting several hundred doughnuts and burying a dead mouse in a loaf of bread—the last trick getting him thrown out on his own. Herriman then got a job on the old *Los Angeles Herald* as an office boy. He put all of his spare time into his cartooning ambitions, sending work off to such magazines as *Life* and *Judge*, where much of it sold. Unable to persuade his *Herald* bosses to upgrade him to staff cartoonist, he rode the rails to New York at 20 and took a sustaining job as a salesman, while he spent most of his time selling himself—hopefully—to New York newspaper editors. Finally he landed a job as staff artist on the *New York World* in 1901, where he did daily art and Sunday full and half comic pages in color (some reprinted in Philadelphia and elsewhere), but did not undertake an actual comic strip.

Seeing little future with the *World*, Herriman tried a short-lived half-page Sunday strip (his first), with the McClure Syndicate, called *Lariat Pete* (about a rough-and-tumble cowhand visiting relatives back East), of which only seven episodes appeared between September 6, 1903, and November 15, 1903; then he turned to sports-page work on the Hearst *New York Journal*, where he shared cartooning honors with the *Journal's* famed Tad Dorgan (and in fact drew a large number of the cartoons signed by Dorgan at that time). Unable to interest his Hearst editors in his strip ideas, Herriman sold three series in 1905 to the World Color Printing Co. of St. Louis (which circulated a four-page color strip section to many newspapers): *Major Ozone's Fresh Air Crusade, Rosy-Posy—Grandma's Girl,* and *Bud Smith. Major Ozone* was a wildly fanciful strip and some of its freewheeling pages resemble those of the later *Krazy Kat* in unbridled imagination, about a contemporary Don Quixote obsessed with clean air; *Rosy-Posy* was a simple gag strip about an eight-year-old girl, and *Bud Smith* focused on a slightly older boy. On the strength of the income from these strips, Herriman left the *Journal* and returned to Los Angeles. Recalled by the *Journal* in 1907, he traveled back to New York to do general cartooning and launch a short-lived daily strip called *Baron Mooch* (essentially continued in his later *Baron Bean*). He followed this in June 1910 with the extraordinary daily strip, *The Dingbat Family*, in which his talents fully flowered in the creation of his most famed characters: the crew of humanized animals who populate the mythic fantasy land of *Coconino County* in *Krazy Kat*. (*Krazy Kat* appeared as a strip of its own in October 1913, to which a Sunday page was added in 1919.)

By January 1916, however, Herriman had dropped *The Dingbat Family* and replaced it with the daily *Baron Bean*, a very funny fantasy strip which ran until December 31, 1918. Herriman followed with two relatively short-lived and unimportant daily strips: *Mary's Home From College,* which ran for the first four months of 1919 and was replaced by *Now Listen, Mabel* (following a love-sick lad yearning for a fickle girl named Mabel Malarkey) which ended at the end of 1919. From this point, Herriman worked only on *Krazy Kat* until December 4, 1922, when he opened *Stumble Inn*. A continuing comedy strip about a Mr. and Mrs. Stumble who run a ramshackle hotel, their bumbling house detective, and the series of weird guests they entertain, *Stumble Inn* was a major comic strip hit of the 1920s and was nearly made into a live-action film. It folded in April 1925, after which Herriman started his last strip independent of *Krazy Kat, Us Husbands.* A Sunday gag strip about married conflict, *Us Husbands* started on July 3, 1926, and ran for little more than half a year, as did its weekly companion piece, *Mistakes Will Happen,* a gag feature without continuing characters. After this page was dropped, Herriman concentrated on *Krazy Kat,* doing only a daily panel called *Embarassing Moments* for a few years in the late 1920s.

In the meantime, Herriman had moved to Los Angeles in 1924 and built a Spanish-style house in the Hollywood hills, where he lived with his wife, children, and dogs until his death. He liked poetry, especially the comic poetry of Don Marquis, whose three *Archy and Mehitabel* books he illustrated with stunning effect in the 1920s. But Herriman's classic work, *Krazy Kat,* speaks more for his fundamental graphic and literary genius than any other undertaking, and any episode from that magnum opus is enough to tell the reader that he is looking at the work of a master in the field of comics. Time eventually ran out for Herriman in Los Angeles on April 26, 1944, and he died quietly in his sleep after a short illness.

B.B.

HERRON, FRANCE EDWARD (1916-1966) American comic book writer and editor born 1916 in New York City. Eddie Herron broke into the comic book business at Fox in 1939, and after a short stint at the Harry "A" Chesler shop, became an editor at Fawcett on October 10, 1940.

Herron's Fawcett assignments came as a result of several excellent *Captain Marvel* scripts he had submitted. In addition to his tightly knit scripts and editing, Herron was responsible for the first of many *Captain Marvel* spin-offs when he and artist Mac Raboy created the *Captain Marvel Jr.* feature for December 1941's *Whiz* number 25. Earlier that year, he and artist Jack Kirby developed the *Mr. Scarlet* strip in *Wow* number one (Spring 1941). Herron was dismissed as Fawcett editor March 1, 1942, for purchasing scripts he had written under a pen name.

While he was still editor at Fawcett, however, Herron freelanced for other companies. Along with artist Al Plastino, he created *The Rainbow* for *Centaur,* a colorful—if short-lived—superhero who made his sole appearance in *Arrow* number three (October 1941). He also created *The Red Skull,* perhaps the most famous comic book villain. The malevolent super-Nazi made his first appearance in Timely's *Captain America* number one (March 1941).

After serving in the armed forces during World War II, Herron returned to comics and wrote several outstanding stories for Quality's *Blackhawk* feature. He later moved to National and scripted stories for *Batman* and *The Boy Commandos,* but then turned his attention to short story writing. He continued working sporadically for National (*Challengers of the Unknown, Blackhawk, Tomahawk*) and on syndicated strips (*Bat Masterson, Davy Crockett*) until his death on September 2, 1966.

J.B.

HERSHFIELD, HARRY (1885-1974) Next to James Swinnterton the longest-lived of the great comic strip

Harry Hershfield.

artists, Harry Hershfield was born of newly arrived Russian immigrants in Cedar Rapids, Iowa, on October 13, 1885. Like many of his peers of the time, Hershfield roamed about the country with his cartooning talent from an early age, doing newspaper sports and feature-story comic art first on the *Chicago Daily News* in 1899 at the age of 14 (where he drew his first strip, *Homeless Hector*, about a big-city street mutt), moving to the *San Francisco Chronicle* in 1907, then to the Hearst *Chicago Examiner* in late 1909 (where he created another dog strip, *Rubber, the Canine Cop*), and finally to the *New York Journal* to begin his first major strip in 1910, *Desperate Desmond*. Later, Desmond, a silk-hatted villain, was switched to another, similar strip called *Dauntless Durham of the U.S.A.*, where his adventures ended in January 1914. Hershfield then immediately began his most successful and longest-lasting strip, *Abie the Agent*, for the same paper, running it both daily and Sunday at various times until 1940, when this notable ethnic comedy finally and lamentably folded. While drawing and writing *Desmond, Durham,* and *Abie*, Hershfield periodically reintroduced *Hector* to readers, for the last time as a Sunday strip accompaniment to *Abie* in the 1920s. During a legal disagreement with the Hearst interests circa 1933-35, Hershfield worked for the *New York Herald-Tribune*, where he drew a Sunday half-page called *According to Hoyle*, about a well-to-do, elderly, walrus-moustached New Yorker named Hugo Hoyle and his modish wife, Hannah.

Hershfield quickly developed a marked reputation as a humorous writer and raconteur quite apart from his repute as a strip artist. For a number of years in the late 1910s, Hershfield wrote weekly short comic pieces, presumably narrated by Abie, under such titles as "Abie on Conversation," "Abie on Summer Snapshots," etc., which ran on the editorial and feature pages of newspapers, many of which did not carry the *Abie* strip at all. In 1932, he became a columnist ("My Week") for the *New York Daily Mirror*, and, later in the 1930s, began to broadcast theatrical criticism, scripted for Hollywood studios, and joined the radio cast of *Can*

You Top This? a 1940s show tailored for comic raconteurs. His ethnic dialect stories, largely about Irish, Jewish, and German types, were marked by wit and good taste. A toastmaster who was always in great demand, Hershfield also authored such books as *Laugh Louder, Live Longer* (Grayson, 1959), a title which seems to have been happily prophetic in his case. He died on December 17, 1974, in New York City.

B.B.

HERZOG, GUY (1923-   ) A Belgian cartoonist born July 11, 1923, in Riga, Latvia, Guy Herzog spent his childhood in a number of foreign countries. A member of the Belgian diplomatic service, Herzog's father returned his family to Belgium in 1940.

In 1945 Herzog founded the arts and letters weekly *Le Faune*, which folded the next year, carrying away all of the young man's savings. From 1946 to 1949 he held a variety of jobs as an advertising man, lathe operator in a plant manufacturing car engines, sports writer, designer, and cartoonist. In 1949 he became editor-in-chief of the weekly publication *Vivre*. In 1950 he moved to Paris and contributed a great many cartoons (under his pseudonym "Bara") to various French publications.

In 1955 Bara created the pantomime strip *Max l'Explorateur* (later simply called *Max*). Syndicated by P.I.B. of Copenhagen, the strip appeared for the first time in the daily *France-Soir* on March 1, 1955; it was later published in newspapers throughout Europe. In addition to his work on *Max,* Bara designed stage sets from 1960 to 1963.

Returning to Belgium in 1963, Bara produced a continuity strip featuring *Max* for the comic weekly *Spirou*. From there he went to *Tintin* in 1969. At *Tintin* he resumed the drawing of *Max* and later did another gag strip, *Ephémère*, about a star-crossed traveler. In 1973 he produced *Cro-Magnon*, featuring a zany tribe of prehistoric cavemen. Bara was also the founder, publisher, and editor of a monthly magazine aimed at the medical profession, *L'Oeuf*, which ran from 1971 to 1973. After leaving *Tintin* in 1977, he contributed to a number of European periodicals, notably *Zack* in Germany, for which he created *Sigi the Frank* (1978), about a feckless warrior of the Middle Ages. His mainstay, however, remains *Max*, which has now passed the 40-year mark.

Bara is one of the most versatile and talented gag cartoonists in Europe. With a few lines and a simple background he is able to create a hilarious situation that he then presents in all of its variations, transformations, and implications. Bara is, without a doubt, the supreme pantomime strip artist, far ahead of even Carl Anderson or Dahl Mikkelsen.

M.H.

HESS, SOL (1872-1941) American comic strip writer born October 14, 1872, on a farm in Northville Township, Illinois. When Sol Hess was eight years old, his parents moved to Chicago; the next year his father died and Sol went to work as an errand-boy for a wholesale jewelry company. Hess eventually became a salesman for the firm and traveled the western United States with a line of watches and jewelry. He did so well that he founded, with two partners, the watch and diamond firm of Rettig, Hess, and Madsen.

Sol Hess's involvement in comics came late and quite by accident. His office was located a block from

Stilson's, a favorite hangout of newspapermen. John Wheeler, former head of the Bell Syndicate, recounted in his memoir *I've Got News For You:* "Sol Hess was a Chicago jeweler who liked to associate with newspapermen and pay the tabs, so he was welcome. Among those he met in this rendezvous were Ring Lardner, Clare Briggs, John McCutcheon, and a struggling cartoonist, Sid Smith."

Sol Hess became a close friend of Sidney Smith, who had just started to draw *The Gumps,* and before long he was supplying most of the dialogues for the strip as a labor of love. When Smith got his famous million-dollar contract in 1922, he asked Hess to stay with him as his ghost-writer for $200 a week. Feeling insulted Hess broke with Smith and proposed a brand-new idea for a family strip to Wheeler, who promptly accepted. For the drawing Hess then turned to W. A. Carlson, with whom he had previously worked on a short-lived series of *Gumps* animated cartoons. In May of 1923 Hess and Carlson finally brought in the new strip, called *The Nebbs* (to which was later added a companion strip, *Simp O'Dill,* about a sap-headed coffee-house owner).

The Nebbs did so well that Sol Hess was able to quit the jewelry business in 1925. A generous, friendly, and much-beloved man in and out of his chosen profession, as well as a creator of small but solid achievement, Sol Hess was greatly missed when he died on December 31, 1941.

M.H.

"Hi and Lois," Dik Browne and Mort Walker. © King Features Syndicate.

HI AND LOIS (U.S.) The quintessential suburban family strip, *Hi and Lois* has climbed steadily but quietly in circulation and popularity since its inception in 1954; it remains one of the most popular comics.

Mort Walker, with three years of a successful *Beetle Baily* under his belt, suggested the story idea to King Features after introducing a sister and brother-in-law on some of Beetle's visits home. He and comic editor Sylvan Byck developed the names and basics and began looking for an artist.

In one of those coincidences that luckily frequent the annals of comic history, Byck noticed Dik Browne's *Tracy Twins* in *Boy's Life* magazine during a dentist visit; Walker saw a candy advertisement of Browne's, one of many for the Johnstone and Cushing agency. Browne topped both their lists and was offered the job of drawing *Hi and Lois.* The first strip appeared in October of 1954.

The family has not changed since inception except for a more sophisticated personality on the part of Trixie, the baby who doesn't walk or talk but thinks and dominates half of the strips. The parents, Hi and Lois Flagston, are typical suburbanites; Hi goes to the Foofram offices every morning and Lois is inevitably cleaning or shopping. She is more of a real housewife than Blondie.

Chip, the early-teen eldest son, is mop-haired, lazy, and at the inevitable awkward age. Nobody but his friends quite understand him. The twins, Dot and Ditto, are first-graders whose main interest in life seems to be outshining—or outmaneuvering—each other. And Trixie, the baby, has been given to thoughts and "conversations" with sunbeams that seem to be the most popular feature of the strip today.

Other incidental characters and settings have become more incidental through the years: Thirsty Thurston, the next-door souse; Hi's boss Mr. Foofram; the Abercrombie and Fitch; neighborhood garbagemen.

The gags are gentle and real (perhaps the strip's most endearing quality) and the art simple and clean. After Dik Browne's death in 1989, his son, Bob "Chance" Browne, took over the drawing duties. Mort's sons, Brian and Greg Walker, are now in charge of the writing.

R.M.

HICKS, REGINALD ERNEST (1915-   ) Born in Kent, England, in 1915, Reginald Ernest Hicks's parents brought him to Melbourne, Australia, in 1921. At the age of 14, Reg Hicks obtained a job learning color stencil designing in a soft goods factory, where he spent the next four years learning his trade and ending up in charge of the art department. During that time he began to study music and learned to play violin. On leaving the factory, he taught violin and attended art training at the National Gallery School under Napier Waller and John Rowell. Hicks became an exhibiting member of the Victorian Artists Society as well as doing freelance caricatures, cartoons, and interviews for various magazines.

In 1934 he produced Australia's first adventure strip of any consequence. This was an adaptation of Erle Cox's *Out of the Silence,* which ran in the *Melbourne Argus* from August 4 to December 21. At the same time he was drawing a single column children's feature, *Kitty's Kapers;* like much of his early comic work these features were signed "Hix." In the following six years he created a multitude of strips for both the *Argus* and the *Age,* including *Robinson Crusoe* (1936), *The Deerslayer* (1936), *Willy and Wally* (1937), *Betty and Bob* (1936-37), *The King's Treasure* (1938), and *The Space Patrol* (1938-40). During this period, he created *The Adventures of Larry Steele,* which ran in the *Age* from October 2, 1937, to October 30, 1940, and became the first Australian adventure strip to prove popular with readers and establish any reasonable lifespan. Reg Hicks had a tremendous capacity for work—while his strips were running in the *Age* (sometimes as many as two dailies and two weeklies at the same time) he was still freelancing as well as working as a story reader for the Australian Broadcasting Commission and doing commercial radio work.

In 1940, Hicks became a member of naval intelligence but was released from service after nine months. He joined Associated Newspapers and created *Tightrope Tim,* which appeared in the *Sydney Sunday Sun* on

Reg Hicks, "Jungle Drums." © The Herald and Weekly Times Ltd.

August 3, 1941. This adventure strip ran until May 29, 1949, setting a record for the genre which wasn't beaten until the advent of *Rod Craig* (1946-1955). He also created a daily domestic strip, *Family Man*, which ran in the *Sydney Sun* for over 12 years. Again, Hicks kept up his frantic outside activities, freelancing for *Rydges*, the *Sydney Morning Herald*, and various advertising agencies, and still found time to produce four *Kid Koals* comic books.

When he left Associated Newspapers in 1958, he became involved in a number of commercial enterprises, including kitchen utilities, plastics, fiberglass, and pottery, yet he still found time to create a strip called *Debbie* for *The New Idea* as well as writing and drawing stories for overseas children's annuals and drawing book covers for Hodders. He is a life member of the A.J.A., an Associate of the Royal Society of Art, and served as vice president of the Adelaide Art Society. Reg Hicks is a remarkably versatile and prolific artist who can rightly lay claim to instigating and popularizing the adventure strip in Australia. He retired in 1977.

J.R.

HIDALGO, FRANCISCO (1929-) Spanish cartoonist and French photographer born in Jaen, Spain, on May 7, 1929. Self-taught in art (although he later studied at the School of Fine Arts in Paris to perfect his skills), Francisco Hidalgo was an avid reader of the comics from the earliest age. "I don't know when I started to get interested in drawing," he said. "I believe I was born a cartoonist." At any rate, he soon developed his own idiosyncratic style, and at age 17 began to see his creations published in the Spanish comics magazines of the period. The influence of American comics is evident even in the titles of these early stories, such as *Skilled* and *Dick Sanders*.

It was in 1948, with *Dr Niebla* ("Dr. Fog"), that Hidalgo achieved his greatest success. Based on a series of paperback novels written by Rafael Gonzalez, *Dr. Niebla* was in the tradition of mysterious defenders of

justice ("No one has ever seen his face. He appears and disappears in the mist"), and his adventures took him from London to New York and throughout the entire world. The artist fleshed out the character, giving him presence and motivation far beyond the conventionality of the scripts (first written by Gonzalez himself, later by Victor Mora). His use of black and white was masterful, and his compositions succeeded in re-creating the atmospheric settings of the *film noirs* of the period. *Dr. Niebla* is now regarded as one of the classics of the Spanish comic strip.

In the 1950s, Hidalgo settled in Paris, where economic circumstances were more favorable for cartoonists than in his native Spain. He soon began contributing a great number of comics to many French magazines, while continuing to draw *Dr. Niebla* until 1959. Among his most notable French contributions were *Bob Mallard* (which he signed "Yves Roy"), an interesting aviation series, and *Teddy Ted*, a Western in which the artist's knowledge of and love for American films served him well. He was equally at ease with the handling of machines, horses, and human characters, and his sense of composition remained as sure as ever.

At the same time, Hidalgo had become fascinated with the medium of photography, and in the mid-1960s, he abandoned the comics (*Pat Patrick* in 1964 was his final contribution to the field) in favor of his new vocation. As a photographer, he has become world famous and he has exhibited widely and received many honors. Yet, as he has often said to interviewers, the comics remain "his one enduring love."

M.H.

HILDEBRANDT, GREG AND TIM (1939-) The fraternal twin brothers Greg and Tim Hildebrandt are best known for their work illustrating J.R.R. Tolkien's *Lord of the Rings*, painting a series of 64 Marvel superheroes for trading cards, and reviving *Terry and the Pirates* in March 1995 for Tribune Media Services.

Francisco Hidalgo, ''Teddy Ted.'' © Editions Vaillant.

Born in Detroit, Michigan, in 1939, at age three the Hildebrant brothers sat on their grandfather's knees as he read them the Sunday funnies. As kids, *Prince Valiant, Tarzan, Tim Tyler's Luck, Dick's Adventures in Dreamland,* and *Terry and the Pirates* were their favorites. The first movie they ever saw was Walt Disney's *Pinocchio* when they were five years old. All through childhood, the twins drew their own comic books, made animated flip books, built models and puppets, and loved anything having to do with cartooning and art.

After a six-month stint at Mienzienger Art School in Detroit, at age 19 Greg and Tim were hired by Jamhandy Company of Detroit, at the time the largest industrial film production house in the world. During their four-year stay at Jamhandy, they progressed to doing storyboards and more advanced work. During this time, they also worked as freelancers illustrating some religious children's books that were published by Franciscan monks in New Jersey. This project brought them to the attention of Bishop Fulton J. Sheen, who had a nationally syndicated weekly television show.

At the time, Dik Browne, of *Hi and Lois* and later *Hägar the Horrible* fame, was the house artist for Bishop Sheen. However, Sheen hired the Hildebrandts to make 16mm documentary films depicting world poverty, which he would use on his television show to educate his viewers about the world beyond the United States. The Hildebrandts traveled to Africa, Asia, and South America, and did very little artwork during this seven-year period. However, constant exposure to the despair of the Third World took its toll,

and they left to pursue a career as a freelance illustration team.

They gained a reputation for always making their deadlines and being able to imitate any style. They drew children's books for Western Publishing's Golden Books, record album covers, and drawings for a myriad of publishers from Doubleday to Random House. Then, on the back of the 1975 Tolkien calendar they noticed a request for artists who would like to draw a *Lord of the Rings* calendar for Ballantine Books. To their surprise, the Hildebrants were the only professional artists to submit work, and they received the job. In all, the Hildebrandts did three calendars for Ballantine, a total of 40 paintings, and they also wrote and illustrated their own fantasy epic, *Ursurak.* Nothing they had done previously equalled the fame the Tolkien paintings brought. Their reputation grew further when they created the original movie poster for *Star Wars* in 1977.

In the early 1980s, after working as a team for their entire lives, Greg and Tim split up. Each pursued independent careers as artists. During that period, Tim drew all the artwork for Parker Brothers' *Clue* games. They merged their talents again in 1992 and continued doing commercial art and paintings of fantasy and comic book heroes. In 1994, Michael Uslan, a driving force behind the successful *Batman* movies, approached the Hildebrandts about a new 1990s version of *Terry and the Pirates.*

The original *Terry* had been continuously syndicated from October 1934 until February 1973. Tribune Media Services launched the second version in March 1995 with characters redesigned by the Hildebrandts and scripts by Uslan. Although newspaper feature editors did not respond well to the new *Terry*, Uslan's stories were sassy, sexy, and action-packed, and the Hildebrandts' drawings of the Dragon Lady, Burma, and Pat Ryan were creative successes. However, the punk-influenced Terry, with his thin face, earring, severe haircut, and backward baseball cap, did not meet with success. Tim and Greg continued drawing the strip for over a year, but not enough newspapers subscribed to justify the Hildebrandts' efforts. Comic book veteran Dan Spiegle took over the artwork and Jim Clark the scripts, and the twins returned to painting and illustration.

B.C.

HILL, ALBERT (1901-1986) British cartoonist Albert Hill was born in Guernsey in the Channel Islands on December 1, 1901. He left school at 13 to become a trainee projectionist at the Electric Cinema, where he became fascinated by the "Lightning Sketch" films of G. E. Studdy, Hy Mayer, and other cartoonists. These films showed the artists' hands quickly sketching cartoons, that then became animated. Always top at art in school and interested in the comic papers, Hill decided to try his hand at cartoons. When the Electric Cinema closed down in 1917 he joined a printing firm as an apprentice and was encouraged by his employer to submit his cartoons to mainland publishers. His first acceptance was a joke drawing for *Merry & Bright*, executed in 1919 but not published until June 5, 1920.

Over the next few years his "singles" appeared in most of the penny comics, and his first strip, a five-panel "one off," was published in *Larks*, on March 9, 1929. When Provincial Comics of Bath published their first weekly, *The Midget Comic* (June 5, 1931), Hill submitted his samples and was immediately given the front-page character, *Sammy Spry*. When the comic changed its format to tabloid and its title to *Merry Midget* (September 12, 1931), Hill moved inside with an additional strip called *Frolics in the Far West*, and was given the large front page of a new companion comic, *Sparkler* (September 12, 1931) on which appeared *Breezy Moments on Wurzel Farm*. This rapid success prompted Hill to think of going freelance, but, unfortunately, Provincial Comics collapsed, leaving Hill unpaid for several strips. He returned to the printing trade as a typesetter.

In 1933 he was contacted by Louis Diamond, the former editor of Provincial Comics, with an offer to contribute to two new comics Diamond was about to publish from Bath. Taking the chance, Hill was soon launched on a cartooning career that quickly enabled him to freelance. Both comics had Hill strips on the front pages, *Crazy Kink the Goofy Gangster* in *Rattler*, and *Charlie Chuckle* in *Dazzler* (both August 19, 1933). These were later replaced by *Willie Wart & Wally Warble* and *Squirt & Squib*.

The comics were such a success that companions were launched, with Hill drawing for them all. *Chuckler* (March 31, 1934) had *Tommy Trot the Tudor Tramp* and *Grizzly Gus the Tricky Trapper*. *Target* (June 15, 1935) had *Tom Tip & Tim Top the Tramps* and *Western Willie the Cowboy Coughdrop*. *Rocket* (October 26, 1935) had *Freddie Freewheel*. *Sunshine* (July 16, 1938) had *P. C. Copperclock the Desert Cop*. *Bouncer* (Fetruary 11, 1939) had *Willie Scribble the Pavement Artist*. These and his other characters were killed when the comics were bought out by Amalgamated Press. Hill made the transfer to Amalgamated, and after taking on a number of strips by other artists, including *The Chimps* (Ray Bailey) and *Will Hay* (Bertie Brown), he created *Puckville Pranks* for *Puck* (1939).

World War II was a bigger setback for Hill than any of the publishers' crises: Guernsey was occupied by the Germans. Affer the war, Hill was quickly in print with the official Liberation cartoon; he then drew *Larry and Len*, a children's strip, for the *Guernsey Star* (1946). He settled in Chichester, England, in 1947, and sent some samples of his work to the minor comic book publisher Gerald G. Swan. He was immediately taken on, and drew *Inspector Slop the Plain Clothes Cop* for *Colored Slick Fun* (January 1949), *Mike the Mule* for *Cute Fun*, and *Betty & Brian* for *Kiddyfun*. His slapstick style was as firm and funny as ever, stronger now that the prewar style of captioned strips had gone. His best work appeared in *Kiddyfun Album*, an annual hardback for which he also painted the covers.

When Swan collapsed in 1951, Hill returned to his printing trade and after retirement took up show-card lettering. He worked in that capacity until his death on October 22, 1986, at age 84.

D.G.

HI NO TORI (Japan) *Hi no Tori* ("The Phoenix," also spelled *Hinotori*), created by Osamu Tezuka, made its first appearance in the January 1967 issue of the monthly *COM* magazine.

Hi no Tori was a legendary bird who lived in a volcano; when a man drank of its blood he became immune to aging and death. No one could kill *Hi no Tori*; it could only burn to death through its own will (later to rise again from the ashes). *Hi no Tori* could understand the language of man and communicate with human beings through telepathy, and it was a symbol of eternity and eternal life.

In his strip, Tezuka tackled the eternal questions: the meaning of life and death and of man's existence and purpose. This was a gigantic theme that challenged the creator and made him rise to new heights of artistry and pathos. The story unfolded freely without regard to the requirements of time and space: moving fron ancient times to the future, and from earth to the farthest recesses of the universe. The main thread con-

Albert Hill, "Bobby Bubble." © *Guernsey Star.*

"Hi no Tori," Osamu Tezuka. © COM.

necting the stories were the humans who came into contact with Hi no Tori and how this phoenix affected their lives.

In the episode titled *Reimei-hen* ("The Chapter of Dawn") for instance, the old queen of Yamatai, Himiko, wanted to drink the blood of Hi no Tori to achieve eternal life and ordered her soldiers to bring the phoenix to her. Hi no Tori was shot down and brought to Himiko, but before the queen could drain its blood, life ran out for her as the phoenix burned before her eyes. When the queen had died, Hi no Tori was reborn from its ashes and flew away. The theme of this particular episode was the deadly peril man places himself in when he tries to challenge the mystery of eternity.

Hi no Tori was conceived by Osamu Tezuka as his life work. It was unfortunately left unfinished when *COM* folded with the August 1973 issue, although two additional installments were published, in *Manga Shōnen* between 1976 and 1980, and in *Yasei no Jidai* in 1986-88. Many mourned the passing of this strip, the most ambitious work undertaken by Tezuka. "Of all the series Tezuka created in his lifetime, *Phoenix* is the only one he referred to as his *raifu waaku*, or his 'life work,'" Fred Schodt wrote in *Dreamland Japan*. "He began drawing it in 1954, and he was still drawing it 35 years later when he died in 1989."

H.K

HIRATA, HIROSHI (1937-   ) A Japanese comic book artist born February 9, 1937, in Itabashi, Tokyo, Hiroshi Hirata became interested in cartooning when he met Masahiro Miyaji, who was drawing four-panel cartoons for his junior high school. He had to drop out of school to carry on the family business, however, when his father died. When he turned 20, he met Miyaji again, who advised him to draw comics: Hirata followed the advice and in 1959 published a short strip, *Aizo no Hissatsuken*, a samurai revenge story for *Mazō*, a rental library comic book. A little later he decided to leave his business and fully devote himself to comic art.

Hirata has published a great number of comic books, the most famous including *Jaken Yaburetari*, the story of a swordsman, in 1959; *Tsunde ha kuzushi*, a revenge story, in 1961; *Hishū no Tachi* ("The Pathetic Sword") and *Musō Ogidachi*, a tragic samurai tale, both in 1963; a host of short-story and novel adaptations from 1966-67; *Soregashi Kojikini Arazu* ("I Am Not a Beggar") in 1970; and *Kubidai Hikiukenin* in 1973. Since the 1980s, he has devoted himself to depicting the bloody tales of Bushido (the samurai code of honor) set in medieval Japan.

Hiroshi Hirata wrote and drew stories for a wide audience and was very popular with boys and young adults in the 1960s. In the early days, his line was very schematic and sketchy, but his style acquired more and more realism and detail. He is probably one of the best illustrative artists in Japan today. His work belongs to the Jidaimono genre (the Japanese equivalent of the American Western) in which he likes to depict samurais of the lower class as miserable, cheerless, and dispirited.

Hiroshi Hirata has influenced a number of young Japanese cartoonists, among them Ken Tsukikage, Shinzō Tomi, Masami Ishii, and Mito Tsukiyama. His younger brother is also a comic book artist.

H.K.

HISTOIRES EN ESTAMPES (Switzerland) The Genevan Rodolphe Töpffer had to renounce his ambition to become a painter because of poor eyesight; instead he became a noted lecturer, scholar, and writer. However, he never abandoned his artistic dreams and illustrated his own humorous accounts of his trips to the Swiss mountainside. For his personal pleasure Töpffer drew a series of illustrated stories which he called "dramas in pictures;" over the years, from 1827 until his death in 1846, he produced eight of them. These are (in chronological order): *Les Amours de M. Vieuxbois* ("The Loves of Mr. Oldwood"), *Les Voyages et Aventures du Docteur Festus* ("The Travels and Adventures of Doctor Festus"), *Monsieur Cryptogame, Histoire de M. Jabot* ("The Story of Mr. Jabot"), *La Veritable Histoire de M. Crépin* ("The True Story of Mr. Crépin"), *L'Histoire d'Albert, M. Pencil*, and *L'Histoire de Jacques*. Töpffer was inspired (as he himself stated) by the cartoon sequences of Hogarth and Rowlandson (whose *Dr. Syntax* was the direct model for Töpffer's own *Dr. Festus*) but his stories were fresh and vibrant, and Töpffer had the uncanny ability to weave a brilliant graphic narrative around his humorous (but largely redundant) text.

In 1844 Töpffer's picture-stories came to the attention of Goethe, who waxed enthusiastic and advised the author to have them published. The first two stories had a limited run of 500 and 800 copies, respectively. In 1845 a German edition was released. The renown of Töpffer's illustrated narratives kept growing by leaps and bounds, and the important French publisher Garnier decided to release all the tales in a collective edition in two volumes that appeared after Töpffer's death (1846 and 1847). This edition (its success was immediate and universal) bore the title by which Töpffer's picture-stories became famous: *Histoires en Estampes* ("Stories in Etchings").

So great was the fame of these stories throughout the 19th century that John Grand-Carteret, in his monumental study *Les Moeurs et la Caricature* ("Mores and Caricature," 1885) simply stated that Töpffer's work was too well known to require illustration.

Ellen Wiese, in her helpful essay on Töpffer, *Enter the Comics* (1965), claims for the author the distinction of having invented the new art form which later came to be called the comics. On the face of it, the claim seems exaggerated, however; Töpffer's work, inspired as it undoubtedly is, is still too overloaded with extraneous literary preoccupations. It signals not the birth of a new form, but the brilliant end of an already outmoded artistic concept.

Töpffer's *Histoires* went through several American editions (all of which are out of print today). The aforementioned *Enter the Comics* reprinted *M. Crépin*, along with the amusing *Petit Essai de Physiognomie* ("Little Essay on Physiognomy").

M.H.

HOBAN, WALTER C. (1890-1939) The strip artist whose fey talent gave birth to *Jerry On The Job* and *Needlenose Noonan* was born Walter C. Hoban in Philadelphia in 1890, into the family of the director of the Philadelphia Municipal Department of Purchases and Supplies—which itself sounds like a comic invention of Hoban's. Raised in a very strict Catholic family—his father, Peter J. Hoban, was a founder of *The Catholic Standard and Times*—the young Hoban attended Catholic schools, graduating from St. Joseph's College and going on to the Philadelphia School of Industrial Art. A precocious student, Hoban was still young when he took his first job as office boy on the Philadelphia *North American*, hoping to become a reporter.

Curiously, he had no special ambitions to be a commercial cartoonist, although he entertained the older reporters with his drawings and as a result was often invited to accompany them to local ball games. At one of these, he made his usual "fun" sketches—and had one of them used on the sports page when it was discovered that no photographs existed of an important aspect of the game. The response to Hoban's cartoon was immediate and enthusiastic, and his sketches became frequent treats in the paper.

Now convinced that his true future lay with his art, Hoban accepted an invitation to join the staff of the Hearst *New York Journal* in 1912, where he ultimately created his best-known strip, a daily and Sunday feature called *Jerry On The Job* for King Features (taking some time off in 1917-18 to serve in Europe as a second lieutenant of artillery). *Jerry On The Job* featured a precocious kid—like Hoban—who was a ticket seller, porter, and jack of all trades at a suburban railway terminal. From the start, the strip was notable for a zany kind of background detail that foreshadowed the later work of cartoonists like Bill Holman (*Smokey Stover*), although the gags themselves were generally routine.

Hoban's strip was never enormously popular with the public—it remained from the start a second-string King Features comic—but his fellow artists enjoyed it greatly, and one, Cliff Sterrett, used Jerry and his train station as elements in his own *Polly and Her Pals* strip, later elaborating upon Hoban by using visually weird settings in his stunning *Polly* Sunday pages of the late 1920s. By the 1930s, however, the public seemed to have lost all interest in *Jerry*, and Hoban undertook a new feature for the new Hearst daily and Sunday *Mirror* tabloid in New York in 1932: *Needlenose Noonan*. *Noonan* was an outright fantastic strip about a rookie cop and his big city predicaments, and Hoban accompanied it on Sundays with a smaller feature called *Discontinued Stories*, in which various humans and animals meet obvious disasters in the undrawn weekly climaxes. This page was popular in the *Mirror*, and appeared briefly in *Puck* in the early 1930s, but it was not a national success and Hoban turned to commercial art, reviving *Jerry* and his train station for a number of nationally printed advertisements in the late 1930s.

He lived in Port Washington, New York, in later life and fathered two daughters. Suddenly becoming ill in the fall of 1939, Hoban was taken to the Post Graduate Hospital in New York where he lingered for two months, visited by dozens of his old cartooning colleagues, and died on November 22, 1939, at the age of 49.

B.B.

HOEST, BILL (1926-1988) American cartoonist born in Newark, New Jersey, on February 7, 1926. Upon graduation from high school, Hoest enlisted in the U.S. Navy; discharged in 1946, he went on to study art at the Cooper Union in New York. His first art job was as a greeting card designer for Norcross from 1948 to 1951. He left to engage in freelance work and was soon contributing cartoons to such publications as the *Saturday Evening Post*, *Collier's*, *Playboy*, and the *Ladies Home Journal*.

Walter Hoban, "Jerry on the Job." © *Int'l Feature Service.*

Hoest's career as an inexhaustible purveyor of comic-strip fare began in the 1950s with the sale to the Chicago Tribune-New York News Syndicate of *My Son John*, a teenage strip that didn't last. He clicked, however, with *The Lockhorns*, distributed by King Features as a daily panel beginning in September 1968 and as a Sunday page from April 1972. Featuring the bickerings of a childless couple, the philandering Leroy and his querulous wife, Loretta, *The Lockhorns* proved a hit with readers.

Hoest followed this initial success with another panel series, *Bumper Snickers*, a string of loosely connected gags about cars and their bumptious drivers, for the *National Enquirer* in 1974. In 1977, he created the daily and Sunday strip *Agatha Crumm* for King. The titular character, a spunky old lady who runs her business empire with an iron hand, is perhaps his most original creation. In 1979 he became cartoon editor for *Parade* magazine; there he produced *Laugh Parade*, a weekly gag feature, in 1980, followed the next year by *Howard Huge*, about a friendly, if overbearing, St. Bernard. *What a Guy!,* a newspaper strip about a young executive on the make, syndicated by King in 1987, turned out to be his last comic strip creation.

A versatile and prolific cartoonist, Hoest varied his graphic style according to the tenor of the strips. *The Lockhorns*, for example, was drawn in a well-rounded, cartoony line, while *Agatha Crumm* was rendered with angular, spindly strokes. He died from cancer at the height of his success, on November 7, 1988. After his death, his widow, Bunny, took over production of the Hoest-originated features in collaboration with her husband's former assistant, John Reiner.

M.H.

HOGARTH, BURNE (1911-1996) American artist and educator born in Chicago on December 25, 1911. Hogarth displayed artistic inclinations as a child and later studied art history and anthropology at Crane College and Northwestern University in Chicago and at Columbia University. He learned to draw at the Chicago Art Institute, the breeding ground of many American artists.

At the age of 15 he became an assistant cartoonist at Associated Editors Syndicate while pursuing his studies at the same time. He was not yet 16 when the syndicate asked him to draw his own panel, *Famous Churches of the World,* and to illustrate two sports features. In 1929 he created his first comic strip, *Ivy Hemmanhaw,* for Bonnet-Brown Company, without success. The following year he started a panel entitled *Odd Occupations and Strange Accidents* for Leeds Features.

In 1935 he was hired by the McNaught Syndicate to draw *Pieces of Eight,* a pirate story written by noted author Charles Driscoll. Hogarth's big chance came in 1936. After Harold Foster announced his decision to leave *Tarzan,* which he had been drawing for United Features Syndicate, Hogarth, among many others, applied for Foster's place. He was accepted on the strength of the sample drawing he had submitted. The first *Tarzan* page signed by Hogarth appeared May 9, 1937.

More than any other artist, Hogarth gave *Tarzan* the mark of his own talent. In 1945, unhappy with the restrictions imposed upon him by United Feature Syndicate, Hogarth left *Tarzan* and gave the Robert Hall Syndicate an original creation, *Drago,* which made its first appearance in November of the same year. However, *Drago* lasted little more than a year, and in 1947 he went back to *Tarzan,* but not before he had obtained more advantageous conditions, including the freedom to write his own scenarios. At the same time, Hogarth created (also for United Feature Syndicate) the short-lived *Miracle Jones*, his only attempt at a humor strip.

A new conflict soon arose between the artist and the syndicate over the foreign rights to *Tarzan,* so when his contract expired Hogarth declined to renew it. He left *Tarzan* and the comic strip field to devote his time to the School of Visual Arts that he had founded with Silas Rhodes in 1947. (It is today one of the most comprehensive centers of art training in the United States.) In 1970 Hogarth retired from the School of Visual Arts in order to devote himself fully to painting, drawing, and writing.

Hogarth produced a number of drawings, paintings, and etchings which have been exhibited in galleries all over the world. He also authored three books of art instruction, *Dynamic Anatomy, Drawing the Human Head,* and *Dynamic Figure Drawing* for Watson-Guptill Publications. Hailed as "the Michelangelo of the comics" in Europe and Latin America, Hogarth's fame was slow in coming in the United States. His renown and influence have grown tremendously in recent years, however.

In 1972 Burne Hogarth went back to *Tarzan* with a totally new pictorial version of Edgar Rice Burroughs's novel *Tarzan of the Apes,* also for Watson-Guptill. His second book based on Burroughs's stories, *Jungle Tales of Tarzan,* came out in 1976.

At an age when most people entertain thoughts of retirement, Hogarth kept pursuing his multifaceted activities at a frenzied pace. He served as president of the National Cartoonists Society in 1977-79, taught art classes at the Parsons School of Design in New York City, and, after his move to California in 1981, taught

Dynamic Anatomy Demonstration, Burne Hogarth. © Burne Hogarth.

at the Otis Art Institute in Los Angeles and the Art Center College of Design in Pasadena. He also published two more art instruction books, *Dynamic Light and Shade* (1981) and *Dynamic Wrinkles and Drapery* (1992).

Hogarth received many distinctions and honors during the last two decades of his life. He was named Artist of the Year at the Pavilion of Humor in Montreal in 1975, received the Lifetime Achievement Award in Lucca, Italy, in 1984, and was the recipient of a special award at the International Festival of Comics and Illustration in Barcelona, Spain, in 1989. He was on his way back from a comics convention in France, where he had been the guest of honor, when he died of a heart attack in Paris on January 28, 1996. At the time of his death he had been working on the concept of a pacifist superhero named Morphos.

M.H.

HOGARTH, WILLIAM (1697-1764) English painter, engraver, and cartoonist born in London, in Ship Court, Old Bailey, on December 10, 1697. William Hogarth's father, Richard Hogarth, had been a schoolmaster in Westmoreland before moving to London, where he worked as a journalist. From his earliest days William Hogarth had a predilection for drawing and he was apprenticed, at his own request, to a silversmith. On the expiration of his apprenticeship he turned to engraving. His first works seem to have been engravings for shop bills and letters for books (1720). In 1726 he became known in his profession with his plates for Samuel Butler's *Hudibras*, and in 1728 he turned to oil painting.

In 1729 William Hogarth eloped with Sir James Thornhill's only daughter, whom he subsequently married. This was followed by a period of intense artistic activity and creativity. This period marked the culmination of Hogarth's fame, with such works as *A Harlot's Progress* (a series of six oil paintings and a corresponding series of six engravings, 1735) and *A Rake's Progress* (a series of six engravings, 1735). Due to pirating of these two works, Hogarth obtained in 1735 an act which vested artists with the exclusive rights to their own designs and restricted their use by others (this act is regarded by law scholars as the first of the modern copyright laws).

William Hogarth is the first artist to whom the term "cartoonist" can be legitimately applied. He was the first artist to draw humorous scenes without recourse to caricature or physical deformities. The backgrounds and details were sufficient to bring out the humor of his compositions; Hogarth's effects were primarily dramatic (and not graphic) and his drawings can be acknowledged as the first direct forerunners of the comic strip. As Alan Gowans perceptively noted in his study *The Unchanging Arts*: "Adapting the theatrical principle of 17th-century Baroque painting, he created distinctive little stage sets, immensely detailed, busy with gesticulating actors, all making a different and distinct contribution to the complex whole." These are, of course, some of the principles later adopted and put to good use by American comic strip artists (notably Outcault and Opper).

William Hogarth died in Chiswick on October 26, 1764.

M.H.

William Hogarth, "The Laughing Audience."

HOGG, GORDON (1912-1973) Born in London in 1912, Gordon Hogg won an art scholarship at the age of 14. He studied art with Ruskin Spear for three years, then became a commercial artist. His first cartoon, a topical gag, appeared in the *Daily Sketch* in 1938, and a series evolved featuring a little man with one big ear listening to wartime whispers.

During World War II he was an official war artist to the Indian Army under General Auchinlek. After the war, he rejoined the *Daily Sketch* as an editorial cartoonist. In 1945, after the retirement of J. Millar Watt, Hogg (who signed "Gog") took over the famous *Pop* daily strip, but later reduced it from four panels to one single picture, which took away the original's special appeal. One book of Gog's *Pop* comics was published, and the cartoon ran for 15 years, concluding January 23, 1960, in the *Daily Mail* after the newspapers merged.

"Gog" then begame "Gay Gordon," the racing tipster, with a daily cartoon tip for readers of the *Sun*, and finally turned to children's comics with *Pop Parade* in *Sunday Extra* (1965), *Glugg* in *Wham* (1966), and *Ronnie Rich* in *Smash* (1966). He died in March 1973.

D.G.

HOKUSAI, KATSUSHIKA (1760-1849) Japanese Ukiyo-e artist born September 23, 1760 in Edo (later called Tokyo).

In 1778 Katsushika Hokusai became a student of the popular Ukiyo-e artist Shunshō Katsukawa and he made his artistic debut in 1779. In 1793 he became a pupil of Yūsen Kanō but soon left him for reasons unknown. In 1794 he was expelled from the Katsukawa family and became acquainted with Tourin Tsutsumi. In addition to Ukiyo-e, he studied many other schools of art such as Yamato-e paintings, Chinese (Kan) painting, and Western painting. In 1778 he took the pen name under which he is most famous: Hokusai (he had earlier used the name Souri).

Jim Holdaway, "Romeo Brown." © *Daily Mirror Newspapers Ltd.*

Hokusai gained fame with his book illustrations after 1806 (he was especially active in this field from 1807 to 1809). His illustrations, full of monsters and violence, were rendered in a highly dramatic style. In 1812 Hokusai produced his first drawing manual, *Ryakuga Hayaoshie*; and in 1814 the first volume of his monumental *Hokusai Manga* ("The Hokusai Cartoons") appeared. A veritable encyclopedia of Hokusai's art, the *Manga* displayed Hokusai's awesome ability in its drawings of people engaged in every possible activity—of faces, manners, animals, fish, insects, natural scenes, monsters, etc. The 15th and final volume of the *Hokusai Manga* was not published until 1878, long after the artist's death. Other famous works by Hokusai are *Hyaku Monogatori* ("The 100 Tales," 1830), *Fugaku Sanjūrnkkei* ("36 Scenes of Mt. Fuji," 1831), *Shokoku Meikyō Kiran* ("Famous Waterfalls in Various Provinces," 1834), *Fugaku Hyakkei* ("100 Scenes of Mt. Fuji," 1834), and *Ehon Musha Burui* (1841).

Hokusai is probably the most famous of Ukiyo-e artists. He drew every conceivable subject—from landscapes to genre compositions to action scenes. He gave fresh impetus to the lethargic tradition of book illustration with his bold and striking compositions. Hokusai was also a pioneer in landscape Ukiyo-e. His works are full of life, vitality, and elan, and display a great inventiveness in composition as well as a keen sense of color. Hokusai has influenced countless numbers of Japanese artists (among his many students were Gyōsai Kawanabe, Kuniyoshi Utagagawa, Yositushi Tsukioka, and others), and his works were introduced in Europe where they exercised a great influence on the Impressionists. He can also be credited with bringing the tradition of the European cartoon to Japan, and thus paving the way for the later acceptance of the Western-style comic strip in Japanese publications.

Hokusai died on April 18, 1849.

H.K.

HOLDAWAY, JAMES (1927-1970) British cartoonist, born at Barnes Common, London, in 1927. He was educated at New Malden Secondary School, winning an art scholarship to the Kingston School of Art. In 1945 he was called for military service in the East Surrey Regiment, serving in Italy, Austria, and Greece, and returning to art school in 1948 on an ex-service grant.

His first professional artwork was designing shoe advertisements in France, and he then worked as a rubber engraver for the Reed Paper Group in Brentford. While there (1950) he began freelancing cartoon work.

In 1951 he joined the art staff of Scion Ltd., a publisher in Kensington, London, that specialized in one-shot comics and science-fiction paperbacks. Here he drew all types of artwork, from comic pages to illustrations, advertisements, and full-color book jackets. As Scion changed their style of comics from the typical British "funny" format of eight pages in two colors to the American style comic book format of 24 pages with full-color covers, Jim Holdaway began to draw more comics. An admirer of the American comic book style, he modeled his technique on Will Eisner, Milton Caniff, and other masters. His first full-length picture stories were for *Gallant Detective* (1952): *Inspector Hayden* in issue number one, *Lex Knight* in number two.

In 1953 he went freelance, working from home for the new independent Sports Cartoons, a division of Man's World Publications. He contributed individual episodes of such regular heroes as *Captain Vigour, Dick Hercules,* and *Steve Samson,* as well as strips for *Football Comic.* Then came more adult strips for the pocket-size "library" comic books, *Tid-Bits Science Fiction Comics,* and a weekly Western featuring the stage and radio cowboy Cal McCord for *Comic Cuts* (1953). *Cal McCord,* his first page for better-class comics, led to *Cliff McCoy* (1955), *The Red Rider* (1956) in *Swift,* and an excellent full-color page in *Mickey's Weekly* adapted from Walt Disney's *Davy Crockett* (1956).

His first daily newspaper strip was *Romeo Brown* in the *Daily Mirror,* which he took over from Albert Mazure and quickly made his own. Suddenly, Jim Holdaway had became Britain's top "girlie" cartoonist! This strip marked his first association with writer Peter O'Donnell, and together they later created the superlative *Modesty Blaise* (1963) for the *London Evening Standard.* Tragically, Jim died in February 1970, but his style lives on in the modern *Modesty.*

D.G.

HOLLANDER, NICOLE (1939-   ) The single girl has had her spokesperson in the comics since Russ Westover's Tillie became a Toiler in 1921, but it was not until Nicole Hollander created the acid-tongued *Sylvia* more than half a century later that the middle-aged woman really had a voice. It isn't a strident voice, but it cuts through the hypocracy and absurdity of modern life as trenchantly as that of any of the younger heroines in comics. Sylvia is today's woman. She is not concerned about diet or failed relationships; her answer to "feminine protection every day" is "use a hand grenade," and one of her answering machine messages is, "I can't come to the phone right now. When you hear the beep, please hang up."

With a Bachelor of Fine Arts degree from the University of Illinois and a M.F.A. ("Master of Feisty Arts," Hollander jokes) from Boston University, Hollander left school expecting to be a painter. She settled for becoming a graphic designer in California, where she styled matchboxes "and other projects of significant social value." After returning to her native Chicago, she worked as an art teacher and art director. She also tried illustrating textbooks and children's books, but, she recalls, people found her illustrations "too weird." It was a job redesigning the Chicago-based national feminist magazine *The Spokeswoman* that led to a career she

Nicole Hollander, "Sylvia." © Sylvia Syndicate.

describes as "cartoonist by surprise." *Sylvia's* first tart observations on popular culture and the status of women appeared in *The Spokeswoman* in 1976. Boldly drawn, in a manner more influenced by German expressionism than by traditional cartoon style, *Sylvia's* astringent dialogue appears without balloons, sprawling throughout the panels like the clutter of its heroine's apartment.

Sylvia was refused by Universal Press Syndicate in 1979 (described by one of its less-perceptive editors as "deep but narrow"), and was taken on by the Toronto Sun Syndicate in Canada. The strip went to Field Enterprises two years later, but Hollander found their promotion of it so lackluster that she took its syndication over herself and soon doubled *Sylvia's* readership. By 1997 it was running in over 80 daily and weekly papers, including the *Boston Globe, Chicago Tribune, Los Angeles Times, Detroit News,* and *Seattle Times.* The first collection of *Sylvia* strips, *I'm in Training to be Tall and Blonde,* was published by St. Martin's Press in 1979; since then a flood of volumes (15 by 1997) have appeared from St. Martin's, Random House, Avon Books, and Dell; all, after the first few, were composed of original work created for book publication.

Hollander also has a line of greeting cards and calendars, provides illustrations for the *New York Times Book Review, Mirabella,* and other magazines, has illustrated two children's books, and does a regular political cartoon for *Mother Jones.* In 1992 her musical comedy, *Sylvia's Real Good Advice,* coauthored with Arnold Aprill and Tom Mula, had an extended run in Chicago and San Francisco, and articles by Hollander have appeared in the *New York Times.*

The audience of *Sylvia* crosses lines of both gender and generation. In *Print* (1988), Tom Gross described the strip as an example of a new genre of comics that are intermediate between the underground and the mainstream. "While they remain well within the mainstream of comic strip sensibility," he wrote, "they represent the leading edge of a more sophisticated and personal perspective."

D.W.

HOLMAN, BILL (1903-1987) An American cartoonist born in 1903 in Crawfordsville, Indiana, Bill Holman exhibited a flair for caricature and the outrageous at an early age. In 1919 he moved to Chicago, where he studied at the Academy of Fine Arts under Carl Ed, and the next year he took a job as copy-boy on the *Chicago Tribune.*

Bill Holman's first comic strip, an animal parody called *Billville Birds,* was released by NEA Service in 1922; it lasted only a few months. Undaunted, Holman

Bill Holman.

went to New York in search of his fortune. His first years there are only fuzzily recorded, but by the late 1920s he was drawing *G. Whizz Jr.* for the Herald Tribune Syndicate and self-syndicating another strip, *Wise Quacks,* about a duck (what else?) giving silly answers in the form of puns to questions asked by readers. Both were failures, however, and Bill Holman turned to the magazine field, contributing innumerable cartoons to *Collier's,* the *Saturday Evening Post, Life, Judge,* and *Everybody's Weekly* in London.

Holman's ceaseless efforts finally found their reward in 1935 when he signed a contract with the News-Tribune Syndicate. On March 10, 1935, *Smokey Stover,* a Sunday feature depicting the antics of a pair of zany firemen, appeared, accompanied by *Spooky,* about a loony cat, and followed by a daily panel called *Nuts and Jolts.*

Bill Holman, whose lifestyle was only slightly less frenzied than that of his fireman hero, once said, "I like to draw firemen because I think they are funny." Holman's art (if it can be called art) was the closest the comics came to burlesque since the days of Opper and Herriman. His devices were the outrageous pun, the raucous aside, the grotesque composition, and the devastating punchline. This is a skill of a special kind that should not be slighted.

Holman served as president of the National Cartoonists Society in 1961-63. He retired after *Smokey Stover* came to an end in 1973, but continued to entertain at charity functions until his death in New York City on February 27, 1987.

M.H.

HOLMES, FRED (1908-   ) One of the best-liked adventure strip artists in British comics, Frederick T. Holmes was born in Linsdale, Buckinghamshire, on November 12, 1908. As with most comic strip artists, he began drawing at an early age. He fondly recalled his love for the full-color cover illustrations of the Aldine series of *Buffalo Bill* novels that he studied and copied long before he was able to read the semiadult stories of life in America's Wild West. In 1923, at the young age of 15, Holmes began to send small sketches into the Children's Page of the *Birmingham Weekly Post*, and five years later he was good enough to illustrate the fiction pages.

While working as an artist for the weekly edition of the *Post*, Holmes improved his artwork by joining the British and Dominions School of Drawing. By the late 1930s he was working full time for the *Post*, drawing cartoon jokes, comic strips, and story headings as well as illustrations. However, he eventually decided his *Post* work was trivial and, deciding to put his talent to a more worthwhile purpose than mere entertainment, took a position as staff artist for the religious publisher Drummonds of Stirling (Scotland). The firm, delighted with his drawing, gave Holmes a lifetime contract; however, it went bankrupt in the post-World War II slump of 1951.

The next year, Holmes's father-in-law found a copy of *Advertiser's Weekly*, and Holmes applied to an advertisement for an artist. He was accepted immediately and asked to illustrate a serial in *Fun Film* titled *Life in Hand*. This led to a commission for another comic magazine, *Comet*. Holmes's *Comet* series, *Claude Duval, the Laughing Cavalier*, started September 19, 1953, and ran until the magazine folded in 1959 (however, later episodes of the series had been drawn by Eric Parker and Patrick Nicolle).

By the mid-1950s, Holmes was illustrating *Buffalo Bill* (his favorite boyhood hero) in *Comet*, *Billy the Kid* in *Sun*, *The Gay Gordons* for *Playhour*, and his longest-running serial, *Carson's Cubs*, a football story, for *Lion*. Holmes drew *Cubs* from 1957 to 1975. From 1960-63, he also drew *Roy of the Rovers*, the front-page football star of *Tiger*. His best work, however, appeared in the 64-page pocket-size monthlies *Thriller Comics Library* and *Tiger Sports Library*, including *Rob Roy*, *Robin Hood of Sherwood*, *Dick Turpin, King of the Highway*, and *Claude Duval and the Traitor Cavalier*.

Holmes was never a strong man—he suffered from bad asthma much of his life—and he was forced to retire in the mid-1970s after 20 years of comic work.

D.G.

HOLROYD, BILL (1919-   ) Bill Holroyd was one of the most prolific strip cartoonists for the Scottish comic publisher D. C. Thomson, working exclusively for Thomson from 1947 until his retirement in 1986. His work always showed good humor, even when he developed his line from pure comedy to adventure serials.

Born in Salford, Lancashire, on March 21, 1919, Holroyd showed an interest in artwork at a young age and developed his abilities at Salford Technical College and Hornsey Art College. His first job was with an advertising agency in Manchester in 1937. Two years later, when World War II broke out, he enlisted in the Royal Artillery and remained in the military until 1946.

Holroyd made his first contact with Thomson toward the end of the war, writing from Italy to ask if there was room for a comic artist on the staff. However, there were no open positions, and after his discharge from the army Holroyd joined the David Hand Studio in Cookham, which had been set up as J. Arthur Rank's film cartoon company. While with David Hand, Holroyd began freelancing in his spare time and had his first series, *Alf Wit the Ancient Brit*, published in the Thomson comic *Beano* on February 22, 1947. He also provided strips for many smaller independent publishers around this period, contributing *The Petrified Valley* to *Sun* (1948), *Big Game Gannon* to *Big Flame*, *Rescue from the Roundheads* to *Big Slide*, *Post Atom* to *Oh Boy* (Paget), *Puppet Land* to *Children's Rocket* (1949), and *Rollo the Gypsy Boy* to *Merry-Go-Round*. The latter series were for J. B. Allen.

But it was with the *Dandy* and *Beano* comics that Holroyd soon found a permanent home. *Plum MacDuff, the Highlandman Who Never Gets Enough*, about a fat fellow with an enormous appetite (a Scottish variation on the popular strip *Hungry Horace*), began in *Dandy* in 1948, followed by *Wuzzy Wiz, Magic is his Biz* (1949). For *Beano*, Holroyd created *Have a Go Jo, Wandering Willie*, and *Ding Dong Belle*. Belle, a tough female sheriff, was notable in a period when female comic strip protagonists were rare.

A touch of the fantastic could be found in Holroyd's serial strips, which began with *Danny Longlegs* (*Dandy*, 1950), about a very tall boy. This was followed by *Tick Tock Tony*, about a robot boy; *The Iron Fish*, about a boy with an incredible one-person submarine; *Tommy's Clockwork Brother*, another robot series; and *Nobby the Enchanted Bobby*, a magical policeman. There was also an experimental series, *Big Hugh and You*, in which the reader of the strip participated in the adventure.

One serial that stands out was *The Fighting Frazers*, which appeared in *Topper* from the first issue (1953). Many years later, Holroyd met a member of the production team for the science fiction movie *Alien*, who told the artist how the strip inspired him in creating the creature from space. Never underestimate the power of a children's comic!

D.G.

HOT ON THE TRAIL (China) This comic book story was published by the People's Art Publications of Shanghai in 1965. Adapted by Hsin Sheng from a short story by An Chung-min and Chu Hsiang-chun, it was drawn by Hao Shih.

The story opens like a classic thriller: in the purse of an old woman who has come to Canton from Hong Kong to visit relatives, a bomb mechanism is found. There follows an investigation conducted by security agent Li Ming-kang and Inspector Hsia Huang of the Canton police. The two men patiently retrace the old lady's path until they come to a likely suspect: a mysterious traveler by the name of Chien Chia-jen. After more detection work the two protagonists unmask

"Hot on the Trail," Hao Shih.

Chien, who is actually a foreign agent assigned to blow up the Canton power plant.

The action is remarkable on several counts: first as a straight spy thriller, complete with shadowy characters, strange happenings, and a general atmosphere of suspense and expectation. The authors make use of every narrative device, including the obligatory chase scene (in this case aboard a motorboat in Canton harbor). Second, there is absolutely no trace of propaganda. Nowhere in the story is there mention of the foreign country for which Chien is working, nor is there any denunciation of class enemies or foreign interlopers. In fact *Hot on the Trail* could have been authored by any number of comic book writers from the United States or Western Europe, with only a few name changes.

The drawings of *Hot on the Trail* are not very remarkable, but are adequate, and the total effect of the strip

(mixing speech balloons with a narrative under the panels) comes closer to that of the English comics of the 1920s than to contemporary American strips. All in all, however, it is quite an entertaining and enlightening experience.

Hot on the Trail was among the comic strips reprinted in *The People's Comic Book* (Doubleday, 1973).

M.H.

HOWARD THE DUCK (U.S.) In the pages of *Adventure Into Fear* issue 19 (December 1973), a Marvel comic book title, Steve Gerber introduced a cantankerous, cigar-chomping duck that had strayed from another dimension into our world, as a kind of Superman-meets-Daffy Duck pastiche. The foul-tempered fowl proved a surprise hit with many readers, so much so that in January 1976 he gained his own comic book, also published by Marvel.

It turned out that Howard (as the palmipede was called) was a denizen of the planet Duckworld, where ducks had evolved instead of humans. Howard was the possessor of a high I.Q., had a sarcastic turn of mind, and could speak fluent English. Fleeing from his arch-nemesis, the monstrous Thog, he landed (of all places) in Cleveland, Ohio, where he saved a comely model named Beverly Switzler from the clutches of the malevolent accountant Pro-Rata. He eventually shacked up with the grateful damsel now out of distress, a case of interspecies miscegeneation that boggles the mind. Setting himself up as a fighter for justice, Howard confronted such menaces as the giant Gingerbread Man, the clangorous Dr. Bong, and the radioactive Morton Erg, all of whom he defeated with the help of Quack-Fu, a lethal form of martial art taught only on Duck-world.

At first the comic book spoofed the absurdities and lunacies of the superhero genre, especially as it was

"Howard the Duck," Steve Skeates and Gene Colan. © Marvel Comics Group.

practiced at Marvel, but soon Gerber cast a wider net, venturing into the sphere of social criticism with his attacks on racial discrimination and political corruption. Following in the footsteps of Pogo Possum, Howard even ran for president in 1976 as a protest candidate on the All-Night Party ticket. All the while, the *Howard the Duck* comic book benefitted from the superlative artwork of such luminaries as Val Mayerik, Gene Colan, Brian Bolland, John Buscema, and Walt Simonson, all of whom seemed to have a good time drawing the strip.

Despite the character's popularity (which caused a *Howard the Duck* newspaper strip to be added in the mid-1970s), and for reasons that are disputed to this day, Gerber and Marvel had a falling-out. In order to recover the rights to the character he had created, Gerber took Marvel to court, subsequently winning the case. During the legal proceedings, however, the object of contention—Howard himself—had quietly expired (1981). He was revived in 1986 in a truly awful movie by George Lucas (with Marvel responsible for the comic book adaptation), after which nothing further has been heard from the crotchety bird.

M.H.

HOWARTH, F. M. (ca. 1870-1908) F. M. Howarth is an important name in comic strip history; his series of strip drawings in *Puck* in the 1890s no doubt paved the way and heightened public acceptance for cartoons in strip form.

Howarth's drawings surfaced in the pages of *Puck, Judge, Life,* and such lesser humor magazines as *Truth* and *Tid-Bits* in the late 1880s. He was then still a talented amateur and his work looked no different than that of the young T. S. Sullivant and James Montgomery Flagg. But in a few short years he found a truly individualistic style and was engaged by *Puck* as a staff artist.

Howarth was the first *Puck* cartoonist who didn't double as an editorial artist; by the 1890s the magazine was toning down its partisan flavor. Howarth's drawings were almost always in sequence, with narration and dialogue underneath.

His two contributions were this narrative innovation—it had been employed by others infrequently before and frequently after Howarth—and a painfully exact stylization. Howarth's characters had enormous heads with exaggerated features (particularly popping eyes), but otherwise everything else in the panels was drawn realistically. Nothing was left to chance; in a day when photoengraving and the heliographic process were permitting cartoonists greater freedom, Howarth achieved success through rigid exactitude.

He drew continuing sequences for *Puck,* but without characters that continued from week to week. This curious fact is contrasted to cartoonists who copied his format but introduced regular weekly characters: James Montgomery Flagg with *Nervy Nat* in *Judge* and Louis Glackens with *Hans* in *Puck.*

In 1903 he had such an opportunity, however, when William Randolph Hearst hired Howarth to work for his Sunday supplement. *Lulu and Leander* was the result, and it quickly became a standby in Hearst's *American-Journal-Examiner* comic sections. (By coincidence, his page-mate was *Foxy Grandpa* by Carl Schultze—the cartoonist who more than any other tried to ape Howarth's style back in the 1890s. By the Hearst days Schultze had settled on his own style.)

Howarth occasionally drew other features, notably *A Lad and His Lass,* which was really no more than a medieval *Lulu and Leander.* By 1907, Hearst and/or the public had tired of Howarth's precisely drawn pictorial narratives, and *Lulu and Leander* was dropped from the Hearst pages. Soon Howarth emerged in the *Chicago Tribune* comic section, doing *Ole Opey Dildock—the Storyteller* in his familiar fashion. This strip about a teller of tales didn't last long—at least with Howarth as artist, for he died in 1908. An artist named Wells continued the strip for the *Tribune.*

Howarth, a man who pioneered the narrative form, ironically never used balloons.

R.M.

HUBERT (U.S.) *Stars and Stripes* was in its earliest stages, a weekly paper published in Ireland, when Dick Wingert submitted his first cartoons. Having just been transferred to Ireland with the U.S. Army and already an aspiring artist stateside, Wingert was able to get in on the ground floor with the army publication. This was in 1942, and when *Stars and Stripes* went to London, so did Wingert.

His earliest cartoons were one-shot gags without a central or continuing character. As cartooning was new to him, he recalls having to copy from the previous week's drawing for his style and format. Soon, however, he introduced a regular character, a short, big-nosed, brash oaf who was named Hubert (by vote of Wingert's buddies).

Hubert, in panel format, became one of the great comic characters of WWII, not as front-line as Mauldin's *Willie and Joe,* but bawdier than any, including Sansone's *Wolf* (a famous gag has two well-dressed Parisian girls saying, as Hubert walks down the street, "Don't look now, but here comes old 'Couchez Avec' again!").

With General Patton's army in France, Wingert met Bill Hearst, who promised to syndicate the feature after the war. So in 1945 *Hubert* changed into his civvies for a daily panel and Sunday page. The transition, consid-

"Hubert," Dick Wingert. © King Features Syndicate.

ering the rakish and freewheeling character Pfc. Hubert had been, was remarkably smooth and successful. He married a pretty blonde named Trudy, battled an impossible mother-in-law (merely a fat, feminine substitute for his previous antagonistic superiors), and had a daughter named Elli who was just starting school, and a large, lazy sheepdog, Freddy, that always got in the way of things. Also in the cast were Charlie the Milkman; Hubert's boss Dexter L. Baxter; and the secretary at the office.

Hubert remained the half-pint, big-nosed bag of seed that he always was, but slightly less grotesque as a suburbanite rather than a serviceman on leave. And his nemeses became crabgrass, broken hammocks, jammed lawnmowers, and nagging motorbikes.

Wingert's art and gag style are one: broad, basic slapstick. For this reason his gags were always more successful in Sunday-page format, where there is more room for development and animation. Even in the daily panel, King Features suggested a novel change—slice the panel in two and let papers run it in strip format. Many chose that option, but this proved less successful with other panels such as *Trudy and Hazel.*

The old slapstick, albeit heavy-handed, managed to survive in the Sunday page, despite the inhibition of spatial restrictions, until 1994.

R.M.

HUBINON, VICTOR (1924-1979) Belgian cartoonist born 1924 in Angleur, near Liège. Upon graduation from high school, Victor Hubinon entered the Liège Academy of Fine Arts where he studied decoration, painting, etching, and drawing, while contributing cartoons and caricatures to several Belgian newspapers and magazines. During the German occupation of Belgium, Hubinon fled to England and enlisted in the Belgian section of the Royal Navy. After the liberation of his homeland, he joined the newspaper *La Meuse* as an advertising artist.

In 1946 Hubinon met Jean-Michel Charlier, who introduced him to the comic weekly *Spirou.* After doing a number of illustrations for *Spirou,* Hubinon created *Buck Danny* in collaboration with Charlier as script-

writer. The story of a U.S. Air Force pilot in the Pacific War, the first episode of *Buck Danny* appeared in January 1947. (With *Buck Danny,* Hubinon found his métier; at first he left the drawing of airplanes to Charlier, a former pilot, but he later earned his own pilot's license and went on to become an aviation expert.)

In addition to *Buck Danny,* Hubinon took over Jijés's *Blondin et Cirage* for a couple of years (1950-52), and did a number of illustrated biographies (Surcouf, Mermoz, Stanley) for *Spirou* in the 1950s. In 1959, again with Charlier writing the scenarios, he produced *Le Démon des Caraïbes* ("The Demon of the Caribbean," title later changed to *Les Aventures de Barbe-Rouge et d'Eric*) for *Pilote;* this excellent sea-adventure strip lasted until 1967. Hubinon also contributed illustrations and cartoons to such publications as *Moustique, La Libre Belgique, Pistolin,* and *Junior. La Mouette* ("The Seagull"), the tale of a female pirate written by Gigi Marechal (who also served as a model for the heroine), was his last comic-strip creation. He died suddenly of a heart attack at his drawing table in January 1979.

Hubinon is not regarded as one of the foremost innovators of the European comics. His early drawings were strongly influenced by Caniff, but he later came into his own agreeable and undemanding graphic style. He occupies a comfortable and honorable position in European comic art.

M.H.

HULK, THE (U.S.) Shortly after the phenomenal success of *Fantastic Four,* Marvel editor Stan Lee was faced with creating a second feature to cash in on the burgeoning Marvel market. His solution was *The Hulk,* which premiered in its own book in May 1962. The script was by the irrepressible Lee and the art was by staff king Jack Kirby.

Early issues by Lee and Kirby exhibited heavy influences of Mary Shelley's *Frankenstein,* but *Hulk* tales also borrowed liberally from *Dr. Jekyll and Mr. Hyde* and *The Hunchback of Notre Dame.* As the original story explained, Doctor Bruce Banner created a highly powerful gamma-ray bomb for the United States government. Shortly before its testing, however, Banner ran

"The Hulk," © *Marvel Comics Group.*

to the test site to rescue a trespassing youth, Rick Jones. In doing so, he was bathed in the rays of the exploding bomb and turned into the snarling, raging, green-skinned (originally gray) Hulk, and like Jekyll and Hyde, changed character at regular intervals; like Frankenstein's monster, he was never understood, always mistaken for evil even when he was simply frightened.

Added to this classical mixture were several strong supporting characters: Rick Jones, the Hulk's only friend although he eventually went on to team up with Captain America and then Captain Marvel; Betty Ross, Banner's lover, who later scorned him for Major Talbot and then shuttled back and forth between the two with fickle regularity; and "Thunderbolt" Ross, Betty's father and Banner's boss, a general who instantly became the Hulk's prime enemy. Lee handled this melange of plot threads and characters until 1969, when he gave way to Roy Thomas, who added even a larger cast and story lines. Archie Goodwin, Gerry Conway, science fiction writer Harlan Ellison, Gary Friedrich, Steve Englehart, and Chris Claremont took turns scripting *The Hulk*, and together they made the feature too complex, inconsistent, and muddled.

Artistically, *The Hulk* did not fare much better. After Kirby and his Frankenstein-like version disappeared, Steve Ditko, Gil Kane, John Buscema, Marie Severin, and finally Herb Trimpe took turns at the strip. Trimpe became the definitive artist, and his mellow, sketchy version appeared regularly for many years in the late 1960s and early 1970s.

The Hulk book lasted only six issues until March 1963, but the feature then began in the 59th issue of *Tales To Astonish* (August 1964). The title was changed to *The Hulk* with April 1968's 102nd issue.

The success of the 1978-82 *Hulk* television series considerably boosted the fortunes of *The Incredible Hulk* (as the comic book was by now officially named). It attracted a number of talented artists to its stable, notably John Byrne, Frank Miller, Todd McFarlane, and Walt Simonson. It also gave rise to a number of spinoffs; to date, these have included *The Savage She-Hulk*, *The Sensational She-Hulk*, *The Rampaging Hulk*, and *Hulk 2099*.

J.B.

HUMAN TORCH, THE (U.S.) *The Human Torch* was created in November 1939 by Carl Burgos and made its first appearance in Timely's *Marvel Comics* number one. (The title of the book was eventually changed to *Marvel Mystery*.) The character quickly became a fantastically successful hero and Timely's first major superheroic strip. By the fall of 1940, *Human Torch* number one had been published, and the strip soon began appearing in *Captain America, All Winners,* and several other Timely titles.

In actuality, the Human Torch wasn't human at all. He was an android, a "synthetic man," created by the visionary Professor Horton. Unfortunately, as soon as Horton released the creation from its protective beaker, it burst into flame and had to be encased in concrete. The fire-man quickly escaped, however, and after accidentally killing his creator and inadvertantly operating in a protection racket, the Torch learned how to control and harness his flaming prowess. After learning how to fly and devising techniques to hurl fireballs and control all types of flame, he became a blue (later red) costumed crime fighter. For a while he even

"The Human Torch." © Marvel Comics Group.

adopted the secret identity of Jim Hammond, but the alter-ego was soon dropped and the Human Torch operated in character throughout the rest of his career. Toro, an orphaned circus performer with an immunity to fire, was eventually introduced as the Torch's sidekick and partner. As the years progressed and the strip continued to grow in stature, the character became more and more human until no further mention was made of his android heritage. He became just another man—albeit a man who could set himself and others ablaze.

The best of the *Human Torch* stories came in three early issues of *Human Torch* (numbers five, eight, and ten). There he was locked in exciting and memorable combat with Timely's water-based character, the vindictive, half-human/half-Atlantean Sub-Mariner. Given the natural dramatic elements inherent in conflicts between fire and water, the epic battles are among the best-remembered stories of the 1940s. Artistically, the strip was never more than average, and after Burgos left for the armed forces in 1942, a long procession of illustrators, including Carmine Infantino, Syd Shores, Don Rico, Mike Sekowsky, and Alex Schomberg, produced the feature.

The Human Torch was another superheroic victim of the post-war comic book bust, however, and the feature's own book folded after the 35th issue (March 1949). By June of that year, the character made its last appearance in *Marvel Mystery* number 92. Atlas Comics Group, Timely's successor, attempted a brief revival of the strip in 1953. After his initial appearance in *Young Men* number 24 (December 1953), the Torch also appeared in several other titles, including his own; by September 1954's *Captain America* number 78, however, *The Human Torch* was again retired.

And although he was one of Timely's high-powered 1940s triumvirate (*Captain America* and *Sub-Mariner* were the other two), he was the only character not totally revived during the superhero boom of the early 1960s. Instead, Marvel Comics gave his powers to Johnny Storm, a teenaged member of the Fantastic Four. This Human Torch was human, however, even if

Hermann Huppen, "Comanche." © Editions du Lombard.

his age made him more akin to Toro than to the original Human Torch. The old-time hero, however, put in one last appearance in *Saga of the Original Human Torch* (1990).

J.B.

HUPPEN, HERMANN (1938-   ) Belgian cartoonist born July 17, 1938, in Beverce, in the disputed Eupen-Malmédy region of Belgium. After graduation from high school and a short stay in Canada, Hermann Huppen tried his hand at different jobs: furniture designer, draftsman, architect's assistant, and decorator. In 1963 he drifted into the comic strip field with a few stories done for a second-rate publisher, and started signing his work simply "Hermann."

In February 1966, Hermann and scriptwriter "Greg" (Michel Régnier) originated an adventure strip, *Bernard Prince*, for the weekly magazine *Tintin*; it was a success and in 1967 *Bernard Prince* became definitively established. Concurrently, he started a historical feature, *Jugurtha*, but it was short-lived. Hermann had more luck in 1971 when, in collaboration with Greg again, he created his acclaimed Western, *Comanche*, also for *Tintin*. In addition to his comic strip work, Hermann is noted for the many illustrations and covers he has contributed to *Tintin* and other publications.

In 1978, Hermann authored his first series, *Jeremiah*, a Western set in a postnuclear world that proved he could write as well as he could draw. After turning out a children's story, *Nic* (1980-83), in 1984 he produced his most celebrated comic series, *The Towers of Bois-Maury*, a medieval fantasy that showed his artistic powers at their peak. All through the 1980s and 1990s he also worked as a book illustrator, poster designer, and movie storyboarder.

A highly regarded cartoonist, Hermann is also a scrupulous and painstaking artist whose work always displays the utmost professionalism, even when his inspiration sometimes flags. Hermann has been the recipient of a number of awards in the cartoon field from organizations in Belgium, France, and Italy.

M.H.

HURTUBISE, JACQUES (1950-   ) Canadian cartoonist born November 5, 1950, in Montreal. It was in the course of his studies toward an engineering degree at the University of Montreal that Jacques Hurtubise first became interested in the problems of the comics. Along with a group of schoolmates, and with a grant from the University, he produced the first issue of a French-language comic magazine, *L'Hydrocéphale Illustre* ("The Illustrated Hydrocephale") in November 1971. After a short study trip to Paris, Hurtubise became more convinced than ever of the need to develop an indigenous French-Canadian comics industry; his efforts and a grant from the Quebec government led to the establishment in 1973 of a cooperative of French-Canadian comic artists, Les Petits Dessins ("The Little Drawings"). In 1974 Les Petits Dessins signed an exclusive contract with the newly founded Montreal daily *Le Jour* for the production of the paper's daily strips.

Among the six new features appearing in *Le Jour* on February 28, 1974, was Hurtubise's own creation, *Le Sombre Vilain* ("The Black-Hearted Villain"), signed with the pseudonym "Zyx." *Le Sombre Vilain* depicts the various schemes of a comic-opera conspirator whose goal is nothing less than the total destruction of the world. Hurtubise's graphic style, very stylized and modern, and his caustic sense of humor put *Le Sombre Vilain* in the forefront of French-Canadian comics. As Jacques Samson noted: "Hurtubise has managed to achieve a synthesis between text and image possibly unique in French-Canadian comic art."

In addition to his work as a cartoonist, Jacques Hurtubise continues to be active in the promotion of comics made in Quebec. In 1975, along with Pascal Nadon and Pierre Huet, he was one of the driving forces behind the First International Comics Festival of Montreal. Two years later, Hurtubise and Huet founded the humor magazine *Croc*. In 1983, Hurtubise created a publication of his own, *Titanic*; however, it only lasted a few issues. In recent years, his career has been devoted mainly to illustration and advertising.

M.H.

Color in the Comics

Paradoxically, color comics came into existence well before the cheaper black-and-white variety. The Sunday color comic supplements started in the mid-1890s and were over 10 years old when the first daily strip (Mutt and Jeff) was successfully established in 1907.

The use of color in the comic books, as well as in the Sunday pages, adds a dramatic dimension to the proceedings and the plot. It can call attention to a special point in the narrative, highlight a twist in the action, or underscore the climax of a sequence; it can also provide a psychological link between different panels in a sequence by carrying the same tonal value from one frame to the next.

The illustrations reproduced herein will give the reader a good idea of the imaginative uses to which color has been put by cartoonists around the globe.

"Anibal 5," Alexandro Jodorowski and Manuel Moro Cid. The creation of filmmaker Jodorowski ("El Topo" and "The Holy Mountain"), the strip was peopled with weird, fantastic creatures. © Editorial Novaro.

"Andy Capp," Reginald Smythe. After making a hit with the British public, Smythe's tough little Cockney conquered the U.S. and the world. © Daily Mirror Ltd.

"Asterix," Rene Goscinny and Albert Uderzo. Europe's most popular strip featured Goscinny's clever dialogue, Uderzo's uncluttered line, and the imaginative, witty use of speech balloons (here filled with hieroglyphics). Since Goscinny's death in 1977, the strip has been done entirely by Uderzo. © Editions Dargaud.

"B.C.," Johnny Hart. Despite its serious intent, "B.C." is studded with rib-splitting slapstick, hilarious dialogue, and a delightful sense of the absurd. © Field Newspaper Syndicate.

Enki Bilal and Pierre Christin, "Partie de Chasse." Yugoslav-born Bilal and his usual accomplice Christin are known for their uncompromising treatment of contemporary political themes (in this case the power struggle between Soviet-bloc leaders at the time of the Cold War). © Dargaud Editeur.

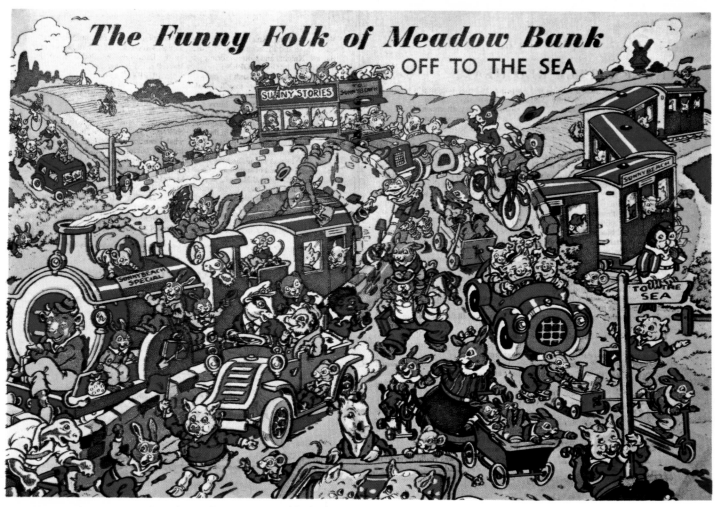

E. H. Banger, "The Funny Folk of Meadow Bank." Banger is noted for his fanciful renditions of animals in absurd situations. © Sunny Stories.

"Barney Google," Billy DeBeck. An earthy example of the traditional comic strip, "Barney Google" exhibits a good-natured humor and a graphic style that is the epitome of the well-crafted cartoon. © King Features Syndicate.

"Batman," Bob Kane. The hooded fighter for justice has achieved a renown exceeded only by that of Superman. © D.C. Comics.

"Buster Brown," R. F. Outcault. This popular and enduring creation has brought the image of Buster and his bulldog, Tige, to shoes, boy's suits, even cigars and whiskey.

BLONDIE
Registered U. S. Patent Office

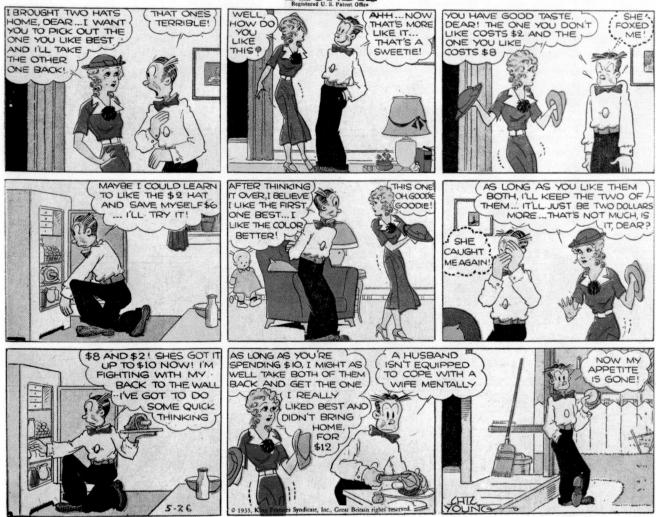

"Blondie," Chic Young. America's perennial favorite, "Blondie" has unrolled a merry chronicle of domestic life for over 60 years, and even the death of its creator has not dimmed its popularity. © King Features Syndicate.

"Bringing Up Father," George McManus. The most striking feature of this strip is its earthy theatricality, in which two lines of dialogue suffice to establish its theme. © King Features Syndicate.

"Beetle Bailey," Mort Walker. A lighthearted satire of military life, Walker's strip is drawn with a spirit and verve that even George Couteline has not surpassed. © King Features Syndicate.

"Buck Rogers," Phil Nowlan and Dick Calkins. The first science-fiction strip of worldwide fame has inspired countless imitations and rivals. © National Newspaper Syndicate.

"Blake et Mortimer," Edgar-Pierre Jacobs. Covering some of the most important themes of post-World War II science fiction, *"Blake et Mortimer"* often ranks with the best of American science-fiction strips. © Editions du Lombard.

"Brick Bradford," William Ritt and Clarence Gray. Without the futuristic vision of "Buck Rogers" or the epic grandeur of "Flash Gordon," "Brick Bradford" displayed undeniable qualities of fantasy, poetry, and imagination that equal its better-known rivals. © King Features Syndicate.

"Captain Marvel," C. C. Beck. In the 1940s Captain Marvel was Superman's most successful rival. © Fawcett Publications.

"Captain America," Joe Simon and Jack Kirby. During World War II Captain America and his boy companion, Bucky, were among the most persistent foes of the Axis and their allies. © Marvel Comics Group.

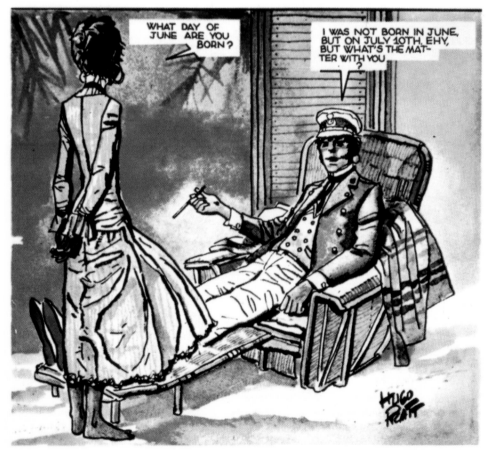

"Corto Maltese," Hugo Pratt. An atmospheric and exotic tale of adventure, "Corto Maltese" is set in the second decade of the 20th century. © Hugo Pratt.

"Captain Easy," Roy Crane. Innovative layout, imaginative situations, and a brisk, unrelenting pace were the hallmarks of "Captain Easy." © NEA Service.

Fingering her jewels, the Nizerine Eleyn watched the Kündüke in their pursuit.

...energy trails binding and tripping the fugitive....

From the ledge above the entangled woman, Akbrum jumped down.

"They want this woman badly." Suddenly the Nizerine hurled her rings and broaches. They streaked through the rubble, leaving trails of energy, homing in on their prey....

...their touch painful as molten wire.

She tried to keep the crystal from him.

Howard Chaykin and Samuel Delany, "Empire." Chaykin was very active in the 1970s and 1980s in the field of science-fiction graphic novels. "Empire," based on the Samuel Delany novel, was one of his early (and most successful) essays in the genre. © Byron Preiss Visual Publications.

c12

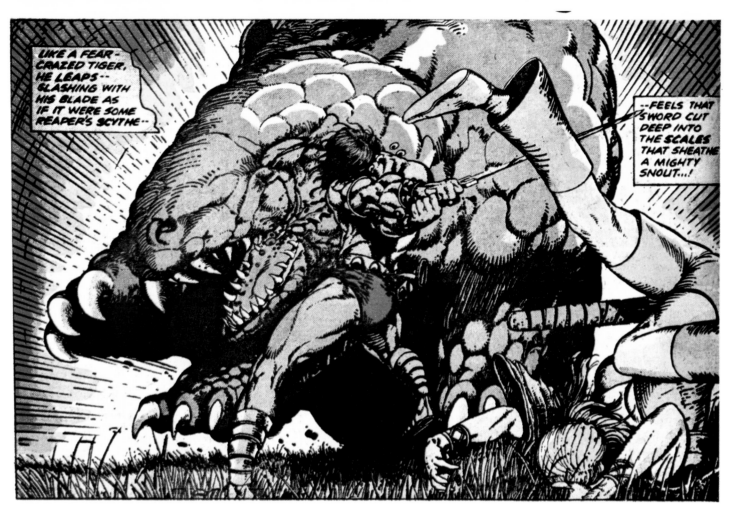

"Conan," Barry Smith. Robert E. Howard's fabled barbarian was given new life in a series of well-rendered tales. © Marvel Comics Group.

Richard Corben, "Cidopey." One of the most talented artists of the underground comics, Corben often draws very violently, but he can also be tender and lyrical. © Richard Corben.

"Connie," Frank Godwin. Frank Godwin's masterpiece blends outstanding draftsmanship, imaginative composition, and dramatic continuity. © Ledger Syndicate.

Robert Crumb, comic book cover. The best-known of underground cartoonists,
Crumb's choice of subject matter is often salacious. © Robert Crumb.

*"Dan Dare," Frank Bellamy. One of England's best-known adventure strips,
"Dan Dare" has seen the handiwork of many distinguished artists, Frank
Bellamy foremost among them. © Odhams Press Ltd.*

"Dzjengis Khan," Jos Looman. This chronicle of the life of the famed Mongol conqueror is one of the finest epic strips to come out of Europe. © Pep.

"Il Dottor Faust," Federico Pedrocchi and Rino Albertarelli. Albertarelli provided remarkable artwork to complement Pedrocchi's tasteful adaptation of the Faust legend. © Mondadori.

Du Jianguo, "The Little Rabbit Feifei." Du Jianguo is one of the foremost authors of children's comics in China, and "The Little Rabbit Feifei," based on a traditional folktale, is his most famous creation. © Du Jianguo.

"Dick Tracy," Chester Gould. The first detective strip to appear in print, *"Dick Tracy"* introduced crime and violence to the comic pages. © Chicago Tribune-New York News Syndicate.

"Doctor Strange," Roy Thomas and Gene Colan. One of the weirdest heroes to appear in comic books, Doctor Strange has known a checkered career, despite the talents of many of the people who worked on the feature. © Marvel Comics Group.

"Donald Duck," Carl Barks. The supreme "duck artist," Barks's cover for one of Donald's adventures is a classic. © Walt Disney Productions.

"Dennis the Menace," Hank Ketcham. "Dennis the Menace" renewed the tradition of the kid strip and became a part of the American idiom. © Field Newspaper Syndicate.

"Fatty Finn," Syd Nicholls. Modelled on the successful American strips, "Fatty Finn" was one of the funniest and most likable of Australian comic strips. © Syd Nicholls.

Fernando Fernandez, "Zora." "Zora," with its striking drawings and innovative
layouts, is one of Fernandez's most representative and most ambitious works.
© Fernando Fernandez.

"Felix the Cat," Otto Messmer. Of Felix's rare poetry and lyricism, French academician Marcel Brion said: "Felix is not a cat; he is the Cat. Or better to say yet, he is a supercat, because he does not fit in any of the categories of the animal kingdom." © King Features Syndicate.

"Flash Gordon," Alex Raymond. Universally regarded as the epitome of the adventure comics, Raymond's strip style has been widely imitated but never equalled. © King Features Syndicate.

"The Fantastic Four," Stan Lee and Jack Kirby. A group of misfit superheroes, The Fantastic Four launched the highly successful line of Marvel comic books in the 1960s. © Marvel Comics Group.

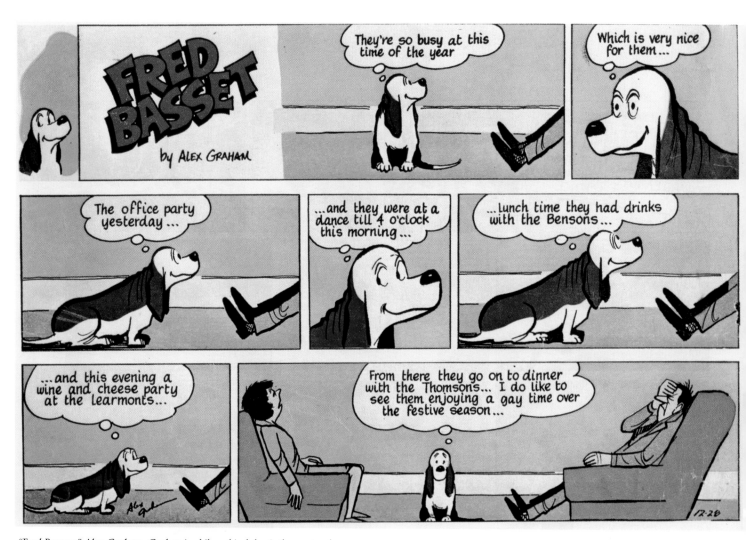

"Fred Bassett," Alex Graham. Graham's philosophical dog is the most endearing canine this side of Snoopy. © Associated Newspapers Ltd.

"Gaki Deka," Tatsuhiko Yamagami. Yamagami's "boy-policeman," the most troublesome brat in Japanese comics, introduced a breath of fresh air into the stale tradition of Japanese child strips. © Shomen Chambion.

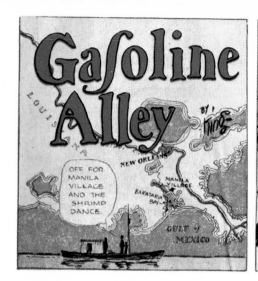

*"Gasoline Alley," Frank King. In "Gasoline Alley" King introduced a funda-
mental innovation: the characters in the strip grew old along with the readers.
© Chicago Tribune-New York News Syndicate.*

*"The Gumps," Sidney Smith. For a long time "The Gumps" was the most pop-
ular of all comic strips, and it was the first to earn its author a million-dollar
syndication contract. © Chicago Tribune-New York News Syndicate.*

*"Happy Hooligan," F. B. Opper. This forlorn hobo was a forerunner of Charlie
Chaplin's "little tramp." © King Features Syndicate.*

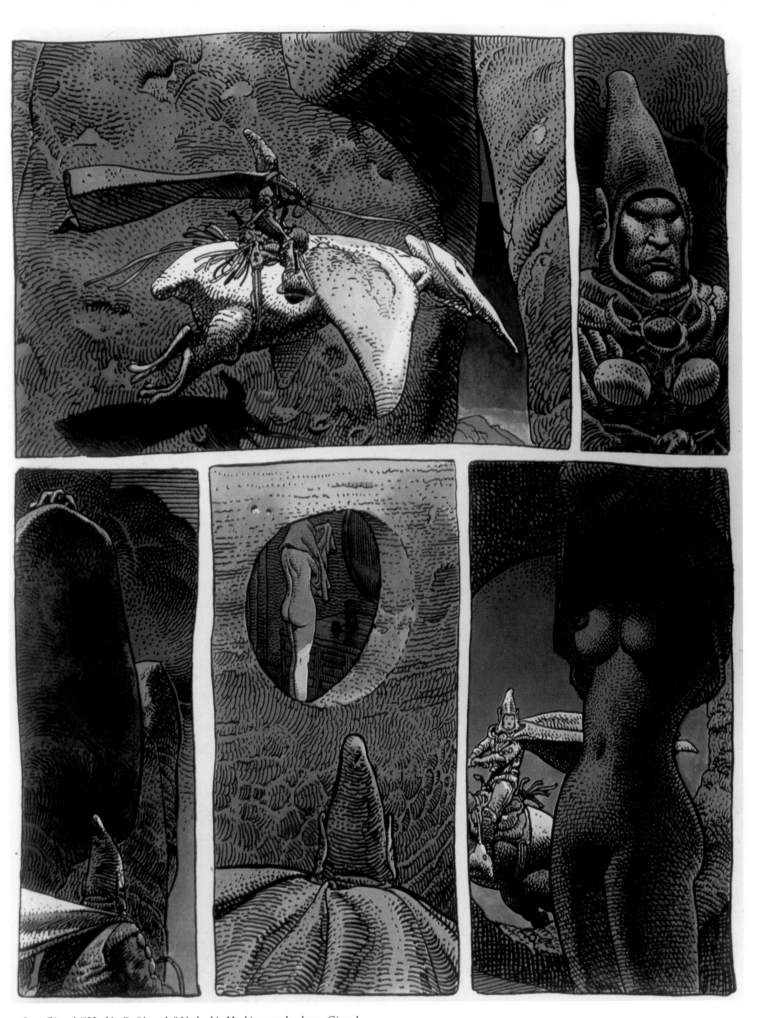

Jean Giraud ("Moebius"), "Arzach." Under his Moebius nomde plume, Giraud
has produced some of the most acclaimed French comic stories of the last two
decades. "Arzach" is probably his most representative creation, a fantasy tale
realized entirely with visuals, without use of text or dialogue. © Humanoides
Associés.

c29

"Happy Days," Roy Wilson. Typical English whimsy was Wilson's stock-in-trade. © Amalgamated Press.

Frank Hampson, "The Road of Courage." Hampson was one of the most noted artists in the British tradition. © Odhams Press Ltd.

Harry Hargreaves, "Ollie of the Movies." Movie comedians were a staple of
the English comic strip. © The Sun.

"The Hawkman." "The Hawkman" was one of the better-
drawn and -written comic books in the National stable. ©
National Periodical Publications.

"Johnny Hazard," Frank Robbins. Unjustly neglected, "Johnny Hazard" was one of the better-drawn and more imaginatively plotted of the post-World War II adventure strips. © King Features Syndicate.

Hiroshi Hirata, "Katame no Gunshi." Hirata is an outstanding draftsman whose forte is the depiction of battle and war scenes. © Hiroshi Hirata.

"The Heart of Juliet Jones," Stan Drake. This strip is one of the best representatives of the soap-opera school of comic writing. © King Features Syndicate.

"The Katzenjammer Kids," Rudolph Dirks. This strip was the first genuine
comic strip and is the oldest still in existence. © King Features Syndicate.

"The Katzenjammer Kids," Harold Knerr. Knerr took over the "Katzies" from Rudolph Dirks in 1914 but maintained the quality, high spirits, and unpredictability of the strip. © King Features Syndicate.

Koo Kojima, comic book illustration. One of Japan's leading illustrators, Kojima is particularly noted for his sexy, glamorous women. © Koo Kojima.

"Kozure Okami," Goseki Kojima. Kojima's strip is a grim tale of murder and revenge set in feudal Japan. © Manga Action.

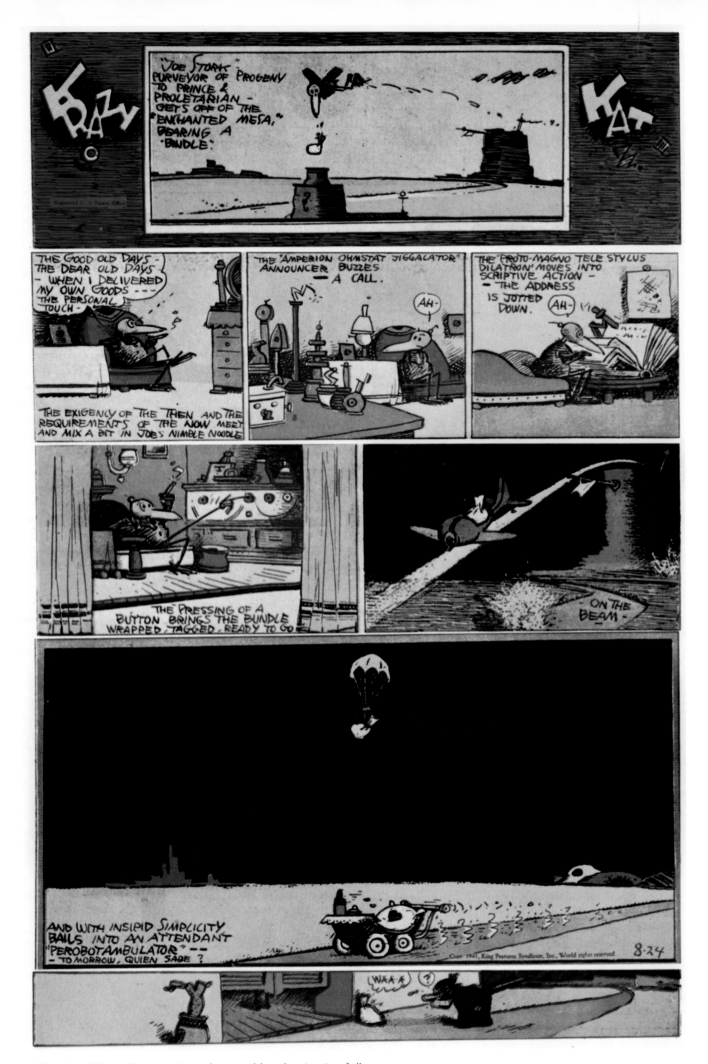

"Krazy Kat," George Herriman. Among the most celebrated comic strips of all time, *"Krazy Kat"* has earned its author the respect and admiration of intellectuals the world over. © King Features Syndicate.

"Lieutenant Blueberry," Jean-Michel Charlier and Gir (Jean Giraud). *This French Western strip is noted for the quality of Gir's artwork.* © Editions Dargaud.

"Li'l Abner," Al Capp. Li'l Abner and his hillbilly family and friends are now part of American folklore. © Chicago Tribune-New York News Syndicate.

"Little Jimmy," James Swinnerton. *"Little Jimmy"* is the best-remembered among Swinnerton's many comic strip creations. © King Features Syndicate.

"Little Orphan Annie," Harold Gray. Most noted for its author's ideological soap-boxing, "Little Orphan Annie" was also moody and suspenseful. © Chicago Tribune-New York News Syndicate.

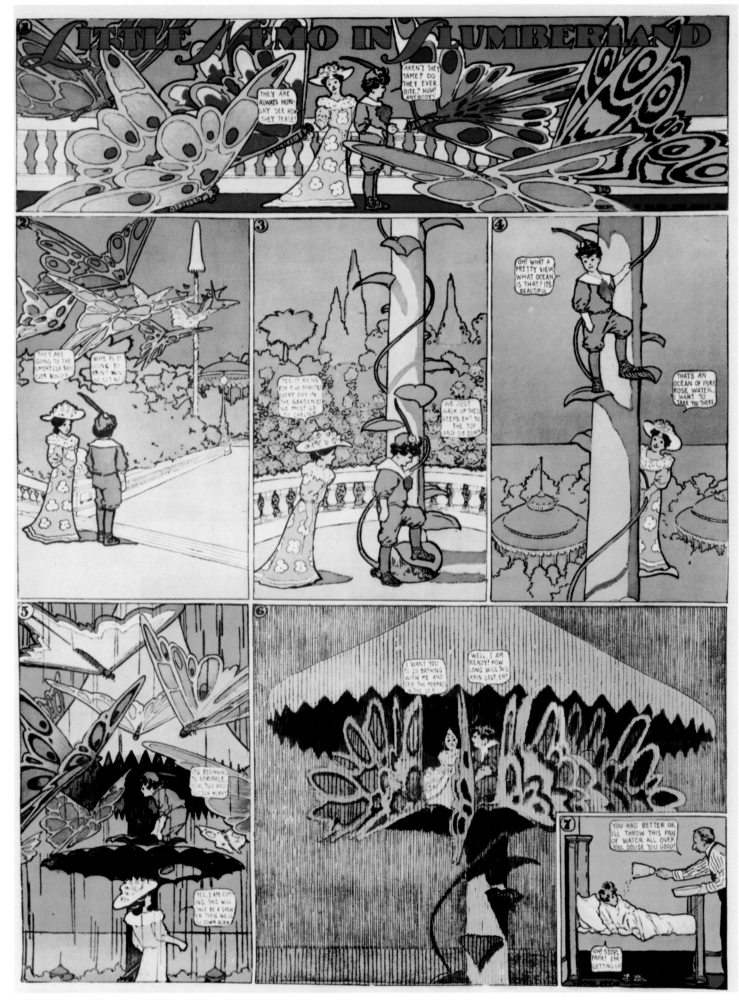

"Little Nemo in Slumberland," Winsor McCay. *"Little Nemo"* is a masterpiece
of design, grace, and light.

"Lucky Luke," Rene Goscinny and Morris (Maurice de Bevere). This parodic Western is one of the funniest of European comic strips. © Editions Dargaud.

"Marmittone," Bruno Angoletta. An Italian "Sad Sack," Marmittone poked fun at Mussolini's military pretensions. © Corriere dei Piccoli.

"Mandrake the Magician," Lee Falk and Phil Davis. Mandrake, the master of magic and illusion, is a frequently imitated strip character. © King Features Syndicate.

"Mallard Fillmore," Bruce Tinsley. "Mallard Fillmore" was created as a conservative counterpoint to "Doonesbury," with which it often appears on the editorial page of a number of newspapers. © King Features Syndicate.

Milo Manara, "The Wall." The fall of the Berlin Wall has inspired a number of comic-strip artists: here is Manara's exuberantly lyrical take on the event. © Carlsen Verlag.

Esteban Maroto, "Wolff." Maroto, who also works for American comic books, is one of the most famous contemporary Spanish cartoonists. © Buru Lan.

Lorenzo Mattotti, "Fuochi." The plot of "Fuochi" ("Fires") is quite simple: a battleship has been ordered to bomb out a little island, but one of the sailors, dazzled by the colors and creatures of the island, tries to prevent its destruction. The story's fascination lies in the artwork, midway between realism and abstraction, and in the narrative tension created by the images and the colors. © Lorenzo Mattotti.

Todd McFarlane, "Spawn." Todd McFarlane made a name for himself working on some of Marvel's most successful comic book titles. He has enjoyed his greatest hit, however, with a creation of his own, "Spawn," about a vengeful black superhero. © Todd McFarlane.

"Mickey Mouse," Floyd Gottfredson. Mickey Mouse began his joyful career in animated cartoons and was adapted into comic strips in 1930. © Walt Disney Productions.

Attilio Micheluzzi, "Titanic." Micheluzzi's narrative talent is much in evidence
in this comicbook telling of the fabled ocean liner's doomed Atlantic voyage.
© Casterman.

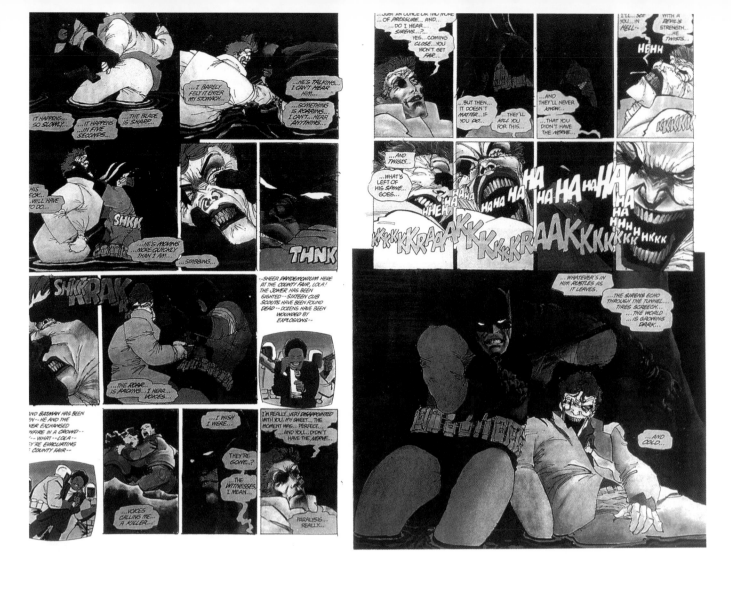

Frank Miller, "The Dark Knight Returns." Of all of Miller's achievements in
the field of comic books, his most notable remains his successful revamping of
the Batman character in the 1980s. © DC Comics.

"Over the Hedge," Michael Fry and T. Lewis. "Over the Hedge" features the
bad boys of the animal world and has proved a huge success with the readers.
The circulation of this dark-humored comic strip has grown consistently since its
inception in 1995. © United Feature Syndicate.

"Moon Mullins," Frank Willard. *Moon Mullins and his friends and relatives are some of the weirdest misfits ever to appear in the comic pages. © Chicago Tribune-New York Times Syndicate.*

"Nus," Enric Sio. "Nus" is typical of Sio's avant-garde comic creations. ©
Salvat Editores.

Pran, "Chacha Chaudhary." India's most popular comic book series. © Pran's Features.

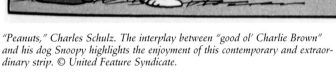

"Peanuts," Charles Schulz. The interplay between "good ol' Charlie Brown" and his dog Snoopy highlights the enjoyment of this contemporary and extraordinary strip. © United Feature Syndicate.

"Polly and Her Pals," Cliff Sterrett. Elements of surrealism and cubism were
often incorporated into Sterrett's highly stylized strips. © King Features
Syndicate.

"Pogo," Walt Kelly. *"Pogo" dealt with some of the most important moral,
social, and political themes of its time.* © Walt Kelly.

Prince Valiant

Registered U. S. Patent Office.

IN THE DAYS OF
KING ARTHUR
BY
HAROLD R. FOSTER

SYNOPSIS: NEVER HAS SUCH A GREAT SAXON FORCE INVADED BRITAIN — AND NEVER IN A STRONGER POSITION. IN DESPERATION THE KING ADOPTS THE MAD, INGENIOUS PLAN THAT VAL UNFOLDS TO THE GRAND COUNCIL OF WAR. VAL HAS PROMISED THAT, WITH 500 MEN, HE WILL DRIVE 20,000 ARMED SAXON WARRIORS IN PANIC BEFORE ARTHUR'S WAITING ARMY.

VAL SHOUTS A COMMAND, A TRUMPET SOUNDS AND IN A MOMENT THE MARSH IS A MASS OF FLAMES.

THE ASTONISHED SAXONS SEE THE BAY QUICKLY ENCIRCLED ON THREE SIDES BY A LEAPING SHEET OF FLAME — THEN SUDDENLY THEY ARE ENVELOPED IN A DENSE CLOUD OF CHOKING SMOKE.

AND OUT OF THAT SMOKE COMES A SHOWER OF FIRE-BALLS THROWN BY AN INVISIBLE ENEMY!

BURNING RAFTS AND FLAMING CANOES DRIFT WITH THE WIND AMONG THE ANCHORED SHIPS..... FIRE AND CONFUSION ARE EVERYWHERE.

"TO SHORE," SCREAMS HORSA, "THE SOUTH BANK IS DEFENDED ONLY BY DUMMIES, LAND THERE AND REORGANIZE."

VAL HEARS THE COMMAND AND IMMEDIATELY CHANGES HIS ATTACK.

AS THE SAXONS LAND TO REFORM THEIR RANKS A DEADLY SHOWER OF ARROWS COMES OUT OF THE SMOKE AND DRIVES THEM INLAND.

THE INVADERS COME STUMBLING OUT FROM BENEATH THE CLOUD OF STIFLING SMOKE AND STINGING ARROWS AND THERE — DRAWN UP IN BATTLE ARRAY, IS THE KING'S ARMY!

· NEXT WEEK ·
PRINCE VALIANT
IS KNIGHTED!

HAL FOSTER

"Prince Valiant," Harold Foster. A breathtaking exercise in virtuosity of drafts-manship, "Prince Valiant" is Foster's most outstanding achievement in comics.
© King Features Syndicate.

"Quadratino," Antonio Rubino. "Quadratino" is the best of Rubino's many comic creations. © Corriere dei Piccoli.

„Jetzt hab ich keine Zeit mehr! Her mit dem Werkzeug, Pelle!"

„Langsam, Petzi! Zuerst müssen wir gut überlegen."

„Du brauchst zuerst eine Zeichnung von dem Schiff!"

„Eine Zeichnung? Das trifft sich gut, ich zeichne auch gern."

„Petzi, wir wußten gar nicht, daß du so gut zeichnen kannst."

„Das bauen wir! Das ist ein schönes Schiff!"

"Rusmus Klump" ("Petzi"), Carla and Vilhelm Hansen. This strip, intended especially for young children, is one of the most endearing. © PIB.

AT MULA SA MABANGIS NA MUKHANG SING-TIGAS NG BATO NA PINAGKUKUYUMAN NG DAMDAMING IBIG SUMAMBULAT SA MATINDING SAMA NG LOOB, AY NAMALISBIS ANG DALAWANG BUTIL NA LUHA, NA HINDI NA MAKAYANG PIGILIN...

LUBOS ANG KAGALAKAN NG HARI NANG IABOT NA MULI ANG SANGGOL SA KAMAY NG DAMA, AT TINUNGO ANG SILID NA KINAHIHIMLAYAN NG MAHAL NA KABIYAK... DATAPUWA'T... PARANG PINAGSUKLUBAN NG LANGIT AT LUPA ANG BUONG KATAUHAN NG KILABOT NANG TUMAMBAD SA KANYANG PANINGIN ANG KAHAMBAL-HAMBAL NA ANYO NG ASAWA NA WALA NANG MALAY AT ISA NANG MALAMIG NA BANGKAY...

SANDALING NAMAGITAN ANG ISANG NAKABIBINGING KATAHIMIKAN SA PANAHON NG PAGKAKALUHOD NG KILABOT NA HARI. TIIM ANG MGA BAGANG AT NANLILISIK ANG MGA MATA'Y DAHAN-DAHANG TUMINDIG, AT...

IGINALA ANG KANYANG PANINGIN SA MGA MUKHANG NAROROON AT HINAHANAP ANG MANGGAGAMOT NA KANYANG INATASANG MANGALAGA SA KALIGTASAN NG MAHAL NA REYNA, AT...

NAGIMBAL ANG LAHAT SA MADUGONG WAKAS NA SINAPIT NG MANGGAGAMOT. AT ANG HARI, SA TINIG NA LIPOS NG HINANAKIT AT PAGDARAMDAM: —WALA PANG SINUMANG NAGDULOT SA AKIN NG GANITONG KASAKLAP NA KABIGUAN...

NANG MAKITA ANG KANYANG HANAP AY BINUNOT ANG TABAK NG PINAKAMALAPIT NA KABIG AT WALANG PAKUNDANGANG...

SA Susunod Ang Hula

Jesus Jodloman, "Ramir." Inspired by "Prince Valiant," "Ramir" is one of the best comic strips from the Philippines. © Halaklak.

c54

"Rose Is Rose," Pat Brady. "Rose Is Rose" is an endearing family strip that has
gained great favor with the public since its humble beginnings in 1984.
© United Feature Syndicate.

COMPLAINTE DES LANDES PERDUES

DUFAUX ✎ — ✎ ROSINSKI

Rosinski, dessinateur de *Thorgal*, et Dufaux, l'un des meilleurs scénaristes actuels, nous font découvrir l'univers de Sioban, princesse sans royaume mais animée d'une extraordinaire soif de vengeance et de reconquête ! Un récit d'inspiration celtique empreint d'une ambiance fantastique et d'un souffle légendaire parfaitement servi par un dessinateur au sommet de son art. En l'espace de trois albums cette série fait déjà partie des indispensables.

3 titres disponibles (voir p. 64)

« SIOBAN »
SÉLECTIONNÉ
PARMI LES
30
INDISPENSABLES
D'ANGOULÊME
94.

Gregor Rosinski and Jean Dufaux, "La Complainte des Landes Perdues."
Polish-born Rosinski became noted for the comic stories he contributed to
Warsaw magazines from the late 1960s to the mid-1970s. Moving to the West
he then demonstrated his graphic mastery in a number of comic series, of which
this is one of the most breathtaking. © Dargaud Editeur.

"Roy Tiger." A revived German comic strip industry produced "Roy Tiger."
© Bastei Verlag.

"Rusty Riley," Frank Godwin. Godwin's last creation is a nostalgic and beautiful paean to youth. © King Features Syndicate.

"Sandman," Neil Gaiman and Sam Kieth. One of the most original of contemporary comic book writers, Gaiman could take even an old warhorse like DC's Sandman and make it seem new. © DC Comics.

Matthias Schultheiss, "Them." Schultheiss is a German comics creator who is better known in France and the U.S. than in his native country. He has published several highly dramatic graphic novels and a number of shorter stories, of which "Them," built around the destruction of the Berlin Wall, is one. © Carlsen Verlag.

"Sheena, Queen of the Jungle," W. Morgan Thomas. Sheena was the first in a long line of sexy, scantily clad comic book heroines. © Fiction House.

"Sturmtruppen," Bonvi (Franco Bonvicini). Set during World War II, this strip was a satire on military life and an example of black, even sick, humor. © Franco Bonvicini.

"Il Signor Bonaventura," Sto (Sergio Tofano). This simple tale of a Good Samaritan is beloved among Italian strips. © Corriere dei Piccoli.

"Sjors," Frans Piet. Begun as the Dutch version of the "Winnie Winkle" Sunday page, "Sjors" later became the most popular kid strip in the Netherlands. © Het Sjorsblod.

"Les Schtroumpfs," Peyo (Pierre Culliford). A race of gentle, civilized, and utterly winsome elves, the schtroumpfs are involved in the most improbable adventures. © Editions Dupuis.

HE WON'T JUMP THROUGH THE HOOP!

OFFER HIM CANDY

HE STILL WON'T!

I WILL!

One of these suspects stole an Egyptian sculpture from the Forest Museum. Slylock Fox is holding a box that contains physical evidence dropped by the thief at the crime scene. What do you think is in the box, and which suspect do you believe is guilty?

One of the raccoon's coat buttons is gone. The box contains his missing button. Slylock suspects the raccoon is the thief.

E-Mail: SLYLOCK F @ AOL.COM

Find six differences between these two panels.

Answer – Cork, earring, air hose, crab leg, fish fin, octopus tentacle.

True or False

CLICK!

Electric lights can cause cats to shed.

True. Even the illumination of a television is enough to trigger shedding.

HOW TO DRAW a dinosaur

Your Drawing

This week's artist, Taylor Santos, age 9, of Pawtucket, RI, receives a free SLYLOCK FOX BRAIN BOGGLERS game.

Send your drawings (b&w) to Slylock Fox and Comics for Kids c/o this newspaper.

"Slylock Fox," Bob Weber Jr. Slylock Fox, a Sherlockian sleuth in vulpine guise, is the star of "Comics for Kids," the highly successful activity strip created by Bob Weber Jr., son of "Moose" creator Bob Weber. © King Features Syndicate.

c62

Reg Perrott, "Song of the Sword." Perrott was an early English adventure strip
artist. © Amalgamated Press.

"Spider-Man," Stan Lee and John Romita. Also known as the "web slinger" and "your friendly neighborhood Spider-Man," this character epitomizes the comic book antihero and is the best-known comic creation of the 1960s. © Marvel Comics Group.

"The Spectre," Murphy Anderson. "The Spectre" was one of the more interesting superhero features. © National Periodical Publications.

"The Spirit," Will Eisner. "The Spirit" was the historical bridge between the comic book and the newspaper strip. © Will Eisner.

"Steve Canyon," Milton Caniff. "Steve Canyon" was one of the few contemporary continuity strips to exhibit some of the spirit and élan of the old adventure stories. © Field Newspaper Syndicate.

"*Superman,*" *Wayne Boring. Despite imitations and variations, since 1938 Superman has been the uncontested champion of the costumed superhero league. © National Periodical Publications.*

"Tarzan," Harold Foster. More than any other, "Tarzan" established the
adventure strip as an autonomous genre. © Edgar Rice Burroughs, Inc.

"Tarzan," Burne Hogarth. After taking over the strip from Harold Foster, Hogarth fashioned "Tarzan" into one of the most celebrated adventure strips in comics history. © Edgar Rice Burroughs, Inc.

CONTINUED ON 3RD PAGE FOLLOWING

"Swamp Thing," Alan Moore and Rick Veitch. Moore constructed genuinely gripping tales around the premise of a scientist turned into a "plant elemental" following the bombing of his laboratory. He was helped in his task by Veitch's often brilliant visuals. © DC Comics.

"Terry and the Pirates," Milton Caniff. More faithfully than any other comic strip, "Terry" reflected the American attitude after Pearl Harbor. © Chicago Tribune-New York News Syndicate.

"Tetsuwan-Atom" ("Astroboy"), Osamu Tezuka. This is Tezuka's most widely circulated comic feature. © Shonen.

"Thimble Theater" ("Popeye"), Elzie Segar. "Thimble Theater" reached its peak of popularity in 1929, when the invincible one-eyed sailor, Popeye, and the intellectual moocher, Wimpy, were introduced. © King Features Syndicate.

"Thor," Stan Lee and Jack Kirby. Thor is another of the superheroes made popular by the dynamic duo, Lee and Kirby. © Marvel Comics Group.

THE BRUIN BOYS GET SOME NEW HATS THIS WEEK.

1. "Now, run along to the shop in the High Street, boys," said Mrs. Bruin, "and get some new hats, and say that they are for me!" "Oh yes, Mrs. Bruin!" Tim cried. "Come along, boys!" And away they all went. "This is much better than doing sums!" said Georgie Giraffe to Jumbo.

2. So off they all went. And at last they came to a shop with the window full of hats. "This must be the place. Come along in, boys!" Tim cried to the others. And in they all went. "Now we shall be all right!" said Jacko to Bobby Bruin. "Oh, I do feel so excited!"

3. Well, I think that Madame Duck, who kept the hat shop, was a little bit surprised when the Bruin Boys came into her shop. "Are you sure that Mrs. Bruin told you to come here?" she asked. "Oh, yes! We want eight hats, please!" Willie Ostrich cried. "And here's the money!" Tim said.

4. So Mrs. Duck put eight hats into some hat-boxes. "There you are, then," she said. "Now do be careful with them!" "I wonder what sort of hats they are?" Georgie Giraffe said later. "I do want to see mine, don't you, Jacko?" "Yes, rather! Of course I do!" Jacko replied.

5. Well, those stupid boys put the boxes down and opened them, and took out all sorts of ladies' hats! "These are funny!" said Fido. "They're not a bit like the hats we had last time!" "Well, let's go back to school and show them to Mrs. Bruin," Willie Ostrich said. "Yes, let's put them on our heads!" laughed Tim.

6. So, wearing the hats, back went all the Bruin Boys. "Goodness!" Mrs. Bruin cried when she saw them. "What ever have you got there?" And didn't they look silly! "The lady gave us these," Jumbo said. "Well," Mrs. Bruin replied, "you just take them back!" "There, I knew they were wrong!" said little Joey.

You will roar with laughter over the funny Bruin Boys' story in "Tiger Tim's Weekly." Now on sale. 2d.

"Tiger Tim" ("The Bruin Boys"), H. S. Foxwell. The dean of British animal strips, "Tiger Tim" has entertained several generations of young readers. © Fleetway Publications Ltd.

"Tintin," Hergé (George Rémi). *"Tintin" has been the most acclaimed comic creation in Europe for more than 65 years.* © Editions Casterman.

Daniel Torres, "Triton." This is an episode in the "astral adventures of Rocco Vargas,"
Torres's half-parody, half-homage to the space-opera genre. © Daniel Torres.

"Valhalla," Peter Madsen. "Valhalla" is a tongue-in-cheek retelling of the old Norse myths and legends. © A/S Interpresse.

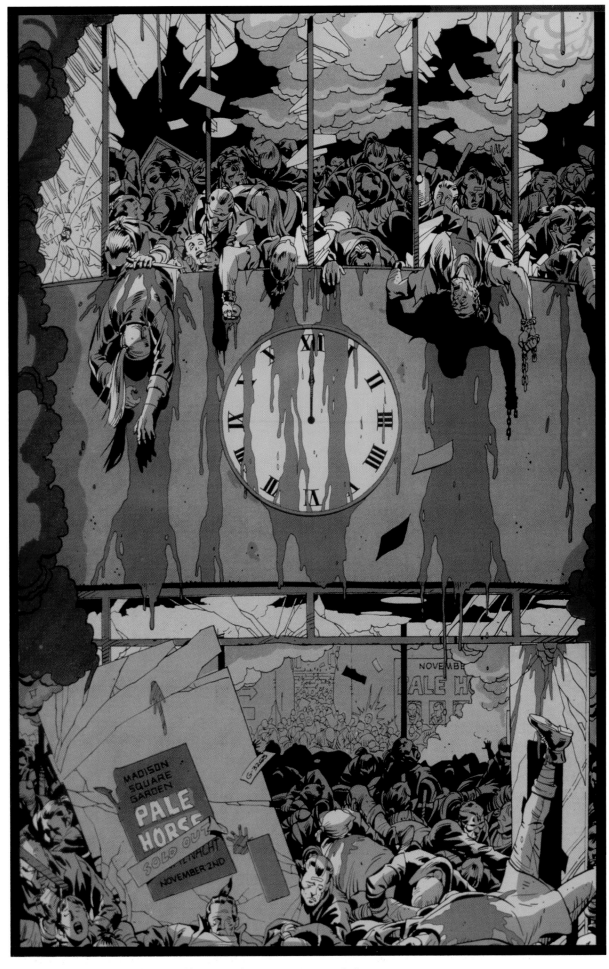

"Watchmen," Alan Moore and Dave Gibbons. "Watchmen" is a unique tour de force whose excellence has not been replicated so far. It lies like an erratic rock in the middle of the great American comic book landscape. © DC Comics

Wee Willie Winkie's World

"Wee Willie Winkie's World," Lyonel Feininger. Feininger skillfully created a world of fantasy and whimsy, of sweetness and shadows, of marvel and terror.

Winnetou

und Old Shatterhand haben Blutsbrüderschaft geschlossen

Vorher hatten die Apatschen Old Shatterhand und seine Gefährten Sam Hawkens, Dick Stone und Will Parker an den Marterpfahl gebunden. Sie waren von Tangua, dem Häuptling der Kiowas, dazu aufgehetzt worden, der in den Bleichgesichtern unbequeme Zeugen seiner eignen Schurkereien beseitigen will.

In einem Zweikampf um das Leben rettet Old Shatterhand sich und seine Gefährten und besiegt Tangua.

"Winnetou," Helmut Nickel. Inspired by Karl May's popular novels, "Winnetou" is the only German Western strip of note. © Walter Lehning Verlag.

"The Wizard of Id," Johnny Hart and Brant Parker. This strip, with its weird cast of characters, can only be called a "black" fairy tale. © Field Newspaper Syndicate.

"Wonder Woman," William Moulton Marston. Hailed in some quarters as a champion of women's liberation, Wonder Woman spent an inordinate portion of her time in chains. © National Periodical Publications.

"White Boy," Garrett Price. "White Boy" was a handsome and offbeat Western whose qualities were unappreciated by readers. © Chicago Tribune-New York News Syndicate.

"The Yellow Kid," Richard Felton Outcault. Not yet a genuine comic strip in 1895, "The Yellow Kid" ushered in the era of the modern Sunday newspaper supplement and was of pivotal importance to the development of the American comic strip.